WITHDRAWN

D1260075

THE STRUCTURE OF EARNINGS AND THE MEASUREMENT OF INCOME INEQUALITY IN THE U.S.

CONTRIBUTIONS
TO
ECONOMIC ANALYSIS

184

Honorary Editor:
J. TINBERGEN

Editors:
D. W. JORGENSON
J..WAELBROECK

NORTH-HOLLAND
AMSTERDAM • NEW YORK • OXFORD • TOKYO

339.2
SL563

THE STRUCTURE OF EARNINGS AND THE MEASUREMENT OF INCOME INEQUALITY IN THE U.S.

Daniel J. SLOTTJE

Department of Economics
Southern Methodist University
Dallas, Texas 75275
U.S.A.

1989

NORTH-HOLLAND
AMSTERDAM • NEW YORK • OXFORD • TOKYO

ELSEVIER SCIENCE PUBLISHERS B.V.
Sara Burgerhartstraat 25
P.O. Box 211, 1000 AE Amsterdam, The Netherlands

Distributors for the United States and Canada:

ELSEVIER SCIENCE PUBLISHING COMPANY INC.
655 Avenue of the Americas
New York, N.Y. 10010, U.S.A.

ISBN: 0 444 88320 7

© ELSEVIER SCIENCE PUBLISHERS B.V., 1989

All rights reserved. No part of this publication may be reproduced, stored in a retrieval system, or transmitted, in any form or by any means, electronic, mechanical, photocopying, recording or otherwise, without the prior written permission of the publisher, Elsevier Science Publishers B.V. / Physical Sciences and Engineering Division, P.O. Box 1991, 1000 BZ Amsterdam, The Netherlands.

Special regulations for readers in the U.S.A. - This publication has been registered with the Copyright Clearance Center Inc. (CCC), Salem, Massachusetts. Information can be obtained from the CCC about conditions under which photocopies of parts of this publication may be made in the U.S.A. All other copyright questions, including photocopying outside of the U.S.A., should be referred to the copyright owner, Elsevier Science Publishers B.V., unless otherwise specified.

No responsibility is assumed by the publisher for any injury and/or damage to persons or property as a matter of products liability, negligence or otherwise, or from any use or operation of any methods, products, instructions or ideas contained in the material herein.

PRINTED IN THE NETHERLANDS

INTRODUCTION TO THE SERIES

This series consists of a number of hitherto unpublished studies, which are introduced by the editors in the belief that they represent fresh contributions to economic science.

The term "economic analysis" as used in the title of the series has been adopted because it covers both the activities of the theoretical economist and the research worker.

Although the analytical methods used by the various contributors are not the same, they are nevertheless conditioned by the common origin of their studies, namely theoretical problems encountered in practical research. Since for this reason, business cycle research and national accounting, research work on behalf of economic policy, and problems of planning are the main sources of the subjects dealt with, they necessarily determine the manner of approach adopted by the authors. Their methods tend to be "practical" in the sense of not being too far remote from application to actual economic conditions. In additon they are quantitative.

It is the hope of the editors that the publication of these studies will help to stimulate the exchange of scientific information and to reinforce international cooperation in the field of economics.

The Editors

ALLEGHENY COLLEGE LIBRARY

89-8362

5-14-90 BNA 30188

*To Kathy Jean Hayes
with love and thanks
for solving many hard problems
that I got credit for.*

PREFACE

This study stems from research I started about five years ago and have continued with since. I am grateful to many people for their help in this project. At various stages of the writing of this book, different individuals were very helpful with comments and criticisms without being implicated for the final results.

For their discussions with me on this subject matter, I would like to thank Bob Basmann, Tom Fomby, Joe Hirschberg, Jerry Scully, and Mike Nieswiadomy. The same holds for Dennis Aigner, John Creedy, Jim McDonald, David Molina, Richard Butler, Peter Gottschalk, Tim Smeeding, Tony Shorrocks, Dan Black, and Mike Baye who were very helpful both formally in critiquing aspects of the book and informally in conversations. Hans Theil has been very supportive of this project and I am very grateful for our conversations over the years. Kin Blackburn was especially considerate in painstakingly pointing out many of my errors with the data, etc. Essie Maasoumi has been a good friend and proffered excellent advice. Ann Caple competently assisted in preparing Chapter 2. Ken King of Mark Co. was very helpful in preparing the tables in Chapter 2. For their excellent typing I am grateful to Pontip Vattakavanich, Sherry Jackson and Janet Thoele. As is always the case, the usual caveat applies.

D.J. Slottje
Dallas, Texas 1989

TABLE OF CONTENTS

Chapter 1

INTRODUCTION

As Harold Lydall noted almost twenty years ago,

The essential problem of economics is how to increase
economic welfare. In a broad sense, this problem can be
divided into two parts: how to increase total output from
given resources; and how to distribute the resulting goods
and services in such a way as to give the community the most
benefit from them. These two aspects are sometimes described
as the problem of 'production' and the problem of 'distribution', respectively. The two parts are not, of course,
independent; and many of the most difficult questions arise
out of the interdependence of production and distribution.
Nevertheless, it is possible to identify some influences
which bear primarily on the side of production and others
which primarily affect distribution. No progress could be
made in the discussion unless we abstracted, at least
temporarily, from some of the considerations which might
eventually be shown to be relevant to one or other side
(Lydall, 1968, 1).

Bronfenbrenner (1971) pointed out that economists generally view the
problem of economic distribution as either the fundamental problem in
economics or as,

uninteresting--the outcome of more basic decisions "up the
line" (Bronfenbrenner, 1971, 1).

Those who considered the issue important were economists such as Ricardo
(1819), J. B. Clark (1899) and Galbraith (1962) among others. These
individuals believed the question important primarily due to class
conflict considerations. Sen (1973) has echoed the same sentiment in
noting that

the correlation between inequality and rebellion is a close
one and it runs both ways (Sen, 1973, 7).

Many economists, of course, consider the problem important for social
justice and moral reasons independent of class struggle rationale. For
whatever reason, clearly economic inequality questions have been
important, are important and will continue to be important to many
economists. On the other hand, many prominent economists felt that the
inequality question should not receive a central emphasis. These
individuals fall into the Pigou (1932) and Simons (1948) camp. Pigou
stated,

It is evident that, provided the dividend accruing to the
poor is not diminished, increases in the size of national
income, if they occur in isolation without anything else
happening, must involve increases in economic welfare
(Pigou, 1932, 82).

and Simons observed that,

Our primary problem is production. The common man or average
family has a far greater stake in the size of our aggregate
income than in any possible redistribution of income (Simons,
1948, 5).

This group of economists were arguing that efficiency gains will "raise
all boats" and total welfare will increase, a positivistic argument that
is difficult to dispute. However, this viewpoint ignores the notion that
people care, and care a great deal, about their relative positions within
the distribution of resources and the status inherent therein.

Frank (1984, 1985) and Sen (1986) have recently made economists
aware of this idea. These two prominent economists have pointed out that
status as measured by one's perceived position in the observed graduation
of income, commodity expenditures and other economic indicators of status
are highly relevant in an individual's assessment of own well-being and
self-esteem. Control over economic resources which makes mobility in
these perceived graduations possible is still determined primarily by an
individual's earnings. These earnings (wages and salaries, fringe benefits and bonuses, etc.) have constituted approximately two thirds to
three fourths of total income in the United States for most people over
the past fifty years.

It is for these reasons that this book will examine the distribution
of labor earnings as well as the distribution of nonlabor earnings and
total income. Analysis of earnings and total income distributions opens
a flood gate that could quickly inundate us with so many diverse aspects
of the problem that a requisite "comprehensive" treatise would be beyond
our capability to study here. Sahota (1978) surveyed one aspect of the
distribution literature and cited hundreds of articles and books. To
keep this current project tractable, we therefore will proceed as
follows. Chapter 2 of this book will be a broad overview of how the U.S.
labor market has changed and what trends have developed in it since the
late 1940's. Changes in the makeup of the labor force, in the way people
co-habit and the education they achieve (to name just a few factors), all
will be important in determining wages individuals are paid and the

attendant distribution of earnings that results from these considerations.

Chapter 3 will give a review of theories of how observed income
distributions are generated and then a brief synopsis of mathematical
statistical distributions that have been used to approximate income
distributions. Finally, Chapter 3 examines the problem of measuring
income inequality and discusses various proffered measures. Chapter 4
resurrects a technique from classical statistics that allows for **a priori**
discrimination amongst statistical distributions in choosing an appropriate form of hypothetical distribution to approximate the income
graduation. In addition, Chapter 4 demonstrates the theoretical link-up
of many well-known statistical distributions that have been used in the
past to approximate the observed income graduation.

Chapter 5 introduces a specific form of statistical distribution to
describe actual income graduations. The form discussed here is the Beta
distribution of the second kind. We demonstrate the flexibility of this
functional form for making comparisons across states, regions (urban/
rural) and races below. We also examine the labor/nonlabor income
distributions. The assumption of a specific functional form in analyzing
earnings distributions arises over and over again. The work of Mincer
and others on human capital models all estimate the return to educaton
and training costs under the assumption of lognormally distributed
earnings, cf. Chiswick (1974). The research here suggests another form
may be more appropriate.

In Chapter 6 we present inequality measures for various demographic
groups and demonstrate that the question of whether inequality has
increased or decreased depends critically on which income-earner group of
the population we are referring to and on which socio-economic characteristics of these groups we are examining. Chapter 7 follows with an
analysis of earnings inequality across occupations for selected years and
describes how the distributions have changed over time. Finally, Chapter
8 summarizes and concludes the study. In the summary we also present
suggestions for future research.

It is not accidental that we first present specific forms of statistical distributions to examine inequality and then begin examining
inequality from Lorenz-based non-parametric measures. Nor is it accidental that we jump from data source to data source and from inequality
measure to inequality measure. We have followed a strategy that

introduces   the   reader   to different models, measures and data so he/she
will realize that results (and therefore conclusions drawn which lead   to
public   policy   implications)   do depend on <u>what</u> measure you use and what
<u>data</u> you use and how you model inequality.

Chapter 2

TRENDS IN THE LABOR MARKETS

A 'careful examination of the structure of earnings necessarily requires a careful discussion of the demographic trends that characterize and shape the demand and supply for labor. Whether one is an avowed human capital theorist or not, there is little disagreement over the major role that demographics play in determining wages and the distribution of these wages. It is well known that changes in labor force participation by women, hours worked by men and educational attainment have greatly affected the structure of earnings for all groups in the economy. The purpose of this chapter is to give a broad overview of what demographic trends have developed in the past forty years. We will discuss the implications of these trends at the appropriate time further on in the book. We begin by examining the changes in the population.

From Table 2.1 we note that the total civilian non-institutional population of the United States has been growing at the fairly steady annual rate of 2.8 percent since 1948. Of that total, 47% of the population were men and 53% women in 1983, with 87% white and 11% black. Although the population as a whole has been growing at a steady rate there is quite a bit of variation among different segments. Since 1972, the first year for which some data is available, the black population has had a 23% increase, from 14.5 million to 18.9 million individuals. During this same period the white population only increased 15% and the total population 17%. The variation in percentage increases between men and women has not been so great. Since 1972 the male population increased 17.8% as compared to 16.8% for women. This is a reversal of the trend since 1948 - from which time the total female population has increased 42% as compared to 39% for males.

Table 2.2 presents information on the labor force participation rate of various groups. The most dramatic changes to occur in the civilian labor force participation rates since 1948 have been the decline in workers age 65 and over and the increase in the participation rate of women. The total participation rate was quite stable for the 20 years from 1948 to 1968, but since 1968 it has steadily increased.

From 1948 to 1983 the total participation rate increased 8%, 6.9% of that increase has been since 1968 alone. Of the total increase, the teenage participation rate (ages 16-19) only increased 1.9% while the rates for those 65 years and older <u>decreased</u> 130.8% since 1948. The rate for those between the ages of 20 and 54 increased 18% on average, with the highest rate of increase occurring for those between the ages of 25 and 34. Their participation in the labor force increased 22.4% from 1948.

The labor force participation rate for men as a whole has been declining steadily from 86.6% in 1948 to 76.4% in 1983. This decrease was especially marked for those aged 65 and over - the participation rate for men in this segment fell 165%, from 46.8% in 1948 to 17.4% in 1983. The only age segment for men for which no decline occurred over this period was for those aged 20 to 24. The participation of this group remained fairly steady at about 85% during the 25 years from 1948 to 1983.

The participation rate for women, on the other hand, grew 38.2% over this same period. The participation of women in the labor force, although growing, is still much less than that of men. The rate for women in 1983 was 52.9% as compared to 76.4% for men. The fastest growing segment for women was for those aged 25 to 34. For this age group the participation rate increased 51.9% - from 33.2% in 1948 to 69% in 1983. The next fastest growing segment was for those women aged 34 to 44; their participation rate increased 46.3% over this same period. Even though women have been entering the labor market in increasing numbers, for those women aged 65 and over, there has been a decline in the labor force participation rate. This segment's total participation in the labor force is so small, however, that this decline (from 9.1% to 7.8%) had little effect on the overall growth in the participation of women.

One interesting difference between the changes in the participation rates of men and women has been those changes in the 45 to 64 age group. While women in this age group have been entering the labor force in increasing numbers (the participation rate of these women increased on average by 42% from 1948 to 1983), men in this same age group have been leaving the labor force. The participation rate of these men fell an average of 17% during this same period.

For white workers as a whole, the participation rate has increased 9.5% since 1954, with the majority of the increase due to the participation of women. The same is true for black workers, whose participation rate increased 2.6% since 1972. In the past, white men have had a slightly higher participation rate than black men, 77.1% compared to 70.6% in 1983. The reverse is true for women. Black women have historically had a higher participation rate than white women, 54.2% compared to 52.7% in 1983, but this difference has been narrowing as a growing number of white women are entering the work force.

Although the total participation rates between white and black workers seem to be moving along similar paths, there are a number of striking differences between various age groups. For example, black men ages 65 and over have had a larger decline than any other age group in their labor force participation rate during the years 1972 to 1983. Their rates fell 72.86% as compared to a drop of 37.9% for white men in this age group. Another group, teenagers, shows a great deal of variation among different groups - black teenagers have had a drop in their participation rate of 7.4% from 1972 to 1983. During this same period white teenager participation increased 4.9%. This increase was due to large numbers of women in this age group entering the labor force. White women between the ages of 16 and 19 increased their participation rates by 11.7% during this period while white men's participation fell 1.2%. For black teenagers, the decrease for men was 16% and black women only increased 2.4%.

As can be seen in Table 2.3, tremendous gains have been made in the educational attainment of the civilian work force. Since 1958 the number of workers who had less than five years of schooling fell 43%, while the number completing four or more years of college increased 54.1%. The largest gains during the period 1959 - 1983 were made by black workers, who make up 10.4% of the work force. Black workers with less than five years of education fell 947.1% during this period, for black women the drop was 1266.7%. At the same time the number of black workers with at least some college increased 73.5%. In 1959 only 16.5% of all black workers had completed four years of high school. By 1948, 41.5% had.

As a group, more women than men in the work force had completed 4 years of high school - 44.4% compared to 37.8% of men in 1984. This was true for blacks, whites and those of Hispanic origin, suggesting that more men leave school early to enter the work force than women. However, this data doesn't include those who left school early who are not in the work force.

Those with the lowest levels of education continue to be those of Hispanic origin. Only 31.8% of Hispanic workers, who represent 5.6% of

the total civilian work force, had completed high school in 1984. This
is compared to the national average of 40.7%.

Table 2.4 presents unemployment rates by age group. We observe that
16-19 year olds have the largest unemployment rates and that those rates
have more than doubled from 1948-1983. The older cohorts have
demonstrated much lower rates but still substantial increases over time.
We will say more about this later.

Data on hours worked is given in Table 2.5. The "40-hour work week"
appears to be a fairly accurate description of the average weekly hours
of production workers in the United States. In 1983 the average weekly
hours of those producing durable and non-durable goods was 40.7 hours and
39.4 hours, respectively. The average weekly hours are calculated by
summing the hours reported by each firm in an industry and dividing by
the total number of workers in that firm. Industry averages are all
weighted averages of the figures for each component firm. The figures
for weekly hours are used by economists as lead indicators of swings in
the business cycle. Trends in average hours worked can indicate
structural changes within industries - the growth or decline in an
industry will often be an indication of future trends. It should be
noted that the data collected is for average hours paid for, rather than
scheduled hours or hours worked. Therefore the data reflect the effects
of factors such as absenteeism, turnover, part-time work and strikes.

The industries with the longest average weekly hours in 1983 were
those of petroleum and coal products and motor vehicles and equipment,
each averaging 43.9 and 43.3 hours per week, respectively. The lowest
were 36.2 hours for apparel and other textile products and 36.8 for
leather and leather products. In general workers in the durable goods
industries have a longer work week than do those in the non-durable goods
industries.

For most of the industries producing durable goods, the swings in
the average weekly hours of its workers have corresponded closely to the
swings in the post WWII business cycles. The average weekly hours tend
to peak just before or right at the peak of the business cycle - a nice
signal for industry watchers. The fit is not quite as good for the non-
durable goods industries. The industry producing chemicals and allied
products has had remarkable steady weekly hours in the post-war period,
averaging 41.6 hours per week, indicating that this industry is not as
vulnerable to swings in the business cycle. The printing and publishing

industry is another one whose hours have not varied much with swings in the business cycle. Instead, the weekly hours in this industry have been more or less steadily falling since 1947, averaging only 37.6 hours per week in 1983, a fall of 6.9% during the post-war period. This is probably indicative of the increasing technology and productivity of workers in this industry, rather than a decline in the industry.

Table 2.6 discusses overtime activity of the work force. The average weekly overtime hours of production workers are calculated in much the same way as the average weekly hours. That is, the sum of the overtime hours reported is divided by the number of production workers in each firm. The average for both durable and non-durable goods industries was 3 hours per week in 1983. The average overtime hours, like average weekly hours reflect swings in the business cycle - with a peak in overtime hours per week occurring just prior to the peak in the business cycle. The industries with the highest average overtime hours are the paper and allied products industry with 4.6 hours per week in 1983 and the stove, clay and glass products industries with 4.1 hours per week in 1983. The lowest overtime hours occurred in the tobacco and apparel industries, each averaging 1.2 hours and 1.3 hours in 1983.

We now turn to changes in the indexes of output per hour and related data given in Table 2.7. These data reflect changes in the efficiency of labor as well as changes in other factors of production that interact with labor input. Changes in technology, capital investment, human capital, energy and raw materials can all have a tremendous effect on productivity. Since 1947, the output per hour (gross domestic product divided by the hours of all persons engaged in production) has increased in the business, non-farm business and manufacturing sectors by 57.9%, 51.7% and 62%, respectively. For all three sectors, the index increased almost every year since there was a slight decline in productivity in 1979 and 1980 in the business and non-farm business sectors, but from 1980 to 1983, the index for these two sectors increased 4.7% for business and 4.9% for non-farm business. Productivity in the manufacturing sector increased 8.9% during this same period.

Another measure of productivity, output per person, has moved in a very similar manner to output per hour, although the gains in productivity measured this way have not been so great. In the post-war period, output per person has increased 50.4% in the business sector,

44.8 percent in the non-farm business sector, and 61.5 percent in the manufacturing sector.

The index for output shows an increase from 1947 to 1983 or 68.5% for the business sector, 69.4% for the non-farm business sector, and 67.5% for the manufacturing sector. The employment index also showed steady increases over this same period of 36.4% in the business sector and 44.7% in the manufacturing sector. While the employment index rose 15.6% during the same 26 year period, the index was subject to swings in the business cycle - the employment index has tended to peak with the business cycle. The same type of swings are apparent in the index of hours, although the movements are not nearly as pronounced in the business and non-farm business sectors as they are in the manufacturing sectors. Overall, the hours index increased 25.2% in the business sector, 36.7% in the non-farm business sector, and only 14.5% in the manufacturing sector during the post-war period.

Unemployment rates are now discussed in Table 2.8. The total unemployment rate for those ages 16 and over reached 9.6 percent in 1983, a drop of one percentage point from 1982's rate of 9.7%, the highest in the post-war era. The highest rate in 1983 was for black men which was 20.3% and the lowest was for white women at 7.9%. The unemployment rate represents the number of unemployed as a percent of the civilian labor force. For obvious reasons, the unemployment rate tends to drop during the recovery phase of the business cycle and to increase during recessions. The lowest unemployment rate in the post-war period was in 1953 when only 2.9% of the civilian work force was unemployed. During the late 50's and early 60's the rate rose, then fell to relatively low levels through the rest of the 60's. Unemployment began to increase in the 1970's, increasing more rapidly through the early 1980's. From 1972 to 1983 the total unemployment rate rose 41.7%, the increase was 49.5% for men, with only 28.3% for women. For black men alone the unemployment rate rose 54.2% during this period. For those workers of Hispanic origin, the unemployment rate rose 45.3%, 50.4% for men and 34.8% for women.

Although movements in the unemployment rate coincide with movements in the business cycle, there has been a secular trend upward in unemployment since the late 1960's.

Table 2.9 looks at the unemployment rate in terms of marital status. This shows that, not surprisingly, the lowest rates of unemployment occur

for those men who are married with their wives present. The highest rate
is for single men. Married women with their spouses present fare almost
as well as the married men category. Among women, single women have the
highest levels of unemployment. In general then, unemployment rates for
both men and women can be ranked from lowest to highest in the three
following segments: married with spouse present; widowed, divorced, or
separated; and single.

Table 2.10 presents unemployment rates by specific occupations. The
years 1982 and 1983 had the highest rates of unemployment in the post-war
era. During these two years the occupation with the highest unemployment
rate was that of construction workers. Although the unemployment rate
for these workers was 28.2% in 1982 and 25.8% in 1983, these unemployed
workers comprise only about 2% of the total unemployed. The occupation
with the next highest rates were for handlers, equipment cleaners,
helpers and laborers who made up about 9% of these unemployed. The group
with the highest percentage of those unemployed were operators,
fabricators, and laborers. With unemployment rates of about 16%, this
classification of worker made up over 30% of those unemployed. The
occupations with the lowest levels of unemployment were for manager,
executives, administrative and those with some professional specialty.
The unemployment rates for these groups were only about 3.3% much lower
than the national average of 9.65%.

Table 2.11 reports unemployment rates by selected industries. The
unemployment rate for experienced wage and salary workers was only
slightly lower at 9.2% than the rate for all civilian workers at 9.6% in
1983. Those classified as experienced wage and salary workers make up
about 85% of all civilian workers. In this category of workers the group
with the lowest rates of unemployment are those employed in finance,
insurance and real estate. The unemployment rate for this group was only
4.5% in 1983 and throughout the post-war period has been well below the
national average. The same is true for government workers, whose
unemployment rate was only 5.3% in 1983. Those experienced workers
employed in the service or transportation and public utilities sectors
also tend to enjoy unemployment rates below the national average. The
sectors with the highest unemployment rates are the construction, mining
and agricultural sectors. For all groups, unemployment has been rising
secularly since 1948.

Table 2.12 presents the number and rate of unemployment by duration. It is very illuminating to see that most of those unemployed were unemployed for a relatively short duration (less than five weeks) in 1948 and a complete flip-flop occurs in 1983 where now the rate has increased dramatically for longer duration rates. This suggests the reasons for unemployment have changed. It appears structural factors are much more important than they were in the late 1940s.

Table 2.13 presents unemployment rates for families. For families with unemployment present, the existence of at least one person in the family who is employed can make a tremendous difference in the urgency of unemployment. For married couple families with children under 18, 76.3% had at least one member of the family employed in 1982, 77.2% in 1983. This percentage was quite similar for white, black and Hispanic families. For families maintained by women with children under 18 years of age, only about 38% had at least one person employed. Of those, only about 28.6% had someone employed full-time present. For families maintained by men with children under 18 about 44% had some employed present. Of the 9.5 million families maintained by women, 17% or 1.6 million have at least one person unemployed. Only 2.4 million families were maintained by men in 1982, and of those only .4 million have one or more persons unemployed. Of the families maintained by women, 69.4% were white, 28.6% were black, and 7.6% were of Hispanic origin in 1982, with 10%, 6.6%, and 1.3% respectively with at least one person unemployed. For those maintained by men 81.3% were white, 15.15% were black, and 7.2% were of Hispanic origin during the same year, and 12.2%, 3.7% and 1.3% respectively, had one or more persons unemployed.

Table 2.14 is a synthesis of unemployment information by educational attainment. Unemployment rates for those workers with four or more years of college are, not surprisingly, lower than those of workers with any other level of educational attainment. In addition, the business cycle swings cause much less variation in this rate than those for other groups. For all workers the employment rate for this group was only 2.8% in 1984. This rate was very similar for both males and females in this category but varied greatly by race. For whites the unemployment rate was 2.6% in 1984, but was 6.3% for blacks and 3.5% for Hispanics.

The unemployment rates were highest for those workers who had between 1 and 3 years of high school education. The rate for this group was 17.1% in 1984 and again was quite similar for men and women, but varied greatly by race. In 1984 the rate for this group was 15.2% for whites, 27.3% for blacks and 18.4% for Hispanics.

Workers with only elementary education have tended to have somewhat lower unemployment rates than those with some high school - at least during the last 25 years. However, this group makes up only a small percentage of the total work force.

Table 2.15 reports the average hourly earnings of workers. These numbers are computed by dividing the reported payroll by the reported hours. For each industry, the figures are weighted averages. The data excludes overtime earnings, which are typically 1 1/2 times the regular rates. Among production workers on manufacturers payrolls, the average hourly earnings have increased about 86% since 1947. The highest paid workers during the 26 years from 1947 to 1983 have been in the petroleum and coal products industry, the motor vehicle and equipment industry and the blast furnaces and basic steel products industry. Workers in each of these industries earned on average $13.29, $12.12, and $12.89 respectively in 1983. The lowest paid workers have typically been in the furniture, textile, and apparel industries. Earnings for workers in these groups averaged $6.62, $6.18, and $5.37 per hour respectively in 1983.

Among industry groups in manufacturing most showed increases in average hourly earnings of 86% from 1947 to 1983. The least gain was made by workers in the apparel industry - their earnings rose only 78.4% during this period. And the greatest gains in earning were made by workers in the tobacco industry where earnings rose 91.3%.

Workers in the durable goods industries tended to have greater cyclical swings in earnings than did those in the non-durable industry, but all varied with the business cycle.

Table 2.16 summarizes the average weekly earning of production workers. For obvious reasons the average weekly earnings of production workers have behaved similarly to average hourly earnings. Again, the average weekly earnings rose about 86% from 1947 to 1983.

Table 2.1

Civilian Non-Institutional Population by Sex, Race and Age — 1948 - 1983

				16 YEARS AND OVER					
	Total	Men	Women	White	Men	Women	Black	Men	Women
1948	103,068	49,996	53,071	---	---	---	---	---	---
1949	103,994	50,321	53,670	---	---	---	---	---	---
1950	104,995	50,725	54,270	---	---	---	---	---	---
1951	104,621	49,727	54,895	---	---	---	---	---	---
1952	105,231	49,700	55,529	---	---	---	---	---	---
1953	107,056	50,750	56,305	---	---	---	---	---	---
1954	108,321	51,395	56,925	97,705	46,462	51,242	---	---	---
1955	109,683	52,109	57,574	98,880	47,076	51,802	---	---	---
1956	110,954	52,723	58,228	99,976	47,602	52,373	---	---	---
1957	112,265	53,315	58,951	101,119	48,119	52,998	---	---	---
1958	113,727	54,033	59,690	102,392	48,745	53,645	---	---	---
1959	115,329	54,793	60,534	103,803	49,408	54,392	---	---	---
1960	117,245	55,662	61,582	105,282	50,065	55,214	---	---	---
1961	118,771	56,286	62,484	106,604	50,608	55,993	---	---	---
1962	120,153	56,831	63,321	107,715	51,054	56,660	---	---	---
1963	122,416	57,921	64,494	109,705	52,031	57,672	---	---	---
1964	124,485	58,847	65,637	111,534	52,869	58,663	---	---	---
1965	126,513	59,782	66,731	113,284	53,681	59,601	---	---	---
1966	128,058	60,262	67,795	114,566	54,061	60,503	---	---	---
1967	129,874	60,905	68,968	116,100	54,608	61,470	---	---	---
1968	132,028	61,847	70,179	117,948	55,434	62,512	---	---	---
1969	134,335	62,898	71,436	119,913	56,348	63,563	---	---	---
1970	137,085	64,304	72,782	122,174	57,516	64,656	---	---	---
1971	140,216	65,942	74,274	124,758	58,900	65,857	---	---	---
1972	144,126	67,835	76,290	127,906	60,473	67,431	14,526	6,538	7,988
1973	147,096	69,292	77,804	130,097	61,577	68,517	14,917	6,704	8,214
1974	150,120	70,808	79,312	132,417	62,791	69,623	15,336	6,875	8,462
1975	153,153	72,291	80,860	134,790	63,981	70,810	15,751	7,060	8,691
1976	156,150	73,759	82,390	137,106	65,132	71,974	16,196	7,265	8,931
1977	159,033	75,193	83,840	139,380	66,301	73,077	16,605	7,431	9,174
1978	161,910	76,576	85,334	141,612	67,401	74,213	16,970	7,577	9,394
1979	164,863	78,020	86,843	143,894	68,547	75,347	17,397	7,761	9,636
1980	167,745	79,398	88,348	146,122	69,634	76,489	17,824	7,944	9,880
1981	170,130	80,511	89,618	147,908	70,480	77,428	18,219	8,117	10,102
1982	172,271	81,523	90,748	149,441	71,211	78,230	18,584	8,283	10,300
1983	174,215	82,531	91,684	150,805	71,922	78,884	18,925	8,447	10,477

Source: Handbook of Labor Statistics, U.S. Dept. of Labor, June, 1985, Bulletin 2217, pp. 10-13

Table 2.2

Civilian Labor Force Participation Rates by Sex, Rate and Age — 1948 - 1983

	16 Years & Over	16 TO 19 YEARS			20 YEARS & OVER						
		Total	16 to 17 Years	18 to 19 Years	Total	20 to 24 Years	25 to 34 Years	35 to 44 Years	45 to 54 Years	55 to 64 Years	65 Years & Over
Total											
1948	58.8	52.5	41.7	63.4	59.4	64.1	63.1	66.7	65.1	56.9	27.0
1949	58.9	52.2	41.2	63.3	59.5	64.9	63.2	67.2	65.3	56.9	27.3
1950	59.2	51.8	40.7	62.6	59.9	65.9	63.1	67.5	66.4	56.2	26.7
1951	59.2	52.2	42.6	62.6	59.8	64.8	63.2	67.6	67.2	56.7	25.8
1952	59.0	51.3	42.7	61.2	59.9	62.2	63.5	68.0	67.5	56.9	24.8
1953	58.9	50.2	40.7	60.9	59.7	61.6	64.2	68.9	68.1	57.5	24.8
1954	58.8	48.3	37.9	59.1	59.6	61.6	64.0	68.8	68.4	58.0	24.3
1955	59.3	48.9	38.5	60.7	59.6	62.7	64.3	68.9	69.7	58.7	23.9
1956	60.0	50.9	41.9	61.2	60.1	64.1	64.8	69.7	70.5	59.5	24.1
1957	59.6	49.6	40.2	60.4	60.7	64.0	64.8	69.5	70.9	60.8	24.3
1958	59.5	47.4	37.3	59.4	60.4	64.3	64.9	69.6	71.5	60.1	22.9
1959	59.3	46.7	36.9	58.9	60.5	64.3	65.0	69.5	71.9	60.5	21.8
1960	59.4	47.5	37.6	59.5	60.4	65.2	65.0	69.4	72.2	61.0	21.1
1961	59.3	46.9	36.3	58.4	60.5	65.3	65.4	69.5	72.1	60.9	20.8
1962	58.8	46.1	34.9	58.2	60.0	65.1	65.2	69.7	72.2	61.5	20.1
1963	58.7	45.2	34.5	58.5	60.1	65.1	65.6	70.1	72.5	61.5	19.1
1964	58.7	44.5	35.1	57.2	60.2	66.1	65.8	70.0	72.9	62.0	17.9
1965	58.9	45.7	35.8	57.1	60.3	66.4	66.4	70.7	72.5	61.9	18.0
1966	59.2	48.2	38.5	58.3	60.5	66.5	67.1	71.0	72.7	61.9	17.8
1967	59.6	48.4	39.0	58.4	60.9	67.1	68.2	71.6	72.7	62.2	17.2
1968	59.6	48.3	39.1	58.5	60.9	67.0	68.6	72.0	72.8	62.3	17.2
1969	60.1	49.4	40.5	59.3	61.3	68.2	69.1	72.5	73.4	62.2	17.3
1970	60.4	49.9	41.0	59.8	61.6	69.2	69.7	73.1	73.5	62.1	17.0
1971	60.2	49.7	40.7	59.6	61.4	69.3	69.9	73.2	73.2	61.8	16.2
1972	60.4	51.9	42.3	62.3	61.7	70.8	70.9	73.3	72.7	61.3	15.6
1973	60.8	53.7	44.5	63.6	62.0	72.6	72.3	74.0	72.5	60.0	14.6
1974	61.3	54.8	45.5	64.8	62.1	74.0	73.6	74.6	72.7	58.4	14.0
1975	61.2	54.0	44.4	64.1	62.4	73.9	74.4	75.0	72.6	57.8	13.7
1976	61.6	54.5	44.6	64.7	63.0	74.7	75.7	76.0	72.5	57.2	13.1
1977	62.3	56.0	46.2	66.2	63.8	75.7	77.0	77.0	72.8	56.6	13.0
1978	63.2	57.8	48.6	67.3	64.3	76.8	78.3	78.1	73.5	56.3	13.3
1979	63.7	57.9	48.6	67.2	64.5	77.5	79.2	79.2	74.3	56.2	13.1
1980	63.8	56.7	46.9	66.5	64.8	77.2	79.9	80.0	74.9	55.7	12.5
1981	63.9	55.4	45.2	65.6	65.0	77.3	80.5	80.7	75.7	55.0	12.2
1982	64.0	54.1	43.2	64.5	65.0	77.1	81.0	81.2	75.9	55.1	11.9
1983	64.0	53.5	41.6	64.6	65.0	77.2	81.3	81.6	76.0	54.5	11.7

See end of table for data source.

ALLEGHENY COLLEGE LIBRARY

Table 2.2 (Continued)

	16 Years & Over	16 TO 19 YEARS			20 YEARS & OVER						
		Total	16 to 17 Years	18 to 19 Years	Total	20 to 24 Years	25 to 34 Years	35 to 44 Years	45 to 54 Years	55 to 64 Years	65 Years & Over
Men											
1948	86.6	63.7	52.1	76.4	88.6	84.6	95.9	97.9	95.8	89.5	46.8
1949	86.4	62.8	51.2	75.4	88.5	86.6	95.8	97.9	95.6	87.5	47.0
1950	86.4	63.2	51.3	75.8	88.4	87.9	96.0	97.6	95.8	86.9	45.8
1951	86.3	63.0	53.0	75.0	88.2	88.4	96.9	97.5	95.9	87.2	44.9
1952	86.3	61.3	51.9	73.5	88.3	88.1	97.5	97.8	96.2	87.5	42.6
1953	86.0	60.7	50.4	73.4	88.0	87.7	97.4	98.2	96.5	87.9	41.6
1954	85.5	58.0	47.1	71.5	87.8	86.9	97.3	98.1	96.4	88.7	40.5
1955	85.4	58.9	48.1	72.2	87.6	86.9	97.6	98.1	96.6	87.9	39.6
1956	85.5	60.5	51.0	72.4	87.6	87.8	97.3	97.9	96.6	88.5	40.0
1957	84.8	59.1	49.3	71.6	86.9	87.1	97.1	97.3	96.3	87.5	37.5
1958	84.2	56.6	46.5	69.7	86.6	86.9	97.1	97.9	96.3	87.8	35.6
1959	83.7	55.8	45.0	70.5	86.3	87.8	97.4	97.8	96.0	87.4	34.2
1960	83.3	56.1	46.0	69.3	88.0	88.1	97.5	97.7	95.7	86.8	33.1
1961	82.9	54.6	44.1	66.8	85.7	87.8	97.5	97.6	95.6	87.3	31.7
1962	82.0	53.8	42.6	66.7	84.8	86.9	97.2	97.6	95.6	86.2	30.3
1963	81.4	52.9	41.8	68.0	84.4	86.1	97.1	97.5	95.7	86.2	28.4
1964	81.0	52.4	42.8	66.6	84.2	86.1	97.3	97.3	95.7	85.6	28.0
1965	80.7	53.8	43.9	65.9	83.9	85.8	97.2	97.3	95.6	84.6	27.9
1966	80.4	55.3	46.3	65.3	83.6	85.1	97.3	97.2	95.3	84.5	27.1
1967	80.4	55.5	47.0	65.6	83.4	84.4	97.2	97.3	95.2	84.4	27.1
1968	80.1	55.1	46.4	65.4	83.1	82.8	96.9	97.1	95.2	84.3	27.3
1969	79.8	55.9	47.3	65.9	82.8	82.8	96.7	96.9	94.9	83.4	27.2
1970	79.7	56.1	47.0	66.7	82.6	83.3	96.4	96.9	94.6	83.0	26.8
1971	79.1	56.1	46.9	66.6	82.1	83.0	95.9	96.5	94.3	82.1	25.5
1972	78.9	58.1	47.9	69.6	81.6	83.9	95.7	96.4	93.9	80.4	24.3
1973	78.8	59.7	49.9	70.7	81.3	85.2	95.8	96.2	93.2	78.2	22.7
1974	78.7	60.7	50.5	72.0	81.0	85.9	95.2	96.0	93.0	77.3	22.4
1975	77.9	59.1	48.6	70.6	80.3	84.5	95.2	95.6	92.2	75.6	21.6
1976	77.5	59.3	48.5	70.8	79.8	85.2	95.3	95.4	92.1	74.3	20.2
1977	77.7	60.9	50.2	72.3	79.7	85.6	95.3	95.7	91.6	73.8	20.0
1978	77.9	62.0	51.8	72.8	79.8	85.9	95.3	95.7	91.1	73.3	20.4
1979	77.8	61.5	51.6	71.9	79.8	86.4	95.2	95.5	91.3	72.8	20.0
1980	77.4	60.5	50.1	71.3	79.4	85.9	94.9	95.4	91.2	72.1	19.0
1981	77.0	59.0	47.9	70.4	79.0	85.5	94.7	95.3	91.4	70.6	18.4
1982	76.6	56.7	45.4	67.9	78.7	84.9	94.2	95.3	91.2	70.2	17.8
1983	76.4	56.2	43.2	68.6	78.5	84.8	94.2	95.2	91.2	69.4	17.4

ALLEGHENY COLLEGE LIBRARY

Table 2.2 (Continued)

Women	16 Years & Over	16 TO 19 YEARS			20 YEARS & OVER						
		Total	16 to 17 Years	18 to 19 Years	Total	20 to 24 Years	25 to 34 Years	35 to 44 Years	45 to 54 Years	55 to 64 Years	65 Years & Over
1948	32.7	42.0	31.4	52.1	31.8	45.3	33.2	36.9	35.0	24.3	9.1
1949	33.1	42.4	31.2	53.0	32.3	45.0	33.4	38.1	35.9	25.3	9.6
1950	33.9	41.0	30.1	51.3	33.3	46.0	34.0	39.1	37.6	27.0	9.7
1951	34.6	42.4	32.2	52.5	34.0	46.5	35.4	39.8	39.7	27.6	8.9
1952	34.7	42.2	33.4	51.3	34.1	44.7	35.4	40.4	40.1	28.7	9.1
1953	34.4	40.7	31.0	50.7	33.9	44.3	34.0	41.3	40.4	29.1	10.0
1954	34.6	39.4	28.7	48.7	34.2	45.1	34.4	41.2	41.2	30.0	9.3
1955	35.7	39.7	28.9	50.9	35.4	45.9	34.9	41.6	43.8	32.5	10.6
1956	36.9	42.2	32.8	51.9	36.4	46.3	35.4	43.1	45.5	34.9	10.8
1957	36.9	41.1	31.1	51.4	36.5	45.9	35.6	43.3	46.5	34.5	10.5
1958	37.1	39.0	28.1	50.8	36.9	46.3	35.6	43.4	47.8	35.2	10.3
1959	37.1	38.2	28.8	49.0	37.1	45.1	35.3	43.4	49.0	36.6	10.2
1960	37.7	39.3	29.1	50.9	37.6	46.1	36.0	43.8	49.9	37.2	10.8
1961	38.1	39.7	28.5	51.0	38.0	47.0	36.4	44.1	50.1	37.9	10.7
1962	37.9	39.0	27.1	50.8	37.8	47.3	36.3	44.9	50.0	38.7	10.0
1963	38.3	38.0	27.1	50.4	38.3	47.5	37.2	45.0	50.6	39.7	9.6
1964	38.7	37.0	27.4	49.2	38.9	49.4	37.2	46.1	51.4	40.2	10.1
1965	39.3	38.0	27.7	49.3	39.4	49.9	38.5	46.8	50.9	41.1	10.0
1966	40.3	41.4	30.7	52.0	40.1	51.5	39.8	48.1	51.7	41.8	9.6
1967	41.1	41.6	31.0	52.4	41.1	53.3	41.9	48.9	51.8	42.4	9.6
1968	41.6	41.9	31.7	52.4	41.6	54.5	42.6	49.9	52.3	42.4	9.9
1969	42.7	43.2	33.7	53.3	42.7	56.7	43.7	51.1	53.8	43.1	9.7
1970	43.3	44.0	34.9	53.6	43.3	57.7	45.0	51.6	54.4	43.0	9.5
1971	43.4	43.4	34.3	53.1	43.7	57.7	45.6	52.0	54.3	42.9	9.3
1972	43.9	45.8	36.7	55.5	44.4	59.1	47.8	53.3	53.9	42.1	8.9
1973	44.7	47.8	39.1	56.8	45.3	61.1	50.4	54.7	53.7	41.1	8.1
1974	45.7	49.1	40.4	58.0	46.0	63.1	52.6	55.8	54.6	40.7	8.2
1975	46.3	49.8	40.2	56.1	47.0	64.1	54.9	57.8	54.6	40.9	8.2
1976	47.3	51.2	40.7	58.9	48.1	65.0	57.3	59.6	55.0	41.0	8.1
1977	48.4	53.7	42.1	60.3	49.6	66.5	59.7	61.6	55.8	40.9	8.3
1978	50.0	54.2	45.4	62.0	50.6	68.3	62.2	63.6	57.1	41.3	8.3
1979	50.9	52.9	45.6	62.7	51.3	69.0	63.9	65.5	58.3	41.7	8.1
1980	51.5	51.8	43.6	61.9	52.1	68.9	65.5	66.8	59.9	41.3	8.1
1981	52.1	51.4	42.5	60.9	52.7	69.6	66.7	68.0	61.1	41.4	8.0
1982	52.6	50.8	41.0	61.2	53.1	69.8	68.0	68.7	61.6	41.8	7.9
1983	52.9	50.8	39.9	60.7	53.1	69.9	69.0	68.7	61.9	41.5	7.8

Table 2.2 (Continued)

	16 TO 19 YEARS			20 YEARS & OVER							
	16 Years & Over	Total	16 to 17 Years	18 to 19 Years	Total	20 to 24 Years	25 to 34 Years	35 to 44 Years	45 to 54 Years	55 to 64 Years	65 Years & Over
White											
1954	58.2	48.8	38.2	60.5	58.9	61.0	63.5	68.0	67.9	58.4	23.7
1955	58.7	49.3	39.0	61.0	59.5	62.4	64.0	68.3	69.2	59.3	23.9
1956	59.4	51.3	42.4	61.5	60.1	64.1	64.0	68.9	70.1	60.6	24.2
1957	59.1	50.3	40.9	61.0	59.8	63.7	64.1	68.8	70.5	59.9	22.8
1958	58.9	47.9	37.8	60.0	59.8	64.1	64.2	68.8	71.0	60.3	21.7
1959	58.7	47.4	37.7	59.7	59.7	63.7	64.3	68.7	71.5	60.7	21.0
1960	58.8	47.9	38.1	59.9	59.8	64.8	64.7	68.6	71.7	60.6	20.8
1961	58.8	47.4	36.9	58.6	59.9	65.5	64.8	68.8	71.7	61.3	20.0
1962	58.3	46.6	35.5	58.4	59.9	65.0	64.4	69.0	71.8	61.3	20.0
1963	58.2	45.7	35.1	58.9	59.4	64.9	64.8	69.4	72.3	61.8	19.0
1964	58.2	45.1	36.0	57.7	59.4	65.8	64.9	69.5	72.5	61.8	17.9
1965	58.4	46.5	36.7	57.7	59.6	65.7	65.6	70.1	72.2	61.7	17.8
1966	58.7	49.1	39.5	58.9	59.7	66.0	66.3	70.4	72.5	61.9	17.7
1967	59.2	49.2	40.2	59.1	59.8	66.6	67.4	71.2	72.7	62.3	17.1
1968	59.3	49.3	40.5	60.2	60.3	66.6	67.9	71.7	73.3	62.1	17.0
1969	59.9	50.6	42.0	61.0	60.4	67.9	68.4	72.3	73.5	62.1	17.1
1970	60.2	51.4	42.8	61.0	60.9	69.2	69.1	72.9	73.4	61.8	17.2
1971	60.1	51.6	42.9	61.2	61.2	69.6	69.3	73.0	72.9	61.3	16.8
1972	60.4	54.1	44.8	64.1	61.1	71.2	70.4	73.2	72.7	60.3	16.1
1973	60.8	56.0	47.3	65.4	61.2	73.3	72.0	73.9	73.0	58.6	15.4
1974	61.4	57.3	48.4	66.8	61.4	74.8	73.4	74.6	73.0	58.0	14.4
1975	61.5	56.7	47.3	66.5	61.9	75.2	74.4	75.1	73.0	57.4	13.9
1976	61.8	57.5	47.9	67.5	62.0	76.0	75.6	76.1	73.2	56.9	13.6
1977	62.5	59.3	49.8	69.0	62.3	77.0	77.0	77.1	73.8	56.6	13.0
1978	63.3	60.8	52.1	69.9	62.9	77.1	78.3	78.1	74.6	56.4	13.0
1979	63.9	61.1	52.2	70.1	63.6	78.1	79.4	79.3	75.4	56.5	12.9
1980	64.1	60.0	50.4	69.5	64.2	78.9	80.2	80.3	76.2	56.0	13.1
1981	64.3	58.9	48.8	68.8	64.5	78.7	81.0	81.0	76.4	55.2	12.9
1982	64.3	57.5	47.0	67.5	64.8	79.1	81.6	81.5	76.5	55.3	12.2
1983	64.3	56.9	45.4	67.7	65.0	79.0	81.8	81.9	76.5	54.7	11.8

Table 2.2 (Continued)

White Men	16 Years & Over	16 TO 19 YEARS			20 YEARS & OVER							
		Total	16 to 17 Years	18 to 19 Years	Total	20 to 24 Years	25 to 34 Years	35 to 44 Years	45 to 54 Years	55 to 64 Years	65 Years & Over
1954	85.6	57.6	47.1	70.5	87.8	86.3	97.5	98.2	96.8	89.1	40.4
1955	85.4	58.6	48.1	71.7	87.5	86.5	97.8	98.2	96.7	88.4	39.6
1956	85.6	60.4	51.3	71.8	87.6	87.6	97.4	98.1	96.8	88.9	40.0
1957	84.8	59.2	49.6	71.5	86.6	86.6	97.2	98.0	96.7	88.0	37.7
1958	84.3	56.5	46.8	69.4	86.6	86.7	97.2	98.0	96.6	88.2	35.7
1959	83.8	55.9	45.4	70.3	86.3	87.3	97.5	98.0	96.3	87.9	34.3
1960	83.0	55.9	46.0	69.0	86.0	87.8	97.7	97.9	96.1	87.2	33.3
1961	83.0	54.5	44.3	66.2	85.7	87.6	97.7	97.9	95.9	87.8	31.9
1962	82.1	53.8	42.9	66.4	84.9	86.5	97.4	97.8	96.0	86.7	30.6
1963	81.5	53.1	42.4	67.8	84.4	85.8	97.4	97.8	96.2	86.6	28.4
1964	81.1	52.7	43.5	66.6	84.2	85.7	97.5	97.6	96.1	86.1	27.9
1965	80.8	54.1	44.6	65.8	83.9	85.3	97.4	97.7	95.9	85.2	27.9
1966	80.6	55.9	47.1	65.4	83.6	84.4	97.5	97.6	95.8	84.9	27.2
1967	80.6	56.3	47.9	66.1	83.5	84.0	97.5	97.7	95.6	84.9	27.1
1968	80.4	55.9	47.7	65.7	83.2	82.4	97.2	97.6	95.4	84.7	27.4
1969	80.2	56.8	48.8	66.3	83.0	82.6	97.0	97.4	95.1	83.9	27.3
1970	80.0	57.5	48.9	67.4	82.8	83.3	96.7	97.3	94.9	83.3	26.7
1971	79.6	57.9	49.3	67.8	82.3	83.2	96.3	97.0	94.7	82.6	25.6
1972	79.6	60.1	50.2	71.1	82.0	84.3	96.0	97.0	94.0	81.1	24.4
1973	79.4	62.0	52.7	72.3	81.6	85.8	96.2	96.8	93.5	78.9	22.7
1974	79.4	62.9	53.3	73.6	81.4	86.6	96.3	96.7	93.0	78.0	22.4
1975	78.7	61.9	51.8	72.8	80.7	85.5	95.8	96.4	92.9	76.4	21.7
1976	78.4	62.3	51.8	73.5	80.3	86.3	95.9	96.0	92.5	75.2	20.2
1977	78.5	64.0	53.8	74.9	80.2	86.8	96.0	96.2	92.1	74.6	20.0
1978	78.6	65.0	55.3	75.3	80.1	87.3	95.9	96.3	92.1	73.7	20.3
1979	78.6	64.8	55.3	74.5	80.1	87.6	96.0	96.4	92.2	73.4	20.0
1980	78.2	63.7	53.6	74.1	79.8	87.2	95.9	96.2	92.1	73.1	19.1
1981	77.9	62.4	51.5	73.5	79.5	87.0	95.8	96.1	92.4	71.5	18.5
1982	77.4	60.0	49.3	70.5	79.2	86.3	95.6	96.0	92.2	71.0	17.9
1983	77.1	59.4	46.9	71.3	78.9	86.1	95.2	96.0	91.9	70.0	17.7

Table 2.2 (Continued)

	16 Years & Over	16 TO 19 YEARS			20 YEARS & OVER						
		Total	16 to 17 Years	18 to 19 Years	Total	20 to 24 Years	25 to 34 Years	35 to 44 Years	45 to 54 Years	55 to 64 Years	65 Years & Over
White Women											
1954	33.3	40.6	29.3	52.1	32.7	44.4	32.5	39.3	39.8	29.1	9.1
1955	34.5	40.7	29.9	52.0	34.0	45.8	32.8	40.0	42.7	31.8	10.5
1956	35.5	43.1	33.5	53.0	35.1	46.5	33.2	41.5	44.4	34.0	10.6
1957	35.7	42.2	32.1	52.6	35.2	45.8	33.6	41.5	45.4	33.7	10.2
1958	35.8	40.1	28.8	52.3	35.5	46.0	33.6	41.4	46.5	34.5	10.1
1959	36.0	39.6	29.9	50.8	35.6	44.5	33.4	41.4	47.8	35.7	10.0
1960	36.5	40.3	30.0	51.9	36.2	45.7	34.1	41.5	48.6	36.2	10.6
1961	36.9	40.6	29.4	51.9	36.6	46.9	34.3	41.8	48.9	37.2	10.6
1962	36.7	39.8	27.9	51.6	36.5	47.1	34.1	42.2	48.9	38.0	10.5
1963	37.2	38.7	27.8	51.3	37.0	47.3	34.8	43.1	49.5	38.9	9.8
1964	37.5	37.8	28.4	49.6	37.5	48.8	35.0	43.3	50.2	39.4	9.4
1965	38.1	39.2	28.7	50.6	38.0	49.2	36.3	44.4	49.9	40.3	9.9
1966	39.2	42.6	31.8	53.1	38.8	51.0	37.7	45.0	50.6	41.1	9.7
1967	40.1	42.5	32.3	52.7	39.8	53.1	39.7	46.4	50.9	41.9	9.4
1968	40.7	43.0	33.0	53.3	40.4	54.0	40.6	47.5	51.5	42.0	9.3
1969	41.8	44.6	35.2	54.6	41.5	56.4	41.7	48.6	53.0	42.6	9.4
1970	42.6	45.6	36.6	55.0	42.2	57.7	43.2	49.9	53.7	42.6	9.7
1971	42.6	45.4	36.3	55.0	42.3	58.0	43.7	50.2	53.6	42.5	9.5
1972	43.2	48.1	39.3	57.4	42.7	59.4	46.0	50.7	53.4	41.9	9.3
1973	44.1	50.1	41.7	58.8	43.5	61.7	48.7	52.2	53.4	40.7	9.0
1974	45.2	51.7	43.3	60.4	44.4	63.9	51.3	53.6	54.3	40.4	8.7
1975	45.9	51.5	42.7	60.4	45.3	65.5	53.8	54.9	54.3	40.6	8.0
1976	46.9	52.8	43.8	61.7	46.2	66.3	56.0	57.1	54.7	40.7	8.0
1977	48.0	54.5	45.8	63.3	47.3	67.8	58.5	58.9	55.3	40.7	7.9
1978	49.4	56.7	48.8	64.6	48.7	69.3	61.2	60.7	56.7	41.1	8.1
1979	50.5	57.4	49.0	65.7	49.8	70.5	63.1	63.0	58.1	41.5	8.1
1980	51.2	56.2	47.2	65.1	50.6	70.6	64.8	65.0	59.6	40.9	7.9
1981	51.9	55.4	46.1	64.2	51.5	71.5	66.4	66.4	60.9	40.9	7.9
1982	52.4	55.0	44.6	64.6	52.2	71.8	67.8	67.5	61.4	41.5	7.8
1983	52.7	54.5	43.9	64.1	52.5	72.1	68.7	68.2	61.9	41.1	7.8

Table 2.2 (Continued)

	16 Years & Over	16 TO 19 YEARS			20 YEARS & OVER						
		Total	16 to 17 Years	18 to 19 Years	Total	20 to 24 Years	25 to 34 Years	35 to 44 Years	45 to 54 Years	55 to 64 Years	65 Years & Over
Black											
1972	59.9	39.1	27.6	51.8	63.3	68.6	74.9	74.4	70.0	56.9	17.5
1973	60.2	39.8	28.1	52.6	63.4	69.7	75.7	74.5	70.3	55.9	16.0
1974	59.8	39.8	28.3	52.6	63.0	69.8	75.8	74.6	69.1	54.7	15.1
1975	58.8	38.2	27.4	50.0	62.0	66.1	75.6	74.1	69.0	54.3	14.9
1976	59.0	37.0	26.1	48.1	62.5	66.8	77.1	74.9	68.6	53.4	14.9
1977	59.8	37.9	25.8	50.7	63.2	68.2	78.3	75.9	69.0	53.7	14.5
1978	61.5	41.0	29.1	53.6	64.5	68.9	79.6	77.4	70.4	54.8	15.3
1979	61.4	40.1	29.1	51.6	64.1	70.0	79.2	77.9	71.1	53.5	14.5
1980	61.0	38.9	27.8	50.4	64.1	69.0	79.5	77.4	71.4	52.6	13.0
1981	60.8	37.7	26.5	49.2	64.2	69.2	78.5	78.4	71.2	52.8	12.0
1982	61.0	36.6	23.9	49.0	64.3	68.6	78.7	79.8	71.1	52.3	11.5
1983	61.5	36.4	22.7	49.5	64.9	68.4	79.8	80.2	72.1	52.5	10.5
Men											
1972	73.6	46.3	34.3	60.2	78.5	82.7	92.7	91.1	85.4	72.5	24.2
1973	73.4	45.7	32.3	61.2	78.4	83.7	91.8	91.0	87.4	69.5	22.3
1974	72.9	46.7	34.0	61.9	77.6	83.6	92.8	90.4	84.0	68.9	21.6
1975	70.0	42.6	29.8	57.2	76.0	78.7	91.6	89.4	83.5	67.7	20.7
1976	70.0	41.3	29.0	55.0	75.4	79.0	90.7	89.9	82.4	65.5	19.8
1977	70.6	43.2	30.2	58.0	75.6	79.2	90.9	91.0	82.0	65.1	20.0
1978	71.5	44.9	31.9	59.7	76.2	78.8	90.8	90.5	83.2	67.9	21.1
1979	71.3	43.6	30.7	58.1	76.3	80.7	90.9	90.4	84.5	64.8	19.5
1980	70.3	43.2	30.9	56.6	75.1	79.9	88.9	89.1	83.0	61.9	16.9
1981	70.0	41.6	29.2	55.0	74.5	79.2	89.2	89.3	82.7	62.1	16.0
1982	70.1	39.8	24.6	55.3	74.7	78.7	89.0	89.8	82.2	61.9	15.9
1983	70.6	39.9	24.7	55.0	75.2	79.4	89.0	89.7	84.5	62.6	14.0
Women											
1972	48.7	32.2	21.0	44.3	51.2	57.0	60.8	61.4	57.2	44.0	12.6
1973	49.3	34.2	23.9	45.1	51.6	58.0	62.7	61.7	56.4	44.7	11.4
1974	49.0	33.4	22.7	44.6	51.4	58.8	62.8	62.2	56.6	42.8	10.4
1975	48.8	34.2	25.0	43.8	51.1	55.9	62.8	62.0	56.8	43.1	10.7
1976	49.8	32.9	23.2	42.6	52.5	56.9	66.7	63.0	57.9	43.7	11.3
1977	50.8	32.9	21.5	44.3	53.6	59.3	68.5	64.1	59.4	43.7	10.5
1978	53.1	37.3	26.4	48.3	55.5	62.7	70.6	67.2	59.6	43.8	11.1
1979	53.1	36.8	27.5	45.9	55.4	61.5	67.2	68.0	59.4	44.0	10.9
1980	53.1	34.9	24.6	45.0	55.6	60.2	70.1	66.1	61.4	44.8	10.2
1981	53.5	34.0	23.3	44.0	56.0	61.1	70.5	69.8	62.0	45.4	9.3
1982	53.7	33.5	23.3	43.3	56.2	60.1	70.0	71.7	62.4	44.8	8.5
1983	54.2	33.0	20.8	44.4	56.8	59.1	72.3	72.6	62.3	44.8	8.2

Source: Handbook of Labor Statistics, U.S. Dept. of Labor, June 1985, Bulletin 2217, pp. 18-21.

Table 2.3

Educational Attainment of Civilian Labor Force

by Sex, Race and Hispanic Origin for Selected Years

| | | | PERCENT DISTRIBUTION | | | | | | |
| | | | ELEMENTARY | | HIGH SCHOOL | | COLLEGE | | |
	Total	Total	Less Than 5 Years	5 to 8 Years	1 to 3 Years	4 Years	1 to 3 Years	4 Years Or More	School Years Completed
Total									
1959	65,842	100.0	5.3	25.2	19.8	30.7	9.3	9.6	12.0
1962	67,988	100.0	4.6	22.4	19.3	32.1	10.7	11.0	12.1
1964	69,926	100.0	3.7	20.9	19.2	34.5	10.6	11.2	12.2
1965	71,129	100.0	3.7	19.6	19.2	35.5	10.5	11.6	12.2
1966	71,958	100.0	3.3	18.9	19.0	36.3	10.8	11.8	12.2
1967	73,218	100.0	3.1	17.9	18.7	36.6	11.8	12.0	12.3
1968	75,101	100.0	2.9	16.8	18.2	37.5	12.2	12.4	12.3
1969	76,753	100.0	2.7	15.9	17.8	38.4	12.6	12.6	12.4
1970	78,955	100.0	2.4	15.1	17.3	39.0	13.3	12.9	12.4
1971	80,128	100.0	2.2	14.1	16.7	39.4	13.9	13.6	12.4
1972	85,832	100.0	2.1	12.9	19.2	38.7	13.6	13.6	12.5
1973	87,958	100.0	2.0	11.6	18.6	39.4	14.2	14.1	12.5
1974	90,477	100.0	1.8	10.9	18.1	39.2	15.1	15.0	12.5
1975	92,328	100.0	1.7	10.0	17.6	39.6	15.5	15.7	12.5
1976	94,329	100.0	1.5	9.1	17.2	39.7	16.1	16.5	12.6
1977	97,243	100.0	1.5	8.6	17.2	39.4	16.4	16.9	12.6
1978	100,125	100.0	1.4	8.2	16.8	39.5	17.1	16.9	12.6
1979	103,478	100.0	1.4	7.5	16.0	39.9	17.6	17.6	12.6
1980	105,449	100.0	1.2	7.1	15.5	40.1	17.9	18.2	12.7
1981	107,721	100.0	1.2	6.7	14.9	40.9	17.9	18.3	12.7
1982	108,762	100.0	1.1	6.2	14.3	41.0	18.0	19.3	12.7
1983	109,814	100.0	1.1	5.7	13.5	40.5	18.7	20.5	12.7
1984	111,943	100.0	1.0	5.5	13.0	40.7	19.0	20.9	12.8

Source: Handbook of Labor Statistics, U.S. Dept. of Labor, June, 1985

Table 2.3 (Continued)

		ELEMENTARY		HIGH SCHOOL		COLLEGE		
				PERCENT DISTRIBUTION				
	Total	Total	Less Than 5 Years	5 to 8 Years	1 to 3 Years	4 Years	1 to 3 Years	4 Years Or More	School Years Completed
All Men									
1959	44,286	100.0	6.1	26.9	20.2	27.2	9.1	10.4	11.5
1962	45,011	100.0	5.4	24.2	19.6	28.7	10.4	11.7	12.0
1964	45,600	100.0	4.4	22.5	19.4	31.1	10.6	12.1	12.1
1965	46,258	100.0	4.4	21.3	19.4	32.0	10.5	12.4	12.2
1966	46,356	100.0	3.9	20.6	19.3	32.6	10.7	12.8	12.2
1967	46,571	100.0	3.7	19.7	18.8	32.9	11.7	13.2	12.2
1968	47,255	100.0	3.4	18.6	18.6	33.8	12.2	13.6	12.3
1969	47,862	100.0	3.2	17.6	18.1	34.4	12.6	13.9	12.3
1970	48,891	100.0	2.9	16.9	17.5	35.1	13.5	14.2	12.4
1971	49,553	100.0	2.7	15.8	16.9	35.7	14.0	14.9	12.4
1972	52,705	100.0	2.5	14.5	19.2	35.0	13.8	15.0	12.4
1973	53,761	100.0	2.4	13.1	18.6	35.8	14.5	15.6	12.4
1974	54,767	100.0	2.3	12.4	18.0	36.0	14.9	16.4	12.5
1975	55,346	100.0	2.2	11.1	17.6	36.2	15.6	17.3	12.5
1976	55,929	100.0	1.9	10.2	17.2	36.4	16.1	18.2	12.6
1977	57,189	100.0	1.9	9.8	17.3	35.9	16.5	18.7	12.6
1978	58,376	100.0	1.8	9.4	17.0	35.9	17.1	18.8	12.6
1979	59,632	100.0	1.6	8.7	16.1	36.6	17.5	19.6	12.6
1980	60,514	100.0	1.5	8.3	16.0	36.5	17.7	20.0	12.7
1981	61,306	100.0	1.5	7.9	15.4	37.5	17.4	20.3	12.7
1982	61,666	100.0	1.4	7.3	14.8	37.9	17.3	21.3	12.7
1983	62,035	100.0	1.4	6.7	14.1	37.5	17.8	22.5	12.7
1984	62,733	100.0	1.2	6.6	13.6	37.8	18.1	22.7	12.8

Table 2.3 (Continued)

All Women	Total	Total	ELEMENTARY		HIGH SCHOOL		COLLEGE		School Years Completed
			Less Than 5 Years	5 to 8 Years	1 to 3 Years	4 Years	1 to 3 Years	4 Years Or More	
1959	21,556	100.0	3.5	21.5	19.1	38.1	9.7	8.1	12.2
1962	22,977	100.0	3.0	18.8	18.8	38.7	11.2	9.5	12.2
1964	24,326	100.0	2.4	17.8	18.8	40.9	10.6	9.5	12.3
1965	24,871	100.0	2.4	16.6	18.7	41.9	10.4	10.0	12.3
1966	25,602	100.0	2.1	15.7	18.4	43.0	11.0	9.9	12.3
1967	26,647	100.0	2.1	14.8	18.5	42.9	11.8	9.9	12.4
1968	27,846	100.0	1.9	14.1	17.6	43.7	12.3	10.5	12.4
1969	28,891	100.0	1.8	13.1	17.3	45.0	12.4	10.4	12.4
1970	30,064	100.0	1.5	12.2	16.9	45.5	13.2	10.7	12.5
1971	30,575	100.0	1.4	11.5	16.4	45.4	13.9	11.4	12.4
1972	33,127	100.0	1.4	10.2	19.2	44.7	13.2	11.4	12.5
1973	34,196	100.0	1.4	9.2	18.6	45.2	13.8	12.0	12.5
1974	35,709	100.0	1.1	8.6	18.1	44.2	15.2	12.8	12.6
1975	36,982	100.0	1.0	8.1	17.6	44.7	15.4	13.3	12.6
1976	38,400	100.0	1.0	7.4	17.2	44.5	16.0	14.1	12.6
1977	40,054	100.0	.9	6.9	17.1	44.5	16.4	14.5	12.6
1978	41,748	100.0	.9	6.5	16.6	44.5	17.2	14.4	12.6
1979	43,845	100.0	1.0	5.8	16.0	44.5	17.9	15.0	12.6
1980	44,934	100.0	.7	5.5	14.9	45.0	18.1	15.9	12.6
1981	46,414	100.0	.8	5.1	14.2	45.5	18.6	15.7	12.7
1982	47,095	100.0	.8	4.8	13.7	45.2	18.9	16.6	12.7
1983	47,779	100.0	.7	4.4	12.9	44.4	19.9	17.8	12.7
1984	49,210	100.0	.7	4.2	12.1	44.4	20.1	18.5	12.7

PERCENT DISTRIBUTION

Table 2.3 (Continued)

| | | | PERCENT DISTRIBUTION | | | | | | |
| | | | ELEMENTARY | | HIGH SCHOOL | | COLLEGE | | |
White	Total	Total	Less Than 5 Years	5 to 8 Years	1 to 3 Years	4 Years	1 to 3 Years	4 Years Or More	School Years Completed
1959	58,726	100.0	3.8	23.9	19.6	32.5	9.8	10.3	12.1
1962	60,451	100.0	3.3	21.4	18.8	33.5	11.3	11.8	12.2
1964	62,213	100.0	2.7	19.8	18.5	36.0	11.1	11.9	12.2
1965	63,261	100.0	2.7	18.9	18.4	36.8	11.0	12.2	12.3
1966	63,958	100.0	2.3	17.8	18.3	37.7	11.2	12.5	12.3
1967	65,076	100.0	2.2	16.9	18.1	37.7	12.4	12.8	12.4
1968	66,721	100.0	1.9	16.1	17.4	38.6	12.8	13.2	12.4
1969	68,300	100.0	2.0	15.1	16.9	39.7	13.0	13.4	12.4
1970	70,186	100.0	1.8	14.4	16.4	40.0	13.9	13.6	12.5
1971	71,182	100.0	1.7	13.5	15.8	40.2	14.5	14.4	12.5
1972	76,302	100.0	1.6	12.2	18.4	39.5	14.1	14.3	12.5
1973	77,903	100.0	1.6	11.0	17.8	40.2	14.6	14.8	12.5
1974	80,083	100.0	1.4	10.3	17.4	39.8	15.4	15.7	12.6
1975	81,789	100.0	1.3	9.5	16.8	40.2	15.9	16.3	12.6
1976	83,351	100.0	1.2	8.6	16.4	40.2	16.5	17.2	12.6
1977	85,820	100.0	1.2	8.0	16.3	40.0	16.8	17.6	12.6
1978	87,947	100.0	1.1	7.7	15.9	40.1	17.4	17.7	12.7
1979	90,858	100.0	1.1	7.1	15.2	40.1	17.8	18.4	12.7
1980	92,693	100.0	1.0	6.8	14.7	40.4	18.0	19.1	12.7
1981	94,303	100.0	1.0	6.4	14.1	40.4	18.0	19.1	12.7
1982	95,107	100.0	1.0	5.8	13.7	41.3	18.0	20.0	12.7
1983	95,657	100.0	1.0	5.5	12.9	41.5	18.8	21.2	12.8
1984	97,617	100.0	.8	5.2	12.4	40.9	19.1	21.6	12.8

Table 2.3 (Continued)

| | | | PERCENT DISTRIBUTION | | | | | | |
| | | | ELEMENTARY | | HIGH SCHOOL | | COLLEGE | | |
	Total	Total	Less Than 5 Years	5 to 8 Years	1 to 3 Years	4 Years	1 to 3 Years	4 Years Or More	School Years Completed
White Men									
1959	39,956	100.0	4.4	26.1	20.2	28.6	9.6	11.2	11.8
1962	40,503	100.0	3.8	23.4	19.3	29.9	11.0	12.6	12.1
1964	41,028	100.0	3.2	21.7	18.8	32.4	11.1	12.7	12.2
1965	41,652	100.0	3.2	20.7	18.8	33.2	11.0	13.1	12.2
1966	41,706	100.0	2.8	19.8	18.7	33.8	11.1	13.7	12.3
1967	41,911	100.0	2.6	18.8	18.3	33.9	12.3	14.1	12.3
1968	42,483	100.0	2.4	17.9	17.9	34.7	12.7	14.4	12.4
1969	43,111	100.0	2.4	16.9	17.4	35.4	13.1	14.7	12.4
1970	43,962	100.0	2.1	16.2	16.7	35.8	14.1	15.0	12.4
1971	44,541	100.0	2.0	15.2	16.1	36.4	14.5	15.8	12.5
1972	47,413	100.0	1.9	13.8	18.5	35.7	14.4	15.8	12.4
1973	48,224	100.0	2.0	12.5	17.8	36.4	15.0	16.4	12.5
1974	49,008	100.0	1.7	11.8	17.3	36.5	15.4	17.2	12.6
1975	49,646	100.0	1.7	10.7	16.8	36.7	15.9	18.1	12.6
1976	50,154	100.0	1.5	9.7	16.4	36.7	16.5	19.0	12.6
1977	51,062	100.0	1.6	9.2	16.5	36.3	16.7	19.6	12.6
1978	52,001	100.0	1.5	8.9	16.2	36.3	17.2	19.8	12.6
1979	53,051	100.0	1.4	8.2	15.3	36.7	17.7	20.6	12.7
1980	53,883	100.0	1.3	8.0	15.2	36.6	17.8	21.0	12.7
1981	54,328	100.0	1.3	7.7	14.6	37.7	17.5	21.3	12.7
1982	54,552	100.0	1.3	6.9	14.2	38.1	17.3	22.3	12.7
1983	54,813	100.0	1.2	6.6	13.4	37.6	17.9	23.4	12.8
1984	55,418	100.0	1.0	6.3	13.0	37.7	18.3	23.7	12.8

Table 2.3 (Continued)

			ELEMENTARY		HIGH SCHOOL		COLLEGE		School Years Completed
	Total	Total	Less Than 5 Years	5 to 8 Years	1 to 3 Years	4 Years	1 to 3 Years	4 Years Or More	
White Women									
1959	18,770	100.0	2.2	9.5	18.5	40.7	10.4	8.6	12.2
1962	19,948	100.0	2.1	17.4	17.9	40.8	11.9	10.0	12.3
1964	21,185	100.0	1.8	16.2	17.8	43.0	11.0	10.1	12.3
1965	21,609	100.0	1.7	15.3	17.7	43.9	11.0	10.3	12.3
1966	22,252	100.0	1.3	14.4	17.5	45.1	11.4	10.3	12.4
1967	23,165	100.0	1.3	13.5	17.6	44.7	12.4	10.4	12.4
1968	24,238	100.0	1.3	12.8	16.7	45.4	12.9	10.9	12.4
1969	25,189	100.0	1.3	11.9	16.2	46.9	12.8	10.9	12.4
1970	26,224	100.0	1.1	11.3	15.8	47.1	13.6	11.1	12.5
1971	26,641	100.0	1.1	10.6	15.3	46.6	14.4	11.9	12.5
1972	28,890	100.0	1.0	9.4	18.3	45.9	13.6	11.8	12.5
1973	29,679	100.0	1.0	8.5	17.7	46.4	14.0	12.3	12.5
1974	31,075	100.0	.8	7.8	17.4	45.2	15.5	13.3	12.5
1975	32,144	100.0	.7	7.5	16.9	45.7	15.6	13.6	12.6
1976	33,197	100.0	.8	6.8	16.4	45.3	16.3	14.5	12.6
1977	34,758	100.0	.7	6.2	16.2	45.5	16.6	14.7	12.6
1978	35,945	100.0	.7	6.1	15.7	45.6	17.3	14.7	12.6
1979	37,807	100.0	.8	5.3	15.2	45.5	17.8	15.4	12.7
1980	38,810	100.0	.6	5.0	14.0	45.8	18.2	16.3	12.7
1981	39,975	100.0	.6	4.7	13.5	46.3	18.7	16.1	12.7
1982	40,554	100.0	.6	4.3	13.0	46.1	18.9	17.0	12.7
1983	40,843	100.0	.6	3.9	12.3	44.8	20.0	18.2	12.7
1984	42,199	100.0	.6	3.8	11.6	45.0	20.0	18.9	12.8

Table 2.3 (Continued)

| | | | ELEMENTARY | | HIGH SCHOOL | | COLLEGE | | School |
| | | | | | | | | | Years |
	Total	Total	Less Than 5 Years	5 to 8 Years	1 to 3 Years	4 Years	1 to 3 Years	4 Years Or More	Completed
Black									
1959	7,116	100.0	17.8	35.5	21.1	16.5	4.9	4.1	8.6
1962	7,537	100.0	15.4	29.8	28.2	21.0	5.7	4.8	9.6
1964	7,713	100.0	11.6	29.2	24.7	22.2	6.6	5.7	10.1
1965	7,868	100.0	11.8	25.7	24.9	24.4	6.1	7.0	10.5
1966	8,000	100.0	11.1	26.7	23.3	24.8	7.1	5.8	10.5
1967	8,142	100.0	10.4	25.5	23.7	27.5	7.2	5.8	10.8
1968	8,380	100.0	9.5	23.5	24.3	28.3	7.7	6.7	11.1
1969	8,453	100.0	8.6	22.6	24.7	28.4	9.0	6.7	11.3
1970	8,769	100.0	7.4	20.6	24.7	31.0	9.0	7.4	11.7
1971	8,912	100.0	6.5	19.5	24.4	32.7	9.5	7.4	11.9
1972	9,462	100.0	6.0	18.6	25.6	32.4	9.4	8.0	12.0
1973	9,953	100.0	5.0	16.4	24.9	33.6	11.0	9.0	12.1
1974	10,258	100.0	5.2	15.6	28.7	34.1	12.1	9.3	12.2
1975	10,369	100.0	4.9	14.0	23.1	34.8	12.4	10.8	12.2
1976	10,773	100.0	4.1	13.1	22.6	36.1	12.8	11.3	12.3
1977	9,596	100.0	3.7	13.9	24.5	35.6	13.4	8.9	12.2
1978	10,124	100.0	3.7	11.8	24.9	35.9	14.9	8.9	12.3
1979	10,386	100.0	3.3	11.4	23.2	37.6	15.0	9.0	12.3
1980	10,472	100.0	2.7	9.7	23.1	39.3	16.1	9.1	12.4
1981	10,894	100.0	2.3	9.5	22.4	39.6	16.9	9.3	12.4
1982	11,067	100.0	2.0	9.5	20.9	39.4	18.0	10.2	12.4
1983	11,352	100.0	2.0	8.3	19.4	41.6	17.7	11.0	12.5
1984	11,696	100.0	1.7	8.3	18.4	41.5	18.5	11.6	12.5

Table 2.3 (Continued)

	Total	Total	ELEMENTARY		HIGH SCHOOL		COLLEGE		School Years Completed
			Less Than 5 Years	5 to 8 Years	1 to 3 Years	4 Years	1 to 3 Years	4 Years Or More	
Hispanic Men									
1974	2,392	100.0	13.7	23.5	21.2	25.4	10.4	5.8	10.8
1975	2,521	100.0	12.6	24.1	20.3	25.0	10.8	7.1	11.0
1976	2,395	100.0	11.9	22.6	20.6	26.9	10.5	7.5	11.3
1977	2,525	100.0	11.9	20.8	21.9	26.2	12.2	6.9	11.4
1978	2,819	100.0	11.1	22.8	20.7	26.2	12.7	6.6	11.3
1979	2,899	100.0	12.0	22.6	19.8	26.8	12.5	6.3	11.3
1980	3,259	100.0	11.0	21.3	19.7	27.8	12.8	7.4	11.7
1981	3,429	100.0	10.3	22.0	20.7	26.7	12.3	8.0	11.6
1982	3,562	100.0	10.0	21.6	18.6	28.7	13.2	7.8	12.0
1983	3,521	100.0	9.9	20.4	17.9	30.4	13.5	7.9	12.1
1984	3,635	100.0	8.7	21.4	19.0	29.0	13.7	8.3	12.0
Hispanic Women									
1974	1,432	100.0	8.6	22.1	19.9	33.3	10.8	5.4	11.9
1975	1,518	100.0	7.6	20.8	19.3	34.0	11.9	6.2	12.1
1976	1,563	100.0	8.1	19.3	18.6	37.0	11.7	5.1	12.1
1977	1,659	100.0	6.7	19.1	20.3	34.3	13.6	5.8	12.1
1978	1,864	100.0	7.1	19.1	19.0	34.7	13.6	6.5	12.1
1979	1,930	100.0	7.3	17.9	17.9	37.4	13.0	6.5	12.2
1980	2,089	100.0	6.3	17.2	18.1	37.4	13.7	7.3	12.2
1981	2,187	100.0	6.0	18.0	17.1	36.9	15.1	7.0	12.2
1982	2,354	100.0	6.2	17.3	17.4	36.8	14.2	8.0	12.2
1983	2,372	100.0	6.2	17.2	17.7	35.9	14.5	8.6	12.3
1984	2,614	100.0	5.7	16.2	17.1	35.7	17.1	8.3	12.3

Source: Handbook of Labor Statistics, U.S. Dept. of Labor, June, 1985, Bulletin 2217, pp. 164-167

Table 2.3 (Continued)

| | Total | Total | ELEMENTARY | | HIGH SCHOOL | | COLLEGE | | School |
			Less Than 5 Years	5 to 8 Years	1 to 3 Years	4 Years	1 to 3 Years	4 Years Or More	Years Completed
Black Men									
1959	4,330	100.0	22.5	35.5	20.4	13.8	4.0	3.8	8.1
1962	4,508	100.0	19.3	31.2	22.2	18.3	5.4	3.6	9.0
1964	4,572	100.0	14.8	29.9	24.5	19.1	5.7	6.1	9.7
1965	4,606	100.0	15.4	26.4	24.4	21.4	6.0	6.4	10.0
1966	4,650	100.0	14.1	28.0	24.3	21.9	6.6	5.1	10.0
1967	4,660	100.0	13.1	27.3	23.3	24.4	6.7	5.3	10.2
1968	4,772	100.0	12.2	24.0	25.0	25.3	7.6	6.0	10.7
1969	4,751	100.0	10.9	24.2	24.7	25.6	8.1	6.5	10.8
1970	4,929	100.0	9.7	22.7	24.6	28.3	8.0	6.8	11.1
1971	4,993	100.0	9.2	21.2	24.5	29.2	9.0	7.0	11.4
1972	5,254	100.0	7.9	20.7	25.6	29.2	8.6	7.9	11.5
1973	5,480	100.0	6.1	18.9	25.4	31.1	9.9	8.5	11.9
1974	5,683	100.0	6.6	17.5	24.0	31.5	10.8	9.5	12.1
1975	5,606	100.0	6.6	15.2	23.8	31.7	11.8	10.8	12.1
1976	5,661	100.0	5.7	15.2	22.8	33.4	12.1	10.7	12.1
1977	5,100	100.0	5.3	15.7	24.9	33.1	13.5	7.4	12.2
1978	5,250	100.0	5.2	13.7	25.3	33.2	14.6	8.0	12.2
1979	5,346	100.0	4.4	13.0	23.8	36.5	13.9	8.1	12.2
1980	5,360	100.0	4.1	10.8	24.1	37.5	15.8	7.6	12.3
1981	5,549	100.0	3.3	10.9	24.1	37.6	15.9	8.2	12.3
1982	5,666	100.0	2.8	10.7	21.9	38.2	16.9	9.5	12.4
1983	5,722	100.0	2.8	9.6	21.5	39.8	15.9	10.3	12.4
1984	5,915	100.0	2.6	9.4	20.5	40.7	16.3	10.6	12.4

PERCENT DISTRIBUTION

Table 2.3 (Continued)

	Total	Total	ELEMENTARY		HIGH SCHOOL		COLLEGE		School Years Completed
			Less Than 5 Years	5 to 8 Years	1 to 3 Years	4 Years	1 to 3 Years	4 Years Or More	
Black Women									
1959	2,786	100.0	12.3	35.1	22.7	20.3	5.1	4.6	9.4
1962	3,029	100.0	9.8	27.8	24.8	24.9	6.0	6.7	10.5
1964	3,141	100.0	7.0	28.2	25.1	26.6	7.8	5.3	10.8
1965	3,262	100.0	6.7	24.9	25.7	28.6	6.3	7.8	11.1
1966	3,350	100.0	7.0	24.9	24.4	28.9	7.9	6.9	11.2
1967	3,482	100.0	6.9	23.1	24.2	31.6	7.9	6.4	11.5
1968	3,608	100.0	5.6	22.7	23.4	32.3	7.9	7.8	11.7
1969	3,702	100.0	4.5	20.7	24.7	31.9	10.1	7.0	11.9
1970	3,840	100.0	3.1	17.8	24.8	34.5	10.3	8.1	12.1
1971	3,919	100.0	3.6	17.4	24.2	37.1	10.1	8.0	12.1
1972	4,208	100.0	3.6	16.0	25.6	36.4	10.3	8.1	12.1
1973	4,472	100.0	3.3	13.4	24.2	36.8	12.4	9.5	12.2
1974	4,574	100.0	3.3	13.4	23.1	37.4	13.6	9.2	12.3
1975	4,763	100.0	2.8	12.7	22.4	38.4	13.1	10.8	12.8
1976	5,113	100.0	2.4	11.0	22.2	38.9	13.6	12.1	12.4
1977	4,497	100.0	1.8	11.9	24.0	38.3	13.4	10.6	12.3
1978	4,874	100.0	2.0	10.2	24.4	38.7	15.1	9.7	12.4
1979	5,041	100.0	2.0	10.0	22.3	38.7	17.3	9.8	12.4
1980	5,112	100.0	1.1	8.5	22.1	41.2	16.4	10.7	12.4
1981	5,346	100.0	1.3	8.0	20.6	41.6	17.9	10.5	12.5
1982	5,401	100.0	1.1	8.3	19.9	40.7	19.2	10.9	12.5
1983	5,631	100.0	1.1	7.0	17.3	43.5	19.5	11.7	12.6
1984	5,781	100.0	.9	7.0	16.3	42.4	20.7	12.6	12.6
Hispanic Origin									
1974	3,823	100.0	11.8	23.0	20.6	28.4	10.6	5.7	11.2
1975	4,038	100.0	10.8	22.9	20.0	28.4	11.1	6.8	11.5
1976	3,959	100.0	10.5	21.3	19.8	30.8	10.9	6.6	11.8
1977	4,185	100.0	9.9	20.1	21.3	29.4	12.7	6.6	11.9
1978	4,683	100.0	9.5	21.4	20.0	29.5	13.0	6.4	11.9
1979	4,829	100.0	10.1	20.7	19.0	31.0	12.6	7.4	12.0
1980	5,348	100.0	9.2	19.7	19.1	31.5	13.1	7.6	12.1
1981	5,616	100.0	8.6	20.4	19.3	30.6	13.4	7.9	12.1
1982	5,916	100.0	8.5	19.9	18.1	32.0	13.6	8.2	12.1
1983	5,893	100.0	8.4	19.1	17.8	32.6	13.9	8.3	12.1
1984	6,249	100.0	7.4	19.2	18.2	31.8	15.1		12.2

Table 2.4
Unemployment Rate by Age, 1948 - 1983

	16+ Years	16-19 Years			20 Years and Over						
	Total	Total	16-17 Years	18-19 Years	Total	20-24 Years	25-34 Years	35-44 Years	45-54 Years	55-64 Years	65 Years & Over
1948	3.8	9.2	10.1	8.6	3.3	6.2	3.2	2.6	2.7	3.1	3.2
1949	5.9	13.4	14.0	13.0	5.4	9.3	5.4	4.4	4.2	5.2	4.9
1950	5.3	12.2	13.6	11.2	4.8	7.7	4.8	3.8	4.2	4.8	4.5
1951	3.3	8.2	9.6	7.1	3.0	4.1	3.0	2.5	2.7	3.1	3.4
1952	3.0	8.5	10.0	7.3	2.7	4.6	2.6	2.3	2.3	2.4	2.9
1953	2.9	7.6	8.7	6.8	2.6	4.7	2.5	2.2	2.3	2.7	2.2
1954	5.5	12.6	13.5	10.7	5.1	9.2	5.3	4.5	4.4	4.2	4.1
1955	4.4	11.0	12.3	10.0	3.9	7.0	3.8	3.4	3.4	3.5	3.6
1956	4.1	11.1	12.3	10.2	3.7	6.6	3.7	3.0	3.2	3.4	3.2
1957	4.3	11.6	12.5	10.9	3.8	7.1	3.9	3.1	3.3	3.4	3.4
1958	6.8	15.9	16.4	15.5	6.2	11.2	6.8	5.4	5.2	5.2	4.8
1959	5.5	14.6	15.3	14.0	4.8	8.5	5.0	4.2	4.2	4.4	4.3
1960	5.5	14.7	15.5	14.1	4.8	8.7	5.2	4.1	4.1	4.2	3.8
1961	6.7	16.8	18.3	15.8	5.9	10.4	6.2	5.2	5.0	5.4	5.1
1962	5.5	14.7	16.3	13.6	4.8	9.0	5.1	4.1	4.0	4.1	4.5
1963	5.7	17.2	19.3	15.6	4.8	8.8	5.2	4.0	3.8	4.1	4.1
1964	5.2	16.2	17.8	14.9	4.3	8.3	4.3	3.6	3.5	3.7	3.8
1965	4.5	14.8	16.5	13.5	3.6	6.7	3.7	3.2	2.8	3.1	3.3
1966	3.8	12.8	14.8	11.3	2.9	5.3	3.1	2.5	2.3	2.4	3.0
1967	3.8	12.9	14.6	11.6	3.0	5.7	3.2	2.2	2.4	2.4	2.8
1968	3.6	12.7	14.7	11.2	2.7	5.8	2.8	2.2	1.9	2.0	2.8
1969	3.5	12.2	14.5	10.5	2.7	5.7	2.8	2.2	1.9	1.9	2.2
1970	4.9	15.3	17.1	13.8	4.0	8.2	4.2	3.1	2.8	2.7	3.2
1971	5.9	16.9	18.7	15.5	4.9	10.0	5.3	3.9	3.4	3.3	3.5
1972	5.6	16.2	18.5	14.6	4.5	9.3	4.6	3.5	3.0	3.2	3.6
1973	4.9	14.5	17.3	12.4	3.9	7.8	4.2	2.7	2.5	2.6	3.0
1974	5.6	16.0	18.3	14.3	4.5	9.1	4.8	3.3	2.9	2.8	3.4
1975	8.5	19.9	21.4	18.9	7.3	13.6	7.8	5.6	5.2	4.6	5.2
1976	7.7	19.0	21.1	17.5	6.5	12.0	7.1	4.9	4.5	4.5	5.1
1977	7.1	17.8	19.9	16.2	5.9	11.0	6.5	4.4	3.9	3.9	5.0
1978	6.1	16.4	19.3	14.2	5.0	9.6	5.3	3.7	3.3	2.9	4.0
1979	5.8	16.1	18.1	14.7	4.8	9.1	5.2	3.6	3.2	3.3	3.4
1980	7.1	17.8	20.0	16.2	6.1	11.5	6.9	4.6	4.0	3.7	3.1
1981	7.6	19.6	21.4	18.4	6.5	12.3	7.3	5.0	4.2	3.7	3.2
1982	9.7	23.2	24.9	22.1	8.6	14.9	9.7	6.9	5.7	5.4	3.5
1983	9.6	22.4	24.5	21.1	8.6	14.5	9.7	7.0	6.2	5.6	3.7

Source: Handbook of Labor Statistics, U.S. Dep. of Labor, June, 1985, Bulletin 2217, pp.

Table 2.5

Average Weekly Hours of Production Workers by Industry For Selected Years

	DURABLE GOODS				PRIMARY METAL INDUSTRIES					TRANSPORTATION EQUIPMENT			
	Total	Lumber & Wood Products	Furni-ture & Fixtures	Stone, Clay & Glass Products	Total	Blast Furnaces & Basic Steel Products	Fabri-cated Metal Products	Machinery Except Elec-trical	Elec-trical & Elec-tronic Equipment	Total	Motor Vehicles And Equipment	Instru-ments & Related Products	Misc. Manu-factur-ing
1947	40.5	40.3	41.5	41.0	39.9	39.0	40.9	41.5	40.3	39.7	39.8	40.4	40.5
1950	41.1	39.5	41.8	41.1	40.9	39.9	41.5	41.9	41.1	41.4	42.1	41.3	40.8
1955	41.3	39.5	41.4	41.4	41.3	40.5	41.7	42.0	40.7	42.3	43.6	40.9	40.3
1960	40.1	39.0	40.0	40.6	39.0	38.2	40.5	41.0	39.8	40.7	41.0	40.4	39.3
1961	40.3	39.5	40.0	40.7	39.5	38.9	40.5	41.0	40.2	40.5	40.1	40.7	39.5
1962	40.9	39.8	40.7	41.0	40.2	39.2	41.1	41.7	40.6	42.0	42.7	40.9	39.7
1963	41.1	40.1	40.9	41.4	41.0	40.2	41.3	41.8	40.3	42.1	42.8	40.8	39.6
1964	41.5	40.4	41.2	41.7	41.7	41.2	41.7	42.4	40.5	42.1	43.0	40.8	39.6
1965	42.0	40.9	41.5	42.0	42.1	41.2	42.1	43.1	41.0	42.6	44.2	41.4	39.6
1966	42.2	40.8	41.5	42.0	42.1	41.0	42.4	43.8	41.2	41.4	42.8	42.1	39.9
1967	41.2	40.2	40.4	41.6	41.1	40.2	41.5	42.6	40.2	42.2	40.8	41.2	40.0
1968	41.4	40.6	40.6	41.8	41.6	41.0	41.6	42.1	40.3	41.5	43.1	40.5	39.4
1969	41.3	40.2	40.4	41.9	41.8	41.3	41.6	42.5	40.4	40.3	41.7	40.7	39.4
1970	40.3	39.5	40.0	41.2	40.4	40.0	40.7	41.1	39.8	40.7	40.3	40.2	39.0
1971	40.3	39.8	39.2	41.6	40.1	39.6	40.4	40.6	39.9	41.7	41.2	39.8	38.7
1972	41.2	40.4	39.8	42.1	41.4	40.6	41.2	42.1	40.4	42.1	43.0	40.6	38.9
1973	41.5	39.9	40.0	41.9	42.3	41.7	41.6	42.8	40.4	40.5	43.5	40.9	39.5
1974	40.7	39.2	39.1	41.3	41.6	41.3	40.8	42.1	39.7	40.4	40.6	40.4	39.0
1975	39.9	38.7	38.0	40.4	40.0	39.5	40.1	40.8	39.7	41.7	40.3	39.5	38.7
1976	40.6	39.9	38.8	41.1	40.8	40.3	40.8	41.2	39.5	42.5	42.9	40.3	38.5
1977	41.0	39.8	39.0	41.3	41.3	40.5	41.0	41.5	40.0	42.2	44.0	40.6	38.8
1978	41.1	39.8	39.3	41.6	41.8	41.5	41.0	42.1	40.4	41.1	43.3	40.9	38.8
1979	40.8	39.4	38.7	41.5	41.4	41.2	40.4	41.8	40.3	40.6	41.1	40.8	38.8
1980	40.1	38.5	38.1	40.8	40.1	39.4	40.3	41.0	39.8	40.9	40.0	40.5	38.7
1981	40.2	38.7	38.4	40.6	40.5	40.4	40.3	40.9	40.0	40.5	40.9	40.4	38.8
1982	39.3	38.0	37.2	40.1	38.6	37.9	39.2	39.7	39.3	40.5	40.5	39.8	38.4
1983	40.7	40.1	39.4	41.5	40.5	39.5	40.6	40.5	40.5	42.1	43.3	40.4	39.1

Table 2.5 (Continued)

NON-DURABLE GOODS

Year	Total	Food & Kindred Products	Tobacco Manufactures	Textile Mill Products	Apparel & Other Textile Products	Paper & Allied Products	Printing & Publishing	Chemicals & Allied Products	Petroleum & Coal Products	Rubber & Misc. Plastic Products	Leather & Leather Products
1947	40.2	43.2	38.9	39.6	36.0	43.1	40.2	41.2	40.6	39.9	38.6
1950	39.7	41.9	38.1	39.6	36.0	43.3	38.9	41.2	40.8	41.0	37.6
1955	39.9	41.5	38.7	40.1	36.3	43.1	38.9	41.1	40.9	41.8	37.9
1960	39.2	40.8	38.2	39.5	35.5	42.1	38.4	41.3	41.1	39.9	36.9
1961	39.3	40.9	39.0	39.9	35.4	42.5	38.2	41.4	41.2	40.3	37.4
1962	39.7	41.0	38.6	40.6	36.2	42.6	38.3	41.6	41.6	41.0	37.6
1963	39.6	41.0	38.7	40.6	36.1	42.7	38.3	41.6	41.7	40.8	37.5
1964	39.7	41.0	38.8	41.0	35.9	42.8	38.5	41.6	41.8	41.8	37.9
1965	40.1	41.1	37.9	41.7	36.4	43.1	38.6	41.9	42.2	41.3	38.2
1966	40.2	41.2	38.9	41.9	36.4	43.4	38.8	42.0	42.4	42.0	38.6
1967	39.7	40.9	38.6	40.9	36.0	42.8	38.4	41.8	42.7	42.0	38.2
1968	39.8	40.8	37.9	41.2	36.1	42.9	38.3	41.8	42.5	41.4	38.3
1969	39.7	40.8	37.4	40.8	35.9	43.0	38.3	41.6	42.6	41.5	37.2
1970	39.1	40.5	37.8	39.9	35.3	41.9	37.7	41.6	42.8	41.1	37.2
1971	39.3	40.3	37.8	40.6	35.6	42.1	37.5	41.7	42.8	40.2	37.7
1972	39.7	40.5	37.6	41.3	36.0	42.8	37.7	41.8	42.7	40.3	38.3
1973	39.6	40.4	38.6	40.9	35.9	42.9	37.7	41.5	42.4	41.1	37.8
1974	39.1	40.4	38.3	39.5	35.2	42.2	37.5	41.0	42.1	40.5	36.9
1975	38.8	40.3	38.2	39.3	35.2	41.6	36.9	41.6	41.2	39.9	37.1
1976	39.4	40.5	37.5	40.1	35.8	42.5	37.5	41.7	42.1	41.0	37.4
1977	39.4	40.0	37.8	40.4	35.6	42.9	37.7	41.9	42.7	40.9	36.9
1978	39.4	39.7	38.1	40.4	35.6	42.9	37.6	41.9	43.6	40.5	37.1
1979	39.3	39.9	38.0	40.4	35.3	42.6	37.5	41.5	43.8	40.0	36.5
1980	39.0	39.7	38.1	40.1	35.4	42.2	37.1	41.6	41.8	40.3	36.7
1981	39.1	39.7	38.8	39.6	35.7	42.5	37.3	40.9	43.2	39.6	36.7
1982	38.4	39.4	37.8	37.5	34.7	41.8	37.1	40.9	43.9	39.6	35.6
1983	39.4	39.5	37.4	40.5	36.2	42.6	37.6	41.6	43.9	41.2	36.8

Source: Handbook of Labor Statistics, U.S. Dept. of Labor, June, 1985, Bulletin 2217, pp. 187-188

Table 2.6

Average Weekly Overtime Hours of Production Workers On Manufacturing Payrolls
by Industry in Selected Years — 1956 - 1983

			DURABLE GOODS									
	Manufacturing	Total	Lumber & Wood Products	Furniture & Fixtures	Stone, Clay & Glass Products	Primary Metal Industries	Fabricated Metal Products	Machinery except Electrical	Electrical & Electronic Equipment	Transportation Equipment	Instruments & Related Products	Misc. Manufacturing
1956	2.8	3.0	2.6	2.3	3.3	2.8	3.1	3.9	2.6	3.1	2.5	2.8
1960	2.5	2.4	2.9	2.5	3.1	1.8	2.6	2.7	1.9	2.7	2.1	2.1
1961	2.4	2.4	2.9	2.4	3.2	1.9	2.4	2.5	1.9	2.5	2.1	2.2
1962	2.8	2.8	3.2	2.9	3.4	2.2	2.9	3.1	2.2	3.5	2.4	2.3
1963	2.8	3.0	3.3	3.0	3.7	2.7	3.0	3.2	2.0	3.6	2.4	2.2
1964	3.1	3.3	3.4	3.2	3.9	3.2	3.4	3.9	2.3	3.9	2.4	2.4
1965	3.6	3.9	3.8	3.6	4.2	3.8	4.0	4.6	2.8	4.8	3.0	2.7
1966	3.9	4.3	4.0	3.8	4.5	4.0	4.5	5.6	3.4	4.7	3.8	3.0
1967	3.4	3.5	3.6	3.0	4.2	3.2	3.8	4.4	2.5	3.7	3.1	2.6
1968	3.6	3.8	3.9	3.4	4.5	3.8	4.1	4.0	2.6	4.6	2.7	2.5
1969	3.6	3.8	3.8	3.3	4.2	4.1	4.2	4.5	2.8	3.8	3.0	2.6
1970	3.0	3.0	3.3	2.3	4.2	3.0	3.3	3.2	2.3	2.9	2.3	2.2
1971	2.9	2.9	3.6	2.6	4.5	3.0	2.8	2.6	2.1	3.1	2.1	2.2
1972	3.5	3.6	4.0	3.1	4.8	3.6	3.5	3.8	2.7	4.9	2.7	2.6
1973	3.8	4.1	3.9	3.1	5.0	4.5	4.1	4.8	3.1	3.4	3.1	2.2
1974	3.3	3.4	3.3	2.4	4.4	3.9	3.5	4.3	2.4	2.8	1.8	1.9
1975	2.6	3.2	2.9	1.8	3.7	2.6	2.6	3.0	1.9	4.2	2.3	2.2
1976	3.1	3.7	3.5	2.0	4.1	3.3	3.2	3.3	2.3	5.0	2.6	2.4
1977	3.5	3.8	3.7	2.4	4.6	3.7	3.6	4.0	2.6	5.0	2.5	2.4
1978	3.6	3.6	3.5	2.7	4.8	4.2	3.8	4.3	2.8	4.2	2.3	2.2
1979	3.3	3.5	3.5	2.2	4.5	3.9	3.4	4.0	2.7	3.2	2.2	1.9
1980	2.8	2.8	2.8	1.7	3.8	2.8	2.8	3.4	2.3	2.7	1.7	1.9
1981	2.8	2.8	2.5	1.8	3.8	3.0	2.7	3.2	2.2	3.9	2.0	1.6
1982	2.3	2.2	2.3	1.5	3.5	2.0	2.0	2.2	1.8	2.7	1.7	2.0
1983	3.0	3.0	3.1	2.3	4.1	3.0	2.9	2.7	2.6	3.9	2.0	2.0

Source: Handbook of Labor Statistics, U.S. Dept. of Labor, June, 1985, Bulletin 2217, pp. 189-190

Table 2.6 (Continued)

NON-DURABLE GOODS

	Total	Food & Kindred Products	Tobacco Manufactures	Textile Mill Products	Apparel & Other Textile Products	Paper & Allied Products	Printing & Publishing	Chemicals & Allied Products	Petroleum & Coal Products	Rubber & Misc. Plastic Products	Leather & Leather Products
1956	2.4	3.1	1.3	2.6	1.0	4.5	3.1	2.1	2.2	2.1	1.4
1960	2.5	3.3	1.0	2.6	1.2	4.1	2.9	2.3	2.0	2.4	1.2
1961	2.5	3.3	1.1	2.7	1.1	4.2	2.7	2.3	2.0	2.7	1.4
1962	2.7	3.4	1.0	3.2	1.3	4.4	2.8	2.5	2.3	3.1	1.4
1963	2.7	3.4	1.1	3.2	1.3	4.5	2.7	2.5	2.3	3.0	1.4
1964	2.9	3.6	1.6	3.6	1.3	4.7	2.9	2.7	2.5	3.5	1.7
1965	3.2	3.8	1.1	4.2	1.4	5.0	3.1	3.0	2.8	4.1	1.7
1966	3.4	4.0	1.4	4.4	1.5	5.5	3.5	3.3	3.2	4.4	1.8
1967	3.1	4.0	1.8	3.7	1.3	5.0	3.2	3.0	3.5	4.0	2.1
1968	3.3	4.1	1.8	4.1	1.4	5.3	3.1	3.3	3.0	4.2	1.9
1969	3.4	4.2	1.4	3.9	1.3	5.5	3.4	3.4	3.6	4.2	2.1
1970	3.0	4.0	1.7	3.3	1.1	4.6	2.8	3.1	3.9	3.3	1.8
1971	3.0	3.8	1.7	3.8	1.2	4.9	2.6	3.1	3.8	3.2	1.7
1972	3.3	4.0	1.6	4.5	1.5	5.2	2.9	3.2	3.7	4.0	1.9
1973	3.4	4.1	2.4	4.4	1.5	4.6	3.0	3.5	3.8	4.2	2.3
1974	3.0	4.1	2.1	3.3	1.2	4.0	2.7	3.3	3.9	3.5	2.1
1975	2.7	3.9	2.0	3.1	1.2	4.8	2.2	2.7	3.9	2.8	1.8
1976	3.0	4.1	1.3	3.4	1.3	4.8	2.5	3.2	3.0	3.5	1.9
1977	3.2	4.1	1.9	3.5	1.3	5.1	2.8	3.4	3.5	3.7	1.9
1978	3.2	4.0	2.1	3.6	1.3	4.8	3.0	3.5	4.0	3.7	1.8
1979	3.1	4.0	1.3	3.5	1.0	5.1	2.8	3.1	4.3	3.0	1.8
1980	2.8	3.8	1.7	3.2	1.0	4.8	2.5	3.3	3.7	2.7	1.4
1981	2.8	3.7	2.0	3.0	1.1	4.3	2.4	3.1	3.8	3.0	1.5
1982	2.5	3.6	1.4	2.2	1.0	4.1	2.3	2.8	3.9	2.6	1.2
1983	3.0	3.6	1.2	3.5	1.3	4.6	2.6	3.1	4.0	3.5	1.4

Source: Handbook of Labor Statistics, U.S. Dept. of Labor, June, 1985, Bulletin 2217, pp. 189-190

Table 2.7
Indexes of Output Per Hour and Related Data Business Sector — 1947 - 1983

	OUTPUT PER HOUR			OUTPUT PER PERSON			OUTPUT			EMPLOYMENT			HOURS		
	Business	Non-Farm Business	Manufac- turing	Business	Non-Farm Business	Manufac- turing	Business	Non-Farm Business	Manufac- turing	Business	Non-Farm Business	Manufac- turing	Business	Non-Farm Business	Manufac- turing
1947	43.7	49.9	42.4	49.9	55.5	42.5	35.0	34.0	33.9	70.2	61.2	79.7	80.1	68.1	79.9
1948	46.1	52.0	45.1	52.3	57.6	44.9	37.2	36.0	35.8	71.1	62.6	79.8	80.7	69.2	79.4
1949	46.7	53.1	46.9	52.4	58.1	45.9	36.5	35.3	33.9	69.5	60.8	74.0	78.0	66.6	72.4
1950	50.4	56.3	49.4	56.6	62.0	49.6	39.8	38.6	38.6	70.3	62.4	77.7	78.9	68.6	78.2
1951	51.8	57.3	51.1	58.1	63.1	51.5	42.1	41.1	43.0	72.4	65.2	83.7	81.2	71.8	84.2
1952	53.5	58.6	52.1	59.7	64.3	52.4	43.5	42.5	44.8	72.9	66.1	84.8	81.3	72.6	85.4
1953	55.2	59.6	52.9	61.3	65.0	53.1	45.4	44.3	47.5	74.0	68.1	89.4	82.2	74.4	89.8
1954	56.1	60.4	53.8	61.7	65.4	53.0	44.6	43.4	44.1	72.2	66.4	83.2	79.4	71.9	82.1
1955	58.3	62.8	56.4	64.6	68.6	56.1	48.1	47.0	48.9	74.5	68.5	86.0	82.4	74.9	86.6
1956	58.9	62.9	56.0	64.8	68.6	55.6	49.3	48.3	49.2	76.2	70.4	87.8	83.7	76.7	87.9
1957	60.4	64.0	57.2	65.5	69.0	56.6	49.8	48.0	49.5	76.1	70.4	87.4	82.5	76.3	86.5
1958	62.3	65.5	56.9	67.0	70.1	59.4	49.0	48.0	45.2	73.2	68.4	81.2	78.7	73.2	79.4
1959	64.3	67.7	59.5	69.6	73.0	59.2	52.6	51.8	50.5	75.5	70.9	84.9	81.8	76.4	84.6
1960	65.2	68.3	60.0	70.3	73.3	61.0	53.5	52.5	50.7	76.0	71.7	85.5	82.0	76.9	84.4
1961	67.4	70.3	61.6	72.3	75.2	64.2	54.4	53.5	50.7	75.2	71.1	83.2	80.7	76.1	82.3
1962	69.9	72.8	64.3	75.3	78.1	69.0	57.4	56.6	55.1	76.2	72.5	85.7	82.1	77.8	85.6
1963	72.5	75.2	68.9	78.1	80.5	72.9	59.9	59.1	59.6	76.7	73.4	86.4	82.6	78.6	86.5
1964	75.6	78.1	72.3	81.2	83.7	76.1	63.5	62.8	63.9	78.1	75.1	87.6	83.9	80.5	88.4
1965	78.3	80.5	74.6	84.3	86.5	77.2	67.8	67.2	69.8	80.4	77.7	97.1	86.6	83.5	93.6
1966	80.8	82.5	75.4	86.5	88.3	76.1	71.5	71.2	75.1	82.7	80.7	97.4	88.6	86.3	99.7
1967	82.6	84.1	75.3	87.2	88.7	78.9	73.1	72.7	75.0	83.8	82.0	98.6	88.5	86.5	99.5
1968	85.3	86.6	78.0	89.8	91.2	80.0	76.8	76.6	79.1	85.6	84.0	100.2	90.0	88.2	101.4
1969	85.5	86.6	79.3	89.5	90.5	78.4	79.0	78.8	81.7	88.3	87.0	102.2	92.4	91.0	103.0
1970	86.2	86.8	79.2	88.9	89.5	83.4	78.4	78.0	77.0	88.1	87.1	98.2	90.4	89.8	97.3
1971	89.3	89.7	84.0	91.7	92.0	88.9	80.7	80.3	78.7	88.0	87.2	94.4	90.4	89.4	93.7
1972	92.4	93.0	88.2	94.9	95.5	94.0	86.1	85.8	86.2	90.7	89.9	97.0	93.2	92.2	97.7
1973	94.8	95.3	93.0	97.2	97.7	94.0	91.7	91.7	95.9	94.4	93.8	102.1	96.8	96.2	103.1
1974	92.5	92.9	90.8	93.7	94.1	90.4	89.9	89.8	91.9	96.0	95.4	101.7	97.2	96.6	101.2
1975	94.6	94.8	93.4	94.8	94.9	91.9	88.2	87.8	85.4	93.0	92.5	93.0	93.2	92.6	91.4
1976	97.6	97.8	97.6	97.8	98.0	97.1	93.8	93.7	93.6	95.9	95.6	96.4	96.0	95.8	95.9
1977	100.0	100.0	100.0	100.0	100.0	100.0	100.0	100.0	100.0	100.0	100.0	100.0	100.0	100.0	100.0
1978	100.5	100.6	100.9	100.2	100.2	101.1	105.5	105.7	105.3	105.4	105.4	104.2	104.9	105.1	104.4
1979	99.3	99.0	101.6	98.5	98.1	101.2	107.8	108.0	108.2	109.5	110.0	106.9	108.6	109.0	106.5
1980	98.8	98.3	101.7	96.9	96.4	100.3	106.5	106.5	103.5	109.9	111.1	103.2	107.8	108.3	101.7
1981	100.7	99.8	104.9	97.5	97.5	103.3	109.2	108.7	106.1	110.9	111.5	102.7	108.4	109.0	101.1
1982	100.9	100.0	107.1	96.6	96.6	103.6	106.3	105.9	99.3	109.1	109.6	95.8	105.4	106.0	92.7
1983	103.7	103.4	111.6	100.7	100.0	110.5	111.0	111.2	104.4	110.3	110.6	94.4	107.1	107.5	93.5

Source: Handbook of Labor Statistics, U.S. Dept. of Labor, June, 1985, Bulletin 2217, p. 228

Table 2.8
Unemployment Rates by Sex, Race, Hispanic Origin and Age — 1948 - 1983

16 YEARS AND OVER

Year	Total	Men	Women	White	Men	Women	Black	Men	Women	Hispanic	Men	Women
1948	3.8	3.6	4.1	—	—	—	—	—	—	—	—	—
1949	5.9	5.9	6.0	—	—	—	—	—	—	—	—	—
1950	5.3	5.1	5.7	—	—	—	—	—	—	—	—	—
1951	3.3	2.8	4.4	—	—	—	—	—	—	—	—	—
1952	3.0	2.8	3.6	—	—	—	—	—	—	—	—	—
1953	2.9	2.8	3.3	—	—	—	—	—	—	—	—	—
1954	5.5	5.3	6.0	5.0	4.8	5.5	—	—	—	—	—	—
1955	4.4	4.2	4.9	3.9	3.7	4.3	—	—	—	—	—	—
1956	4.1	3.8	4.8	3.6	3.4	4.2	—	—	—	—	—	—
1957	4.3	4.1	4.7	3.8	3.6	4.3	—	—	—	—	—	—
1958	6.8	6.8	6.8	6.1	6.1	6.2	—	—	—	—	—	—
1959	5.5	5.2	5.9	4.8	4.6	5.3	—	—	—	—	—	—
1960	5.5	5.4	5.9	5.0	4.8	5.3	—	—	—	—	—	—
1961	6.7	6.4	7.2	6.0	5.7	6.5	—	—	—	—	—	—
1962	5.5	5.2	6.2	4.9	4.6	5.5	—	—	—	—	—	—
1963	5.7	5.2	6.5	4.9	4.7	5.8	—	—	—	—	—	—
1964	5.2	4.6	6.2	4.6	4.1	5.5	—	—	—	—	—	—
1965	4.5	4.0	5.5	4.1	3.6	5.0	—	—	—	—	—	—
1966	3.8	3.2	4.8	3.4	2.8	4.3	—	—	—	—	—	—
1967	3.8	3.1	5.2	3.4	2.7	4.6	—	—	—	—	—	—
1968	3.6	2.9	4.8	3.2	2.6	4.3	—	—	—	—	—	—
1969	3.5	2.8	4.7	3.1	2.5	4.2	—	—	—	—	—	—
1970	4.9	4.4	5.9	4.5	4.0	5.4	—	—	—	—	—	—
1971	5.9	5.3	6.9	5.4	4.9	6.3	—	—	—	—	—	—
1972	5.6	5.0	6.6	5.1	4.5	5.9	10.4	9.3	11.8	—	—	—
1973	4.9	4.2	6.0	4.3	3.8	5.3	9.4	8.0	11.1	7.5	6.7	9.0
1974	5.6	4.9	6.7	5.0	4.4	6.1	10.5	9.8	11.3	8.1	7.3	9.4
1975	8.5	7.9	9.3	7.8	7.2	8.6	14.8	14.8	14.8	12.2	11.4	13.5
1976	7.7	7.1	8.6	7.0	6.4	7.9	14.0	13.7	14.3	11.5	10.8	12.7
1977	7.1	6.3	8.2	6.2	5.5	7.3	14.0	13.3	14.9	10.1	9.0	11.9
1978	6.1	5.3	7.2	5.2	4.6	6.2	12.8	11.8	13.8	9.1	7.7	11.3
1979	5.8	5.1	6.8	5.1	4.5	5.9	12.3	11.4	13.3	8.3	7.0	10.3
1980	7.1	6.9	7.4	6.3	6.1	6.5	14.3	14.5	14.0	10.1	9.7	10.7
1981	7.6	7.4	7.9	6.7	6.5	6.9	15.6	15.7	15.6	10.4	10.2	10.8
1982	9.7	9.9	9.4	8.6	8.8	8.3	18.9	20.1	17.6	13.8	13.6	14.1
1983	9.6	9.9	9.2	8.4	8.8	7.9	19.5	20.3	18.6	13.7	13.5	13.8

Source: Handbook of Labor Statistics, U.S. Dept. of Labor, June, 1985, Bulletin 2217, pp. 69-73

Table 2.9
Unemployment Rates by Sex and Marital Status — 1955 - 1983

	All Civilian Workers	MEN				WOMEN			
		Total	Single	Married Spouse Present	Widowed/ Divorced/ Separated	Total	Single	Married Spouse Present	Widowed/ Divorced/ Separated
1955	4.4	4.2	8.6	2.6	7.1	4.9	5.0	3.7	5.0
1956	4.1	3.8	7.7	2.3	6.2	4.8	5.3	3.6	5.0
1957	4.3	4.1	9.2	2.8	6.8	4.7	5.6	4.3	4.7
1958	6.8	6.8	13.3	5.1	11.2	6.8	7.4	6.5	6.7
1959	5.5	5.2	11.6	3.6	8.6	5.9	7.1	5.2	6.2
1960	5.5	5.4	11.7	3.7	8.4	5.9	7.5	5.2	5.9
1961	6.7	6.4	13.1	4.6	10.3	7.2	8.7	6.4	7.4
1962	5.5	5.2	11.2	3.6	9.9	6.2	7.9	5.4	6.4
1963	5.7	5.2	12.4	3.4	9.6	6.5	8.9	5.4	6.7
1964	5.2	4.6	11.5	2.8	8.9	6.2	8.7	5.1	6.4
1965	4.5	4.0	10.1	2.4	7.2	5.5	8.2	4.5	5.4
1966	3.8	3.2	8.6	1.9	5.5	4.8	7.9	3.7	4.7
1967	3.8	3.1	8.3	1.8	4.9	5.2	7.5	4.5	4.6
1968	3.6	2.9	8.0	1.6	4.2	4.8	7.6	3.9	4.2
1969	3.5	2.8	8.0	1.5	4.0	4.7	7.3	3.9	4.0
1970	4.9	4.4	11.2	2.6	6.4	5.9	9.0	4.9	5.2
1971	5.9	5.3	13.2	3.2	7.4	6.9	10.5	5.7	6.3
1972	5.6	5.0	12.4	2.8	7.0	6.6	10.1	5.4	6.1
1973	4.9	4.2	10.4	2.3	5.4	6.0	9.4	4.7	5.8
1974	5.6	4.9	11.8	2.7	6.2	6.7	10.5	5.3	6.3
1975	8.5	7.9	16.1	5.1	11.0	9.3	13.0	7.9	8.9
1976	7.7	7.1	14.9	4.2	9.8	8.6	12.1	7.1	8.7
1977	7.1	6.3	13.5	3.6	8.2	8.2	12.1	6.5	7.9
1978	6.1	5.3	11.7	2.8	6.6	7.2	10.9	5.5	6.9
1979	5.8	5.1	11.1	2.8	6.5	6.8	10.4	5.1	6.7
1980	7.1	6.9	13.6	4.2	8.6	7.4	10.9	5.8	7.2
1981	7.6	7.4	14.6	4.3	9.1	7.9	11.9	6.0	8.1
1982	9.7	9.9	17.7	6.5	12.4	9.4	13.6	7.4	9.5
1983	9.6	9.9	17.3	6.5	13.0	9.2	13.1	7.0	9.9

Source: Handbook of Labor Statistics, U.S. Dept. of Labor, June, 1985, Bulletin 2217, p. 74

Table 2.10

Unemployed Persons and Unemployment Rates by Occupation — 1982 - 1983

	1982		1983	
	Un-employed	Unemploy-ment Rate	Un-employed	Unemploy-ment Rate
Total, 16 years and over	10,678	9.7	10,717	9.6
Managerial and professional specialty	789	3.3	795	3.3
Executive, administrative & managerial	398	3.6	396	3.5
Professional specialty	391	3.0	399	3.0
Technical, sales & administrative support	2,014	6.1	2,116	6.3
Technicians and related support	135	4.3	152	4.7
Sales occupations	743	6.2	850	6.7
Administrative support, including clerical	1,136	6.4	1,114	6.4
Service occupations	1,628	10.8	1,697	10.9
Private household	69	6.2	79	7.4
Protective service	116	6.7	120	6.7
Service, except private household & protective	1,444	11.8	1,498	11.8
Precision production, craft, and repair	1,403	10.6	1,466	10.6
Mechanics and repairers	316	7.5	344	7.6
Construction trades	714	15.3	709	14.2
Other precision production, craft & repair	372	8.7	412	9.6
Operators, fabricators, and laborers	3,314	16.7	2,955	15.5
Machine operators, assemblers, & inspectors	1,623	17.1	1,411	15.4
Transportation & material moving occupations	626	13.0	596	12.4
Handlers, equipment cleaners, helpers & laborers	1,066	19.2	948	18.6
Construction laborers	220	28.2	207	25.8
Other handlers, equipment cleaners, helpers & laborers	846	17.8	740	17.2
Farming, forestry, and fishing	349	8.5	407	9.9
No previous work experience	1,190	--	1,218	--

Source: Handbook of Labor Statistics, U.S. Dept. of Labor, June, 1985, Bulletin 2217, p. 75

Table 2.11
Unemployed Persons and Unemployment Rates by Industry — 1948 - 1983

(In Thousands)

	All Civilian Workers	Total	Agriculture	WAGE AND SALARY WORKERS IN PRIVATE NON-AGRICULTURAL INDUSTRIES — Total	Mining	Construction	MANUFACTURING Total	Durable Goods	Non-Durable Goods	Transportation & Public Utilities	Wholesale & Retail Trade	Finance, Insurance & Real Estate	Services	Government
1948	2,276	2,046	96	1,832	28	232	678	339	339	149	415	30	300	118
1949	3,637	3,310	132	3,003	73	380	1,242	652	590	252	578	36	442	175
1950	3,288	2,990	162	2,650	61	348	981	466	515	189	580	40	451	178
1951	2,055	1,857	71	1,675	36	218	637	271	366	95	373	27	289	111
1952	1,883	1,707	73	1,531	35	218	573	266	307	95	326	33	251	103
1953	1,834	1,671	81	1,490	45	227	536	253	283	90	315	34	243	100
1954	3,532	3,230	133	2,946	106	386	1,232	720	512	231	549	46	396	151
1955	2,852	2,568	124	2,304	69	337	821	436	385	163	464	49	401	140
1956	2,750	2,443	126	2,199	50	313	832	448	384	127	459	39	379	118
1957	2,859	2,542	118	2,285	41	349	901	502	399	139	461	42	352	139
1958	4,602	4,096	180	3,726	72	523	1,605	1,036	569	246	705	68	507	190
1959	3,740	3,252	158	2,919	59	466	1,055	611	444	178	617	63	481	175
1960	3,852	3,337	159	2,987	59	463	1,103	626	477	193	637	63	469	191
1961	4,714	4,061	173	3,676	67	544	1,376	835	541	218	783	91	597	212
1962	3,911	3,342	127	3,027	46	466	1,045	575	470	166	678	82	544	188
1963	4,070	3,415	158	3,056	41	456	1,061	573	488	170	689	75	564	201
1964	3,786	3,134	158	2,778	37	390	941	498	443	143	649	75	543	198
1965	3,366	2,732	114	2,427	29	364	775	382	393	118	585	70	486	191
1966	2,875	2,331	89	2,048	20	286	651	325	326	88	528	62	413	194
1967	2,975	2,489	96	2,183	19	257	775	418	357	100	521	80	431	210
1968	2,817	2,356	86	2,052	16	247	691	368	323	87	513	74	424	218
1969	2,832	2,372	76	2,067	15	225	705	382	323	99	530	73	420	229
1970	4,093	3,526	94	3,150	16	380	1,195	719	475	150	732	102	575	282
1971	5,016	4,300	100	3,811	23	428	1,401	841	559	178	948	128	706	388
1972	4,882	4,122	103	3,611	19	450	1,154	653	501	168	994	138	687	409
1973	4,365	3,646	95	3,166	19	407	939	500	439	143	896	117	644	385
1974	5,156	4,391	110	3,839	20	486	1,257	703	554	162	1,058	139	718	442
1975	7,929	6,970	151	6,198	31	807	2,333	1,431	902	278	1,493	217	1,039	620
1976	7,406	6,387	180	5,509	37	694	1,700	987	714	246	1,527	200	1,106	698
1977	6,991	5,915	171	5,067	33	593	1,474	805	669	242	1,473	186	1,065	677
1978	6,202	5,220	142	4,439	37	530	1,244	661	583	201	1,295	161	971	637
1979	6,137	5,217	148	4,461	45	541	1,306	702	603	206	1,250	165	949	608
1980	7,637	6,634	175	5,777	65	740	1,991	1,254	736	280	1,443	188	1,071	681
1981	8,273	7,129	201	6,161	70	809	1,915	1,139	777	304	1,609	199	1,257	767
1982	10,678	9,275	260	8,216	154	1,031	2,771	1,788	983	397	2,066	276	1,521	799
1983	10,717	9,276	300	8,101	182	1,005	2,454	1,562	892	424	2,109	272	1,657	875

EXPERIENCED WAGE AND SALARY WORKERS

Table 2.11 (Continued)

(Percent)

EXPERIENCED WAGE AND SALARY WORKERS

WAGE AND SALARY WORKERS IN PRIVATE NON-AGRICULTURAL INDUSTRIES

	All Civilian Workers	Total	Agri-culture	Total	Mining	Construc-tion	Manufacturing Total	Durable Goods	Non-Durable Goods	Transpor-tation & Public Utilities	Wholesale & Retail Trade	Finance, Insurance & Real Estate	Services	Govern-ment
1948	3.8	4.3	5.5	4.5	3.1	8.7	4.2	4.0	4.4	3.5	4.7	1.8	4.8	2.2
1949	5.9	6.8	7.1	7.3	8.9	14.0	8.0	8.1	7.8	5.9	6.2	2.1	6.8	3.1
1950	5.3	6.0	9.0	6.3	6.9	12.2	6.2	5.7	6.7	4.6	6.0	2.2	6.4	3.0
1951	3.3	3.7	4.4	3.9	4.0	7.2	3.9	3.1	4.7	2.3	3.9	1.5	4.2	1.8
1952	3.0	3.4	4.8	3.6	4.6	6.7	3.5	3.0	4.1	2.3	3.5	1.8	3.6	1.6
1953	2.9	3.2	5.6	3.4	4.6	7.2	3.1	2.6	3.8	2.2	3.4	1.8	3.4	1.5
1954	5.5	6.2	9.0	6.7	14.4	12.9	7.1	7.3	6.9	5.6	5.7	2.3	5.5	2.0
1955	4.4	4.8	7.2	5.1	9.1	10.9	4.7	4.4	5.2	3.0	4.7	2.4	5.2	2.0
1956	4.1	4.4	7.4	4.7	6.8	10.0	4.7	4.4	5.1	3.0	4.5	1.8	4.6	1.7
1957	4.3	4.6	6.9	4.9	5.9	10.0	5.1	4.9	5.3	3.3	4.5	1.8	4.2	1.9
1958	6.8	7.3	10.3	7.9	11.0	15.3	9.3	10.6	7.7	6.1	6.8	2.9	5.7	2.5
1959	5.5	5.7	9.1	6.1	9.7	13.4	6.1	6.2	6.0	4.4	5.5	2.5	5.3	2.2
1960	5.5	5.7	8.3	6.1	9.7	13.5	6.2	6.4	6.1	4.6	5.8	2.4	5.1	2.4
1961	6.7	6.8	9.6	7.5	11.1	15.7	7.8	8.5	6.8	5.3	5.9	3.3	6.2	2.5
1962	5.5	5.6	7.5	6.1	7.8	13.5	5.8	5.7	6.0	4.1	7.3	3.0	5.5	2.1
1963	5.7	6.0	9.2	6.1	7.2	13.3	5.7	5.5	6.0	4.2	6.3	2.7	5.3	2.2
1964	5.2	5.4	9.7	5.4	6.7	11.2	5.0	4.7	5.4	3.5	6.2	2.6	5.3	2.1
1965	4.5	4.6	7.6	4.6	5.4	10.1	4.0	3.5	4.7	2.9	5.7	2.3	4.6	1.9
1966	3.8	3.8	6.6	3.8	3.7	8.0	3.2	2.8	3.8	2.1	5.0	2.1	3.9	1.8
1967	3.8	3.9	6.9	3.9	3.7	7.4	3.7	3.4	4.1	2.4	4.4	2.5	3.7	1.8
1968	3.6	3.5	6.3	3.5	3.4	6.9	3.3	3.0	3.7	2.0	4.2	2.2	3.5	1.8
1969	3.5	3.5	6.1	3.5	3.1	6.0	3.3	3.0	3.7	2.2	4.0	2.1	3.5	1.9
1970	4.9	5.2	7.5	5.2	2.9	9.7	5.6	5.7	5.4	3.2	4.1	2.8	4.7	2.2
1971	5.9	6.2	7.9	6.2	3.1	10.4	6.8	7.0	6.5	3.8	5.3	3.4	5.6	2.9
1972	5.6	5.7	7.7	5.7	4.0	10.3	5.6	5.5	5.8	3.5	6.4	3.4	5.3	3.0
1973	4.9	4.9	7.0	4.9	3.2	8.9	4.4	3.9	5.0	3.3	5.7	2.7	4.8	2.7
1974	5.6	5.7	7.5	5.7	2.9	10.7	5.8	5.4	6.3	3.6	6.5	3.1	5.3	3.0
1975	8.5	9.1	10.4	9.1	3.0	18.0	10.9	11.3	10.4	5.6	8.7	4.9	7.1	4.1
1976	7.7	7.9	11.8	7.9	4.1	15.5	7.9	7.7	8.2	5.0	8.6	4.3	7.2	4.4
1977	7.1	7.1	11.2	7.1	3.8	12.7	6.7	6.2	7.4	4.7	8.0	3.8	6.6	4.2
1978	6.1	6.1	8.9	6.6	4.2	10.6	5.5	5.0	6.3	3.7	6.9	3.1	5.7	3.9
1979	5.8	5.8	9.3	5.6	4.9	10.3	5.6	5.0	6.5	3.7	6.5	3.4	5.5	3.7
1980	7.1	7.4	11.0	7.4	4.9	14.1	8.5	8.9	7.9	4.9	7.4	3.0	5.9	4.1
1981	7.6	7.7	12.1	7.7	6.4	15.6	8.3	8.2	8.4	5.2	8.1	3.5	6.6	4.7
1982	9.7	10.1	14.7	10.1	13.4	20.0	12.3	13.3	10.8	6.8	10.0	4.7	7.6	4.9
1983	9.6	9.9	16.0	9.9	17.0	18.4	11.2	12.1	10.0	7.4	10.0	4.5	7.9	5.3

Source: Handbook of Labor Statistics, U.S. Dept. of Labor, June 1985, Bulletin 2217, p.10-13

Table 2.12
Unemployment Rate By Duration Of Unemployment, 1948 - 1983

	Total	Less Than 5 Weeks	5-14 Weeks	15 Weeks And Over			Average (Mean) Duration	Median Duration
				Total	15-26 Weeks	27 Weeks+		
Percent Distribution								
1948	100.0	57.1	29.4	13.6	8.5	5.1	N/A	N/A
1949	100.0	48.3	32.8	18.8	11.8	7.0	N/A	N/A
1950	100.0	44.1	32.1	23.8	12.9	10.9	N/A	N/A
1951	100.0	57.3	27.9	14.7	8.1	6.7	N/A	N/A
1952	100.0	60.3	27.4	12.3	7.9	4.5	N/A	N/A
1953	100.0	62.3	26.3	11.5	7.2	4.3	N/A	N/A
1954	100.0	45.4	31.6	23.0	14.0	9.0	N/A	N/A
1955	100.0	46.8	28.6	24.6	12.8	11.8	N/A	N/A
1956	100.0	51.3	29.3	19.4	10.9	8.4	N/A	N/A
1957	100.0	49.2	31.2	19.6	11.2	8.4	N/A	N/A
1958	100.0	38.1	30.3	31.6	17.1	14.5	N/A	N/A
1959	100.0	42.4	29.8	27.8	12.5	15.3	N/A	N/A
1960	100.0	44.6	30.5	24.8	13.1	11.8	N/A	N/A
1961	100.0	38.3	29.2	32.5	15.4	17.1	N/A	N/A
1962	100.0	42.5	29.0	28.6	13.7	15.0	N/A	N/A
1963	100.0	43.0	30.2	26.7	13.1	13.6	N/A	N/A
1964	100.0	44.8	29.5	25.7	13.0	12.7	N/A	N/A
1965	100.0	47.7	29.9	22.4	12.0	10.4	N/A	N/A
1966	100.0	54.7	27.1	18.3	10.0	8.3	N/A	N/A
1967	100.0	54.9	30.0	15.1	9.1	5.9	N/A	N/A
1968	100.0	56.6	28.8	14.6	9.1	5.5	N/A	N/A
1969	100.0	57.5	29.2	13.2	8.5	4.7	N/A	N/A
1970	100.0	52.3	31.5	16.2	10.4	5.8	N/A	N/A
1971	100.0	44.8	31.6	23.7	13.3	10.4	N/A	N/A
1972	100.0	45.9	30.2	23.9	12.3	11.6	N/A	N/A
1973	100.0	51.0	30.1	18.9	11.1	7.9	N/A	N/A
1974	100.0	50.5	31.0	18.5	11.1	7.4	N/A	N/A
1975	100.0	37.1	31.3	31.6	16.4	15.2	N/A	N/A
1976	100.0	38.4	29.6	32.0	13.8	18.2	N/A	N/A
1977	100.0	41.8	30.5	27.8	13.1	14.7	N/A	N/A
1978	100.0	46.2	31.0	22.8	12.3	10.5	N/A	N/A
1979	100.0	48.1	31.7	20.2	11.5	8.7	N/A	N/A
1980	100.0	43.2	32.3	24.5	13.8	10.7	N/A	N/A
1981	100.0	41.7	30.7	27.6	13.6	14.0	N/A	N/A
1982	100.0	36.4	31.0	32.6	16.0	16.6	N/A	N/A
1983	100.0	33.3	27.4	39.3	15.4	23.9	N/A	N/A

Source: Handbook of Labor Statistics, U.S. Dep. of Labor, June, 1985, Bulletin 2217, pp.

Table 2.12 (Continued)

Number Employed	Total	Less Than 5 Weeks	5-14 Weeks	15 Weeks And Over			Average (Mean) Duration	Median Duration
				Total	15-26 Weeks	27 Weeks+		
1948	2,276	1,300	669	309	193	116	8.6	(1)
1949	3,637	1,756	1,194	684	428	256	10.0	(1)
1950	3,288	1,450	1,055	782	425	357	12.1	(1)
1951	2,055	1,177	574	303	166	137	9.7	(1)
1952	1,883	1,135	516	232	148	84	8.4	(1)
1953	1,834	1,142	482	210	132	78	8.0	(1)
1954	3,532	1,605	1,116	812	495	317	11.8	(1)
1955	2,852	1,335	815	702	366	336	13.0	(1)
1956	2,750	1,412	805	533	301	232	11.3	(1)
1957	2,859	1,408	891	560	321	239	10.5	(1)
1958	4,602	1,753	1,396	1,452	785	667	13.9	(1)
1959	3,740	1,585	1,114	1,040	469	571	14.4	(1)
1960	3,852	1,719	1,176	957	503	454	12.8	(1)
1961	4,714	1,806	1,376	1,532	728	804	15.6	(1)
1962	3,911	1,663	1,134	1,119	534	585	14.7	(1)
1963	4,070	1,751	1,231	1,088	535	553	14.0	(1)
1964	3,786	1,697	1,117	973	491	482	13.3	(1)
1965	3,366	1,628	983	755	404	351	11.8	(1)
1966	2,875	1,573	779	526	287	239	10.4	(1)
1967	2,975	1,634	893	448	271	177	8.7	2.3
1968	2,817	1,594	810	412	256	156	8.4	4.5
1969	2,832	1,629	827	375	242	133	7.8	4.4
1970	4,093	2,139	1,290	663	428	235	8.6	4.9
1971	5,016	2,245	1,585	1,187	668	519	11.3	6.3
1972	4,882	2,242	1,472	1,167	601	566	12.0	6.2
1973	4,365	2,224	1,314	826	483	343	10.0	5.2
1974	5,156	2,604	1,597	955	574	381	9.8	5.2
1975	7,929	2,940	2,484	2,505	1,303	1,203	14.2	8.4
1976	7,406	2,844	2,196	2,366	1,018	1,348	15.8	8.2
1977	6,991	2,919	2,132	1,942	913	1,028	14.3	7.0
1978	6,202	2,865	1,923	1,414	766	648	11.9	5.9
1979	6,137	2,950	1,946	1,241	706	535	10.8	5.4
1980	7,637	3,295	2,470	1,871	1,052	820	11.9	6.5
1981	8,273	3,449	2,539	2,285	1,122	1,162	13.7	6.9
1982	10,678	3,883	3,311	3,485	1,708	1,776	15.6	8.7
1983	10,717	3,570	2,937	4,210	1,652	2,559	20.0	10.1

(1) Not Available.

Table 2.13

Unemployment in Families by Type of Family, Race, and Presence of
Employed Family Members — 1982 - 1983

	1982					1983				
		FAMILIES WITH UNEMPLOYMENT					FAMILIES WITH UNEMPLOYMENT			
			PERCENT WITH:					PERCENT WITH:		
	Total Families	Total	No Employed Person	At Least One Employed Person	At Least One Person Employed Full-time	Total Families	Total	No Employed Person	At Least One Employed Person	At Least One Person Employed Full-time
Total										
Total families	61,614	7,956	30.2	69.8	59.5	61,080	7,836	30.5	69.5	59.5
W/children under 18 years of age	31,159	4,864	32.2	67.8	57.3	30,649	4,709	32.5	67.5	57.2
Married-couple families	49,648	5,939	23.3	76.7	66.5	49,330	5,793	23.2	76.8	66.9
W/children under 18 years of age	24,523	3,732	23.7	76.3	65.5	23,998	3,545	22.8	77.2	66.3
Families maintained by women	9,554	1,623	52.8	47.2	36.5	9,624	1,664	53.4	46.6	36.4
W/children under 18 years of age	5,801	994	61.7	38.3	28.8	5,878	1,032	62.4	37.6	28.5
Families maintained by men	2,412	394	41.9	58.1	49.0	2,125	379	41.5	58.5	49.5
W/children under 18 years of age	835	138	51.8	48.2	41.7	774	131	58.8	41.2	34.4
White										
Total families	53,573	6,246	27.9	72.1	61.7	53,152	6,102	28.3	71.7	61.7
W/children under 18 years of age	26,244	3,763	29.3	70.7	59.8	25,829	3,595	29.4	70.6	59.8
Married-couple families	44,982	4,993	23.1	76.9	66.6	44,796	4,877	23.6	76.4	66.4
W/children under 18 years of age	21,763	3,104	23.5	76.5	65.4	21,392	2,943	23.3	76.7	65.7
Families maintained by women	6,628	958	49.1	50.9	39.7	6,647	952	48.7	51.3	40.5
W/children under 18 years of age	3,797	552	57.8	42.2	31.0	3,811	553	57.5	42.5	32.2
Families maintained by men	1,962	295	40.3	59.7	50.2	1,709	274	40.1	59.9	50.4
W/children under 18 years of age	684	107	49.1	50.9	45.3	625	99	55.6	44.4	37.4

Table 2.13 (Continued)

	1982					1983				
		FAMILIES WITH UNEMPLOYMENT					FAMILIES WITH UNEMPLOYMENT			
			PERCENT WITH:					PERCENT WITH:		
	Total Families	Total	No Employed Person	At Least One Employed Person	At Least One Person Employed Full-time	Total Families	Total	No Employed Person	At Least One Employed Person	At Least One Person Employed Full-time
Black										
Total families	6,686	1,501	39.6	60.4	50.6	6,490	1,517	39.2	60.8	51.3
W/children under 18 years of age	4,062	963	43.6	56.4	47.8	3,909	969	43.2	56.8	48.1
Married-couple families	3,580	778	23.5	76.5	66.5	3,388	756	20.1	79.9	70.1
W/children under 18 years of age	2,050	512	23.5	76.5	67.1	1,856	490	18.8	81.2	71.0
Families maintained by women	2,731	633	58.5	41.5	31.9	2,765	674	59.8	40.2	31.0
W/children under 18 years of age	1,883	422	66.9	33.1	25.5	1,927	453	68.4	31.6	24.5
Families maintained by men	375	90	47.3	52.7	45.1	338	88	44.3	55.7	46.6
W/children under 18 years of age	130	29	--	--	--	125	26	--	--	--
Hispanic Origin										
Total families	3,384	618	33.4	66.6	56.1	3,420	623	33.4	66.6	56.6
W/children under 18 years of age	2,301	435	36.6	63.4	54.0	2,314	433	36.9	63.1	53.0
Married-couple families	2,488	463	27.9	72.1	62.2	2,471	465	27.3	72.7	62.8
W/children under 18 years of age	1,718	344	30.2	69.8	60.8	1,685	340	29.7	70.3	60.4
Families maintained by women	723	123	53.7	46.3	32.5	787	125	55.2	44.8	33.6
W/children under 18 years of age	525	81	63.8	36.2	26.3	573	83	63.9	36.1	26.5
Families maintained by men	174	32	--	--	--	162	33	--	--	--
W/children under 18 years of age	57	11	--	--	--	57	11	--	--	--

Source: Handbook of Labor Statistics, U.S. Dept. of Labor, June, 1985, Bulletin 2217, p. 89

Table 2.14
Unemployment Rates by Educational Attainment, Sex,
Race, and Hispanic Origin, Selected Years — 1959 - 1984

Total

	Total	ELEMENTARY		HIGH SCHOOL		COLLEGE	
		Less Than 5 Years	5 to 8 Years	1 to 3 Years	4 Years	1 to 3 Years	4 Years Or More
1959	6.2	9.5	8.1	8.5	4.8	3.5	1.4
1962	6.0	10.3	7.6	8.3	5.1	3.7	1.4
1964	5.5	8.2	7.4	7.2	4.8	4.3	1.5
1965	4.7	7.1	5.6	7.4	4.1	3.3	1.4
1966	3.7	5.4	4.8	5.3	3.1	3.0	1.1
1967	3.6	5.1	4.6	5.5	3.2	2.7	.9
1968	3.4	5.2	4.2	5.4	3.1	2.6	1.0
1969	3.1	2.9	3.8	4.9	2.9	2.5	.9
1970	4.2	5.5	4.8	6.3	3.9	3.9	1.5
1971	5.8	6.5	6.9	8.7	5.5	5.6	2.3
1972	6.1	6.1	7.0	10.1	5.6	4.9	2.5
1973	5.2	4.4	6.4	8.9	5.6	4.0	2.1
1974	5.3	4.8	6.2	9.6	4.8	4.2	2.0
1975	9.2	12.9	11.6	15.2	9.1	6.9	2.9
1976	8.1	8.5	10.0	13.6	8.2	6.3	2.8
1977	7.9	9.4	10.3	13.8	7.5	6.0	3.3
1978	6.6	7.7	8.5	12.4	6.2	4.6	2.5
1979	6.1	7.7	7.7	12.2	5.8	4.3	2.3
1980	6.8	9.0	9.9	13.0	6.7	5.0	2.1
1981	7.9	10.5	11.9	15.3	8.1	5.1	2.4
1982	9.7	16.9	13.6	18.0	10.3	6.9	3.2
1983	10.9	16.8	16.1	20.6	11.7	8.1	3.8
1984	8.2	12.9	12.9	17.1	8.6	5.9	2.8

Table 2.14 (Continued)

Men	Total	ELEMENTARY		HIGH SCHOOL		COLLEGE	
		Less Than 5 Years	5 to 8 Years	1 to 3 Years	4 Years	1 to 3 Years	4 Years Or More
1959	6.3	9.3	8.3	8.1	4.9	3.3	1.9
1962	6.0	11.0	7.9	7.8	4.8	4.0	1.4
1964	5.2	8.7	7.3	6.6	4.1	3.8	1.5
1965	4.4	6.4	5.7	6.7	3.4	3.1	1.4
1966	3.4	5.5	4.8	4.9	2.6	2.8	1.0
1967	3.1	5.0	4.3	4.6	2.5	2.2	.7
1968	3.0	4.9	3.7	4.8	2.5	2.3	.7
1969	2.6	2.7	3.5	4.2	2.0	2.2	.9
1970	3.7	5.8	4.2	5.6	3.4	3.8	1.3
1971	5.5	6.6	6.7	8.0	5.0	5.6	2.0
1972	5.9	6.1	6.8	9.7	5.4	4.8	2.2
1973	4.7	3.7	6.2	8.4	4.0	3.9	1.8
1974	4.8	4.9	5.7	8.9	4.3	3.8	1.8
1975	9.0	13.5	11.7	14.7	9.1	6.3	2.5
1976	7.8	8.6	9.7	13.5	8.0	6.6	2.4
1977	7.5	9.2	9.7	13.4	7.2	5.5	2.8
1978	6.3	7.4	8.4	12.1	5.9	4.3	2.2
1979	5.8	7.0	7.1	11.9	5.5	4.3	1.9
1980	6.8	8.8	9.8	12.8	6.9	5.0	1.8
1981	8.1	11.0	11.5	15.6	8.8	5.2	2.1
1982	10.3	16.7	13.2	19.4	11.3	7.5	3.2
1983	11.9	18.2	16.3	21.4	13.6	9.3	3.6
1984	8.6	13.1	12.9	17.6	9.4	5.7	2.8

Table 2.14 (Continued)

		ELEMENTARY		HIGH SCHOOL		COLLEGE	
	Total	Less Than 5 Years	5 to 8 Years	1 to 3 Years	4 Years	1 to 3 Years	4 Years Or More
Women							
1959	6.0	10.4	7.8	9.3	4.7	3.8	1.3
1962	6.0	7.9	6.9	9.2	5.7	3.2	1.5
1964	6.1	6.6	7.7	8.5	5.6	5.2	1.6
1965	5.3	9.4	5.4	8.6	5.0	3.6	1.3
1966	4.1	4.8	4.8	6.1	3.8	3.3	1.3
1967	4.5	5.5	5.4	7.0	4.1	3.6	1.4
1968	4.2	6.1	5.5	6.6	3.8	3.0	1.6
1969	4.0	3.7	4.6	6.2	3.9	3.0	1.1
1970	4.9	4.5	6.2	7.4	4.6	4.0	2.0
1971	6.4	6.6	7.3	9.8	6.0	5.7	2.9
1972	6.5	6.1	7.4	10.7	5.8	5.0	3.1
1973	5.8	6.1	6.6	9.7	5.3	4.3	2.7
1974	6.0	4.7	7.2	10.6	5.4	4.7	2.3
1975	9.5	10.8	11.6	15.9	9.1	7.4	3.6
1976	8.5	8.2	10.8	13.7	8.4	6.5	3.5
1977	8.5	9.9	11.4	14.3	7.8	6.8	4.2
1978	7.0	8.3	8.6	12.9	6.6	5.1	3.0
1979	6.6	9.6	9.2	12.7	6.1	4.3	3.0
1980	6.7	9.6	10.2	13.3	6.4	4.9	2.5
1981	7.6	9.1	12.7	15.0	7.4	5.0	3.0
1982	8.9	17.4	14.6	16.0	9.2	6.1	3.3
1983	9.7	13.5	15.7	19.6	9.7	6.8	4.0
1984	7.7	12.5	12.9	16.2	7.6	6.1	2.7

Table 2.14 (Continued)

	Total	ELEMENTARY Less Than 5 Years	ELEMENTARY 5 to 8 Years	HIGH SCHOOL 1 to 3 Years	HIGH SCHOOL 4 Years	COLLEGE 1 to 3 Years	COLLEGE 4 Years Or More
White							
1962	5.2	8.0	--	7.2	4.6	--	--
1964	5.0	9.3	--	6.4	4.3	--	--
1965	4.3	7.4	--	6.4	3.7	--	--
1966	3.3	6.1	4.5	4.5	2.8	2.8	1.0
1967	3.2	4.4	4.2	4.6	2.9	2.5	.8
1968	3.0	5.4	4.0	4.6	2.7	2.5	1.0
1969	2.8	3.2	3.6	4.4	2.6	2.3	.9
1970	3.9	5.3	4.7	5.7	3.6	3.7	1.5
1971	5.5	7.2	6.6	8.1	5.1	5.4	2.2
1972	5.5	5.9	6.5	9.2	5.1	4.5	2.5
1973	4.7	4.7	6.1	8.0	4.1	3.6	2.1
1974	4.8	5.4	5.7	8.7	4.3	3.9	1.8
1975	8.5	15.2	10.9	14.0	8.4	6.6	2.8
1976	7.4	8.6	10.0	12.6	7.5	5.7	2.8
1977	7.2	8.7	9.9	12.7	6.8	5.5	3.2
1978	5.8	7.6	8.3	10.7	5.5	4.1	2.3
1979	5.4	7.5	7.4	10.9	5.0	3.8	2.1
1980	6.0	8.7	9.8	11.6	5.9	4.4	1.9
1981	7.0	10.0	11.7	13.5	7.2	4.4	2.3
1982	8.6	15.2	13.2	17.0	9.1	5.8	2.9
1983	9.7	15.1	16.1	19.0	10.3	7.0	3.4
1984	7.2	12.9	12.2	15.2	7.4	5.1	2.6

Table 2.14 (Continued)

		ELEMENTARY		HIGH SCHOOL		COLLEGE	
	Total	Less Than 5 Years	5 to 8 Years	1 to 3 Years	4 Years	1 to 3 Years	4 Years Or More
Black							
1962	12.1	12.6	--	15.3	12.4	--	--
1964	10.0	7.8	--	12.5	10.1	--	--
1965	8.5	7.8	--	13.5	8.2	--	--
1966	7.0	5.5	6.6	9.7	7.0	6.3	1.9
1967	7.3	6.3	6.9	10.6	6.5	5.8	1.9
1968	6.5	4.9	5.7	9.8	6.7	3.9	1.6
1969	5.7	2.7	5.0	7.6	6.4	4.8	1.2
1970	6.7	5.7	5.3	9.5	7.2	6.1	1.4
1971	8.8	5.2	8.4	11.8	8.8	9.0	3.3
1972	10.4	6.6	9.4	15.5	9.6	9.7	2.8
1973	8.9	3.6	7.5	13.6	8.8	8.8	2.3
1974	9.3	3.9	8.5	14.7	8.9	6.9	3.4
1975	14.7	8.6	15.8	22.0	15.2	10.1	3.9
1976	13.1	8.2	10.4	19.0	14.3	12.5	3.0
1977	14.7	12.2	12.0	20.0	14.4	12.5	5.0
1978	13.2	8.2	8.9	21.6	12.7	10.4	4.7
1979	12.6	9.1	10.3	19.6	12.6	8.8	4.2
1980	13.4	8.5	11.6	20.5	13.1	10.8	4.4
1981	15.9	11.7	13.2	24.7	16.4	11.8	4.0
1982	18.9	23.4	16.1	24.1	20.7	15.8	8.3
1983	21.0	21.8	16.2	29.5	22.8	17.3	8.5
1984	17.2	15.7	16.7	27.3	18.3	12.0	6.3
Hispanic Origin							
1973	7.2	6.6	6.7	10.2	6.0	5.7	5.0
1974	8.1	6.5	9.0	12.2	7.1	5.0	4.8
1975	12.8	16.5	14.2	18.4	10.5	7.9	3.6
1976	11.4	9.4	12.3	15.5	11.6	8.2	4.4
1977	11.4	10.9	11.9	17.2	10.0	8.2	5.0
1978	9.5	10.5	10.0	14.0	7.4	7.3	7.3
1979	8.7	8.2	7.0	14.6	8.2	6.5	3.6
1980	9.2	9.2	12.8	14.3	7.1	5.9	3.7
1981	11.2	11.1	14.4	17.0	9.7	6.3	2.8
1982	13.4	16.2	15.4	21.8	11.4	7.1	4.9
1983	16.3	20.6	18.6	23.9	14.4	10.9	6.8
1984	11.6	17.8	12.9	18.4	9.6	7.2	3.5

Source: Handbook of Labor Statistics, U.S. Dept. of Labor, June, 1985, Bulletin 2217, pp. 169-171

Table 2.15

Average Hourly Earnings or Production Workers on
Manufacturing Payrolls by Industry, Selected Years

DURABLE GOODS

	Total	Lumber & Wood Products	Furniture & Fixtures	Stone, Clay & Glass Products	PRIMARY METAL INDUSTRIES			Machinery Except Electrical	Electrical & Electronic Equipment	TRANSPORTATION EQUIPMENT			Misc. Manufacturing
					Total	Blast Furnaces & Basic Steel Products	Fabricated Metal Products			Total	Motor Vehicles And Equipment	Instruments & Related Products	
1947	$1.276	$1.089	$1.097	$1.194	$1.388	$1.443	$1.264	$1.344	$1.246	$1.435	$1.473	$1.197	$1.105
1950	1.517	1.297	1.281	1.437	1.647	1.700	1.518	1.600	1.443	1.722	1.778	1.448	1.275
1955	1.99	1.62	1.62	1.86	2.24	2.39	1.96	2.08	1.84	2.21	2.29	1.87	1.61
1960	2.42	1.89	1.88	2.28	2.81	3.04	2.43	2.55	2.28	2.74	2.81	2.31	1.89
1961	2.48	1.95	1.91	2.34	2.90	3.16	2.49	2.62	2.35	2.80	2.86	2.38	1.92
1962	2.56	1.99	1.95	2.41	2.98	3.25	2.55	2.71	2.40	2.91	2.99	2.44	1.98
1963	2.63	2.04	2.00	2.48	3.04	3.31	2.61	2.78	2.46	3.01	3.10	2.49	2.03
1964	2.70	2.11	2.05	2.53	3.11	3.36	2.68	2.87	2.51	3.09	3.21	2.54	2.08
1965	2.79	2.17	2.12	2.62	3.18	3.42	2.76	2.96	2.58	3.21	3.34	2.62	2.14
1966	2.89	2.25	2.21	2.72	3.28	3.53	2.88	3.09	2.65	3.33	3.44	2.73	2.22
1967	3.00	2.37	2.33	2.82	3.34	3.57	2.98	3.19	2.77	3.44	3.55	2.85	2.35
1968	3.19	2.57	2.47	2.99	3.55	3.76	3.16	3.36	2.93	3.69	3.89	2.98	2.50
1969	3.38	2.74	2.62	3.19	3.79	4.02	3.34	3.58	3.09	3.89	4.10	3.15	2.66
1970	3.55	2.96	2.77	3.40	3.93	4.16	3.53	3.77	3.28	4.06	4.22	3.34	2.83
1971	3.80	3.17	2.90	3.67	4.23	4.49	3.77	4.02	3.49	4.45	4.72	3.50	2.97
1972	4.07	3.33	3.08	3.94	4.66	5.08	4.04	4.32	3.71	4.81	5.13	3.66	3.11
1973	4.35	3.61	3.29	4.22	5.04	5.51	4.29	4.60	3.91	5.15	5.46	3.83	3.29
1974	4.70	3.89	3.53	4.54	5.60	6.27	4.61	4.94	4.21	5.54	5.87	4.11	3.53
1975	5.15	4.26	3.78	4.92	6.18	6.94	5.05	5.37	4.64	6.07	6.44	4.53	3.81
1976	5.58	4.72	3.99	5.33	6.77	7.59	5.49	5.79	4.96	6.62	7.09	4.93	4.04
1977	6.06	5.10	4.34	5.81	7.40	8.36	5.91	6.26	5.39	7.29	7.85	5.29	4.36
1978	6.58	5.60	4.68	6.33	8.20	9.39	6.35	6.78	5.82	7.91	8.50	5.71	4.69
1979	7.13	6.07	5.06	6.85	8.98	10.41	6.85	7.32	6.32	8.53	9.06	6.17	5.03
1980	7.75	6.55	5.49	7.50	9.77	11.39	7.45	8.00	6.94	9.35	9.85	6.80	5.46
1981	8.54	6.99	5.91	8.27	10.81	12.60	8.19	8.81	7.62	10.39	11.02	7.40	5.97
1982	9.04	7.43	6.31	8.87	11.33	13.35	8.77	9.26	8.21	11.11	11.62	8.06	6.42
1983	9.38	7.79	6.62	9.27	11.34	12.89	9.11	9.55	8.65	11.66	12.12	8.46	6.80

Table 2.15 (Continued)

NON-DURABLE GOODS

Year	Total	Food & Kindred Products	Tobacco Manufactures	Textile Mill Products	Apparel & Other Textile Products	Paper & Allied Products	Printing & Publishing	Chemicals & Allied Products	Petroleum & Coal Products	Rubber & Misc. Plastic Products	Leather & Leather Products
1947	$1.145	$1.063	$0.904	$1.035	$1.161	$1.153	$1.475	$1.220	$1.501	$1.299	$1.038
1950	1.347	1.262	1.076	1.227	1.239	1.398	1.831	1.496	1.841	1.472	1.169
1955	1.67	1.66	1.34	1.38	1.37	1.81	2.26	1.97	2.37	1.96	1.39
1960	2.05	2.11	1.70	1.61	1.59	2.26	2.68	2.50	2.89	2.32	1.64
1961	2.11	2.17	1.78	1.63	1.64	2.34	2.75	2.58	3.01	2.38	1.68
1962	2.17	2.24	1.85	1.68	1.69	2.40	2.82	2.65	3.05	2.44	1.72
1963	2.22	2.30	1.91	1.71	1.73	2.48	2.89	2.72	3.16	2.47	1.76
1964	2.29	2.37	1.95	1.79	1.79	2.56	2.97	2.80	3.20	2.54	1.83
1965	2.36	2.44	2.09	1.87	1.83	2.65	3.06	2.89	3.28	2.61	1.88
1966	2.45	2.52	2.19	1.96	1.89	2.75	3.16	2.98	3.41	2.67	1.94
1967	2.57	2.64	2.27	2.06	2.03	2.87	3.28	3.10	3.58	2.75	2.07
1968	2.74	2.80	2.48	2.21	2.21	3.05	3.48	3.26	3.75	2.92	2.23
1969	2.91	2.96	2.62	2.35	2.31	3.24	3.69	3.47	4.00	3.07	2.36
1970	3.08	3.16	2.91	2.45	2.39	3.44	3.92	3.69	4.28	3.20	2.49
1971	3.27	3.38	3.16	2.57	2.49	3.67	4.20	3.97	4.57	3.39	2.59
1972	3.48	3.60	3.47	2.75	2.60	3.95	4.51	4.26	4.96	3.61	2.68
1973	3.70	3.85	3.76	2.95	2.76	4.20	4.75	4.51	5.28	3.81	2.79
1974	4.01	4.19	4.12	3.20	2.97	4.53	5.03	4.88	5.68	4.06	2.99
1975	4.37	4.61	4.55	3.42	3.17	5.01	5.38	5.39	6.48	4.39	3.21
1976	4.70	4.98	4.98	3.69	3.40	5.47	5.71	5.91	7.21	4.66	3.40
1977	5.11	5.37	5.54	3.99	3.62	5.96	6.12	6.43	7.83	5.17	3.61
1978	5.53	5.80	6.13	4.30	3.94	6.52	6.51	7.02	8.63	5.52	3.89
1979	6.01	6.27	6.67	4.66	4.23	7.13	6.94	7.60	9.36	5.97	4.22
1980	6.55	6.85	7.74	5.07	4.56	7.84	7.53	8.30	10.10	6.52	4.58
1981	7.18	7.44	8.88	5.52	4.97	8.60	8.19	9.12	11.38	7.17	4.99
1982	7.74	7.92	9.79	5.83	5.20	9.32	8.74	9.96	12.46	7.64	5.33
1983	8.08	8.20	10.35	6.18	5.37	9.94	9.11	10.59	13.29	7.99	5.54

Source: Handbook of Labor Statistics, U.S. Dept. of Labor, June, 1985, Bulletin 2217, pp. 194-195

Table 2.16
Average Weekly Earnings of Production Workers on Manufacturing Payrolls by Industry, Selected Years

DURABLE GOODS

				PRIMARY METAL INDUSTRIES					TRANSPORTATION EQUIPMENT			
Total	Lumber & Wood Products	Furniture & Fixtures	Stone, Clay & Glass Products	Total	Blast Furnaces & Basic Steel Products	Fabricated Metal Products	Machinery Except Electrical	Electrical & Electronic Equipment	Total	Motor Vehicles And Equipment	Instruments & Related Products	Misc. Manufacturing
$51.68	$43.89	$45.53	$48.95	$55.38	$56.51	$51.70	$55.78	$50.21	$56.97	$58.63	$48.36	$44.75
62.35	51.23	53.55	59.06	67.36	67.95	63.00	67.04	59.31	71.29	74.85	59.80	52.02
82.19	63.99	67.07	77.00	92.51	96.80	81.73	87.36	74.89	93.48	99.84	76.48	64.88
97.04	73.71	75.20	92.57	109.59	116.13	98.42	104.55	90.74	111.52	115.21	93.32	74.28
99.94	77.03	76.40	95.24	114.55	122.92	100.85	107.42	94.47	113.40	114.69	96.87	75.84
104.70	79.20	79.37	98.81	119.80	127.40	104.81	113.01	97.44	122.22	127.67	99.80	78.61
108.09	81.80	81.80	102.67	124.64	133.06	107.79	116.20	99.14	126.42	132.68	101.59	80.39
112.05	85.24	84.46	105.50	129.69	138.43	111.76	121.69	101.66	130.09	138.03	103.63	82.37
117.18	88.75	87.98	110.04	133.88	140.90	116.20	127.58	105.78	137.71	147.63	108.47	85.39
121.96	91.80	91.72	114.24	138.09	144.73	122.11	135.34	109.18	141.86	147.23	114.93	88.80
123.60	95.27	94.13	117.31	137.27	143.51	123.67	135.89	111.35	142.42	144.84	117.42	92.59
132.07	104.34	100.28	124.98	147.68	154.16	131.77	141.46	118.08	155.72	168.09	120.69	98.50
139.59	110.15	105.85	133.66	158.42	166.03	138.94	152.15	124.84	161.44	170.56	128.21	103.74
143.07	116.92	108.58	140.08	158.77	166.40	143.67	154.95	130.54	163.62	170.07	134.27	109.52
153.14	126.17	115.42	152.67	169.62	177.80	152.31	163.21	139.25	181.12	194.46	139.30	115.53
167.68	134.53	123.82	165.87	192.92	206.25	166.45	181.87	149.88	200.58	220.59	148.60	122.85
180.53	144.04	131.60	176.82	213.19	229.77	178.46	196.88	157.96	216.82	237.51	156.65	128.31
191.29	152.49	138.02	187.50	232.96	258.95	188.09	207.97	167.14	224.37	238.32	166.04	136.61
205.49	164.86	143.64	198.77	247.20	274.13	202.51	219.10	183.28	245.23	259.53	178.94	146.69
226.55	188.33	154.81	219.06	276.22	305.88	223.99	238.55	198.40	276.05	304.16	198.68	156.75
248.46	202.98	169.26	239.95	305.62	338.58	242.31	259.79	217.76	309.83	345.40	214.77	169.17
270.44	222.88	183.92	263.33	342.76	389.69	260.35	285.44	234.55	333.80	368.05	233.54	181.97
290.90	239.16	195.82	284.28	371.77	428.89	278.80	305.98	254.70	350.58	372.37	251.74	195.16
310.78	252.18	209.17	306.00	391.78	448.77	300.98	328.00	276.21	379.61	394.00	275.40	211.30
343.31	270.51	226.94	335.76	437.81	509.04	330.06	360.33	304.80	424.95	450.72	298.96	231.64
355.27	282.34	234.73	355.69	437.34	505.97	343.78	367.62	322.65	449.96	470.61	320.79	246.53
381.77	312.38	260.83	384.71	459.27	509.16	369.87	386.78	350.33	490.89	524.80	341.78	265.88

(Years, top to bottom: 1947, 1950, 1955, 1960, 1961, 1962, 1963, 1964, 1965, 1966, 1967, 1968, 1969, 1970, 1971, 1972, 1973, 1974, 1975, 1976, 1977, 1978, 1979, 1980, 1981, 1982, 1983)

Chapter 3

ON THE GENERATION, MEASUREMENT AND DESCRIPTION
OF THE SIZE DISTRIBUTION OF INCOME

A rigorous analysis of the structure of labor earnings distributions necessarily requires us to discuss three important aspects of this structure. We discuss below theories on how observed distributions are generated, given that they are generated how do we measure inequality in them and what hypothetical statistical distributions best approximate the observed income distributions. The three concepts are intimately related and must be analyzed together to even begin to understand the complexity of the income distribution question.

The lack of a satisfactory theory of personal income distribution is a problem that economists have pondered for most of the twentieth century. In 1912 Irving Fisher wrote:

> No other problem has so great a human interest as this [the distribution of personal income], and yet scarcely any other problem has received so little scientific study (Fisher, 1922, 33).

Analyzing problems associated with the distribution of personal income is crucial, for as Sen (1973) points out, the relation between economic inequality and rebellion is indeed a close one, and it runs both ways. Theories of personal income distribution can be divided into three major categories. Models explaining the generation of income distributions are one important aspect of the theory and, as Sahota (1978) demonstrates in his survey article, literally hundreds of pieces have been written on this topic. The first part of this chapter will discuss major theories on the generation of income distributions. Another important aspect of the theory of personal income distribution regards measures of inequality given the income distribution. The second and third portions of this chapter will discuss various measures of economic inequality. Finally, the last part of this chapter will explore studies that have been done on trying to relate a hypothetical distribution to the actual empirical distribution of income.

3.1 Hypotheses on How Observed Distributions Are Generated

The ability theory is one of the oldest of all the generation theories of personal income distribution. Sir Francis Galton postulated that differences in workers' productivity and hence earnings were due to differences in ability. It was believed that abilities were normally distributed; hence, Galton expected income to be normally distributed. Pareto, however, found in his empirical work in 1847 that incomes were lognormally distributed with a skewness to the right, indicating substantial unequal distribution. Pigou (1932) attempted to explain that the discrepancy between ability and income was due to a skewed distribution of inherited wealth. While Pigou's conjecture did explain some of the variation between ability and income, this theory is considered too simplistic and mechanistic (See Sahota, 1978, p.4) to throw useful light on the causes and remedies of inequalities and poverty. The stochastic theory of distribution is another proffered hypothesis. This theory hypothesizes that the skewed income distribution is caused solely by chance, luck, and random occurrences. The theory states that even if a generation started from a state of strict equality of incomes and wealth, stochastic forces could emerge to the degree that the Pareto distribution results. We discuss both Gibrat's (1931) and Champernowne's (1937) expositions. Gibrat (1931) formulated his theory based on the law of proportionate effect. Gibrat's model is a first-order Markov chain model. The variables are expressed in their logarithms where the log of income is dependent on the log of income lagged a period and random events. The theory holds that, as time goes by, the distribution of income approaches the distribution of the random disturbance. Taubman (1975) tested the assumptions of Gibrat's stochastic theories under a large longitudinal survey and found significant evidence against the models.

In 1937, Champernowne based his stochastic theory on Markov chains which generated a Pareto distribution. Later, in 1953, he suggested a random model based on the language of transition probabilities, but this model has the same problem as Gibrat's. Champernowne imposed a stability condition on the chief characteristic equation of his transition probability matrix which could be explained in terms of a birth and death process. He assumed a constant number of incomes in his model. Similar variations of these stochastic models were compiled by Rutherford (1955), Aitchison and Brown (1957), and Steindl (1965). Empirical studies

supporting their results have been confirmed by Fase (1970) for Holland
data and by Creedy (1972) for British data.

One critique by Shorrocks (1973) about the simple stochastic models
noted that the process required an incredibly long period of time to
attain an equilibrium or a stationary state distribution. Instead of the
comparative static approach, Shorrocks used rigorous dynamic models which
also consider real time, economic theory, and random processes. His
models interpret the actual situations as the result of a "nonequilibrium
time-dependent process".

The individual choice theory was postulated by Milton Friedman in
1953. The basic premise of this theory is that incomes are determined by
individual choice among opportunities that yield both different
combinations of cash income and non-pecuniary advantages, and different
profiles of cash income over time. Friedman believed that inequality of
income reflects "equalizing differences" in occupational choice and risk
preferences. Another theory which is closely related to the individual
choice model and attempts to explain the generation question is the human
capital approach. Adam Smith first presented the human capital theory in
1776 by saying wages vary with the cost of learning the business. T. W.
Schultz formulated modern human capital theory in the 1950's. The basic
premise of this theory is that individuals' investment in themselves is
the result of rational optimizing decisions made on the basis of
estimates of the probable present value of alternative life-cycle income
streams, discounted at some appropriate rate. Many criticisms exist of
the human capital theory. The major criticism of the theory is that
discounted-value maximization behavior is too far-fetched. While some
lifelong economic considerations do play a part in individuals' lives,
the probabilities of a maximization of discounted lifetime earnings at
uniform discount rates is unrealistic. Educational theories abounded in
the 1960's which linked the personal income distribution to education
levels. Joseph Hunt (1961) was among the first to postulate this theory.
Hunt provided theoretical and empirical support for the belief that
within genetically given physical limitations of the individual,
environmental circumstances are the primary cause of learning behavior.
At the same time Hunt derived his theory, Schultz was employing the
human-capital approach in analyzing the economic effects of education.
Thus, these theorists believed that income depends on schooling and

ability. The theories mentioned above are all concerned with earned income. Another theory which is more general encompasses inheritances.

The inheritance theory can be traced back to Ricardo and Marx. Kaldor (1957) presented a clear exposition of this theory. According to this theory, capitalists perpetuate their economic positions: the more they have, the more they invest and accumulate, the more profits they earn, the more they can save and reinvest, and so the spiral goes on. In the limiting case, workers get income exclusively from their labor and do not save; hence inequality occurs. In this model human capital is ignored and capitalists do not labor or consume. Obviously, this model has major flaws in it. Another model is based on the life-cycle earnings of individuals; this is called the life-cycle theory. Earnings have been observed to rise with age and then decline near the age of retirement. Measured at a point in time, therefore, earnings' inequalities will naturally be overstated. Accordingly, a life-cycle of income rather than income at a point in time is a proper measure of inequality, especially when individual rather than family incomes are compared. The life-cycle model can be traced to Kuznets' pioneering 1953 study. A problem with this theory is that a choice of the appropriate distribution of lifetime earnings must be presented to look at the overall personal income distribution. The last theory of personal income distribution which will be discussed here is Becker's (1967) supply-demand model of human capital investment. The model employs a general approach and offers reinterpretations of several partial theories, such as the stochastic theory, the ability theory, the inheritance theory, and others. As Sahota (1978) describes the model, it is formalized to incorporate various forces determining the distribution, the shapes, and the elasticities of the supply and demand curves of human capital investment. The interdependence of supply and demand schedules is brought out as one of the crucial sources of earnings' inequality. A problem with this model is that it isn't comprehensive in the sense that earnings inequality is studied only from the supply side; i.e., the model treats demand as exogenous and only is concerned with the supply of human capital as being determinant.

3.2 Measuring Inequality

All of the aforementioned theories are concerned with why the personal income distribution looks as it does or how it was generated.

Measuring the personal income distribution and attendant inequality is another matter. As Sen (1973) points out, measures of inequality can be divided into normative and positive categories. The normative measures are concerned with measuring inequality in terms of a notion of social welfare so that a higher degree of inequality corresponds to a lower level of social welfare for a given total of income. Among the normative measures, Dalton's (1920) measure is best known. Dalton based his measure on the sum of individual utilities. His measure is based on a comparison between actual levels of aggregate utility and the level of total utility that would be obtained if income were equally divided. Dalton took the ratio of actual social welfare to the maximal social welfare as his measure of equality. Atkinson (1970) pointed out that Dalton's measure is not invariant to positive linear transformations of the utility function; his measure implies cardinal utility which means any positive linear transformation would do just as well, so Dalton's measure takes arbitrary values depending on which particular transformation is chosen. Atkinson's own approach is to redefine the measure in such a way that the actual numbers used in measuring the level of inequality would be invariant with respect to permitted transformations of the welfare numbers. Atkinson defines what he calls "the equally distributed equivalent income" of a given distribution of total income, and this is defined as that level of per capita income which, if enjoyed by everybody, would make total welfare exactly equal to the total welfare generated by the actual income distribution. Putting y_e as "the equally distributed equivalent income," we see that:

$$y_e = y \,|\, [nU(y) = \sum_{i=1}^{n} U(y_i)] \tag{3.1}$$

The sum of the actual welfare levels of all individuals equals the welfare sum that would emerge if everyone had y_e income. Since each $U(y)$ is taken to be concave, y_e cannot be larger than the mean income μ. Further, it can be shown that the more equal the distribution the closer will y_e be to μ. Atkinson's measure of inequality is:

$$A = 1 - (\frac{y_e}{\mu}). \tag{3.2}$$

If income is equally distributed then y_e is equal to μ, and the value of Atkinson's measure will be 0. The most obvious problem with this measure is that it is totally dependent on the form of the welfare function. Also, of course, the values of U of each person are simply added together to arrive at aggregate social welfare.

This work has led, however, to the axiomatic approach to analyzing inequality, and we will discuss this approach more fully below. The problems with this approach speak for themselves. The measures which will now be described are positive measures in the sense that they make no explicit use of any concept of social welfare. The following measures will be discussed following Sen (1973). The first measure to be described is the range. Consider distributions of income over n persons, i - 1, ..., n, and let y_i be the income of person i. Let the average level of income be μ, so that:

$$\sum_{i=1}^{n} y_i = n\mu \ . \tag{3.3}$$

The relative share of income going to person i is x_i. That is:

$$y_i = n\mu x_i \ . \tag{3.4}$$

so the range measure is based on comparing the extreme values of the distribution, i.e., the highest and the lowest income levels. The range can be defined as the gap between these two levels as a ratio of mean income. The range E is defined by:

$$E = \frac{(Max_i \ y_i - Min_i \ y_i)}{\mu} \ . \tag{3.5}$$

If income is divided absolutely equally, then E = 0. If one person receives all the income, then E = n. The problem with the range is that it ignores the distribution in between the extremes. A measure that examines the entire distribution is the relative mean deviation. This measure compares the income level of each individual with the mean income, it sums the absolute values of all the differences, and then looks at that sum as a proportion of total income. The relative mean deviation takes the form:

$$M = \frac{\sum_{i=1}^{n} |\mu - y_i|}{n\mu} \ . \tag{3.6}$$

With perfect equality $M = 0$ and with all income going to one person, $M = 2(n - 1)/n$. The major flaw with the relative mean deviation is that it is not sensitive to transfers from a poorer person to a richer person as long as both lie on the same side of the mean income. A very common statistical measure of the variation is the variance:

$$V = \frac{\sum_{i=1}^{n} (\mu - y_i)^2}{n} \ . \tag{3.7}$$

The problem with looking at the variance is that it depends on the mean income level, and one distribution may show much greater relative variation than another and still end up having a lower variance if the mean income level around which the variations take place is smaller than the other distribution. A measure that doesn't have this deficiency and concentrates on relative variation is the coefficient of variation, which is simply the square root of the variance divided by the mean income level:

$$C = \frac{V^{\frac{1}{2}}}{\mu} \ . \tag{3.8}$$

A question that arises with the coefficient of variation asks whether it is best to measure the difference of each income level from the mean only, or should the comparison be carried out between every pair of incomes? By utilizing pairwise comparisons, everyone's income difference from everyone else's is taken into account. The standard deviation of logarithms is a measure of inequality that eliminates the arbitrariness of the units and therefore of absolute levels, since a change of units, which takes the form of a multiplication of the absolute values, comes out in the logarithmic form as an addition of a constant, and therefore disappears when pairwise differences are being taken. The standard deviation of the logarithm takes the form:

$$H = [\ \sum_{i=1}^{n} \frac{(\log \mu - \log y_i)^2}{n}\ ]^{\frac{1}{2}} \tag{3.9}$$

The H measure depends on the arbitrary squaring formula and shares with
the variance and coefficient of variation the limitation of taking
differences only from the mean.

A measure of economic inequality that has been widely used is the
Gini coefficient attributed to Gini (1912). The Gini measure may be
viewed in terms of the Lorenz curve. We will rigorously discuss the
Lorenz curve below. The Lorenz curve was devised by Lorenz (1905),
whereby the percentages of the population arranged from the poorest to
the richest are represented on the horizontal axis and the percentages of
income enjoyed by the bottom x percent of the population are shown on the
vertical axis. A Lorenz curve runs from one corner of the unit square to
the diametrically opposite corner. If everyone has the same income the
Lorenz curve is simply the diagonal. If bottom income groups have a
proportionately lower share of income, the Lorenz curve will obviously
lie below the diagonal. The Gini coefficient is the ratio of the
difference between the line of absolute equality (the diagonal) and the
Lorenz curve--to the triangle underneath the diagonal. The Gini
coefficient may be defined as exactly one half of the relative mean
difference, which is defined as the arithmetic average of the absolute
values of differences between all pairs of incomes. From Sen (1973),

$$G = (\frac{1}{2} n^2 \mu) \sum_{i=1}^{n} \sum_{j=1}^{n} |y_i - y_j|$$

$$= 1 - (\frac{1}{n^2 \mu}) \sum_{i=1}^{n} \sum_{j=1}^{n} \text{Min} (y_i, y_j) \qquad (3.10a\text{-}c)$$

$$= 1 = (\frac{1}{n}) - (\frac{2}{n^2 \mu}) [y_1 + 2y_2 + \ldots + ny_n]$$

for $y_1 \geq y_2 \geq y_3 \ldots \geq y_n$.

Notice that the Gini avoids the total concentration on differences vis-a-
vis the mean which C, V, or H has. It also avoids the squaring
procedures of C, V, and H. But the most appealing property of the Gini
is that it looks at differences between every pair of incomes, cf. Morgan
(1962). Kakwani (1980) has proposed a measure which is best explicated
based on the Lorenz curve so we defer discussion of it to the section 3.5
below.

3.3 Axiom-based Inequality Measurement and Theil's Entropy Measures

While the inequality measures just discussed are positivistic, they do not possess properties that are considered desirable by the new breed of inequality theorists or the so-called "Axiomatic Approach" school. This group is led by the pioneering work of Atkinson, Cowell, Foster, Sen and Shorrocks, cf. Jenkins (1988) for a discussion of their work. This group has gone back to the belief that welfare should serve as a basis for inequality analysis and especially with respect to comparisons between various distributions where one is trying to make the unambiguous statement that one distribution embodies a higher level of welfare vis-a-vis another. This group has taken the approach that inequality measurement (or more specifically a given inequality measure) should fulfill certain criteria and then a measure should be found that is consistent with these criteria.

We will briefly list some of these properties here:

1) Symmetry
2) Pigou-Dalton Principle of Transfers
3) Mean Independence
4) Pareto Dominance
5) Rank Dominance
6) General Lorenz Dominance

These properties have been discussed at length elsewhere but briefly: 1) implies anonymity so if two individuals in the graduation switch places, the value of the measure should not change; 2) simply means a transfer of income from a richer to poorer person should have a clear effect on the inequality measure and 4) is a stronger version of the same. 3) implies that if the population doubles (or all incomes double) by each person being replicated, the inequality measure's value should not change. If 1) and 4) are met, then 5) is valid. This means that the income vector x rank dominates y iff the poorest person in x, etc. has a higher income than the poorest person in y, etc. If the Lorenz curve for x lies everywhere above y and we scale them both by the mean income level then 6) holds. Bishop, Formby and Thistle (1988) give a very nice discussion of these properties as well.

The problem then becomes, of course, one of finding a class of inequality measures that satisfies these criteria. Of all the forms proposed, only one class comes close. This class is known as the generalized entropy or GE class. The relationship between the axioms and

entropy can be traced to Shorrocks (1980,1983), Maasoumi (1986) and
others.   The concept of using entropy to measure inequality, however,
goes back to Theil.

Let x be the probability that a certain event will occur, the
information content h(x) of noticing that the event has in fact   occurred
is a decreasing function of x--the more unlikely an event, the more
interesting it is to know that that thing has really happened.   Theil
considered one case of this,

$$h(x) - \log \frac{1}{x} .$$ (3.11)

When there are n possible events 1, ..., n, we take the respective
probabilities x_1, ..., x_n such that $x_i \geq 0$ and $\sum_{i=1} x_i - 1$. The entropy or
the expected information content of the situation can be viewed as the
sum of the information content of each event weighted by the respective
probabilities.

$$H(x) - \sum_{i=1}^{n} x_i h(x_i)$$

(3.12a-b)

$$= \sum_{i=1}^{n} x_i \log (\frac{1}{x_i})$$

The closer the n probabilities x_i are to $(\frac{1}{n})$, the greater is the entropy.
Interpreting x_i as the share of income belonging to the   ith individual,
H(x) is a measure of equality. When each x_i equals $\frac{1}{n}$, H(x) attains its
maximum value of log n. To get the index of inequality, we subtract   the
entropy H(x) of an income distribution from its maximum value of log n,
we then get an index of inequality. Theil's measure takes the form

$$T - \log n - H(x)$$

(3.12a-b)

$$= \sum_{i=1}^{n} x_i \log nx_i$$

Theil has applied his measure to many interesting   applications but
perhaps one of the most ingenious is that the measure allows for regional
inequality analysis with only per   capita   and   population   data.   In a
recent paper, Theil (1988) notes,

When this measure is applied to the per capita incomes of our 116 countries, it can be written as

(1) $$J = \sum_{i-1}^{116} p_i \log \frac{p_i}{y_i}$$

where p_i is the population share of country i and y_i is its income share (the shares of i in world population and in total world income, respectively).

The advantage of (1) is its convenient additive decomposition, which may be explained as follows. Let $R_1, \ldots, R_G$ be regions so that each country is in exactly one region. Let P_g and Y_g be the population and income shares of region R_g: $P_g = \Sigma_i p_i$ and $Y_g = \Sigma_i y_i$, where the summations are over $i \in R_g$. Then the extension of (1) to regions is

(2) $$J_R = \sum_{g=1}^{G} P_g \log \frac{P_g}{Y_g}$$

which measures the inequality among regions, while

(3) $$J_G = \sum_{i \in R_G} \frac{P_i}{P_g} \log \frac{P_i/P_g}{Y_i/Y_g}$$

measures the inequality among the countries of region R_g. The additive decomposition is then

(4) $$J = J_R + \bar{J} \quad \text{where} \quad \bar{J} = \sum_{g=1}^{G} P_g J_g$$

Thus, total inequality among the 116 countries equals regional inequality plus the average within-region inequality, the average being a weighted average with the population shares $P_1, \ldots, P_G$ as weights. Note that these weights are identical to those of the regional per capita incomes....

Since we confine ourselves to the per capita incomes of the 116 countries, we ignore the income inequality within these countries. Thus, J of equation (1) is not "world income inequality" but it is "international income inequality", where "international" means that the individual incomes in each country have been replaced by that country's per capita income. We obtain world inequality from international inequality by adding the average within-country inequality; this is a decomposition similar to (4) (Theil, 1988, 5-7).

Thus, the entropy class of measures not only satisfies most welfare-based axioms but the class also has members that have powerful decomposition properties.

While Theil's measure is ingenious, the problem remains, however, that the formula is arbitrary and, as Sen (1973) points out, taking the

average of the logarithms of the reciprocals of income shares weighted by
income shares is not a measure that is exactly overflowing with intuitive
sense. Many other lesser known measures do exist. Elteto and Frigyes
(1968) proposed a measure that is also based on the relative mean
deviation.

All of these measures yield information on the inequality present in
a given distribution. One should be careful in choosing one over
another, however, because they measure different aspects of the given
distribution. In this book, we utilize several different measures of
inequality as descriptions of inequality in the various empirical income
distributions we examine. We do so because we want to emphasize that the
information content of all the measures differs and we want to provide as
much information as possible.

3.4 Approximating the Observed Income Distribution: Parametric Forms

Next, the choice of an appropriate hypothetical distribution to
approximate the empirical distribution of income will be discussed. As
was noted earlier, theories of how a particular income distribution was
generated can be traced as far back as Smith (1776). Pareto (1897),
however, was one of the first individuals to actually hypothesize the
size distribution of income and then to actually see how well it fit the
empirical distribution. Pareto presented his law of income distribution,
without, however, considering that he was stating the outcome of a
stochastic (probabilistic) process. He began by examining the
quantitative aspects of the personal distribution of income. His
analysis depends on the observed regularity and permanence of the
elasticity of the upper tail of the income distribution. The formula for
the Pareto distribution of income is given by:

$$z(x) = 1 - F(x) = (\frac{x_0}{x})^{\alpha} \qquad\qquad x > x_0 \qquad\qquad (3.14a)$$

$$= 1 \qquad\qquad\qquad\qquad x < x_0$$

where $F(x) = Pr(X \leq x)$ is called the probability distribution function,
with Pr representing probability. $F(x)$ is defined to be the probability
that a unit chosen randomly will take on a value less than or equal to x.
$Z(x)$ is the proportion of income-recipient units with income greater or

equal to x. x_0 is the "threshold" income level. α is the Pareto parameter.

The functional form of (3.14a) can be transformed to a logarithmic form:

$$\log Z(x) - \alpha\log x_0 - \alpha\log x \qquad (3.14b)$$

This equation implies that $-\alpha$ is the elasticity of $Z(x)$ with respect to x, i.e., if income x increases by 1%, the percentage change of income-recipient units would decrease by α. Hence the α can be regarded as the elasticity of a reduction in the number of units when moving to a higher income class.

Brown commented on the Pareto law:

> There are, of course, two elements to his law, which Pareto, however, did not separately discuss. The first is the algebraic formula itself, and the second is the numerical value of the parameter α which directly controls all the well-known measures of income inequality. It would indeed be sufficiently remarkable evidence of economic stability if all income distributions could be fitted with the same algebraic formula, even though the numerical values of the parameter α might vary from place to place or from time to time. But the general sense of Pareto's writing seems to indicate that he himself was most impressed by the fact that parameter α in fact varied very little over the data available to him (Brown, 1976, 7).

Many researchers have used the Pareto law and model when studying the theoretical and empirical distribution of income. (cf. Aigner and Goldberger (1970), Gastwirth (1972), and Kakwani and Podder (1973)).

The idea of income being lognormally distributed was developed by Kapteyn (1903), subsequently by Edgeworth (1924), and then led to Gibrat's work (1931). Gibrat proposed the "law of proportionate effect", which yields a positively skewed distribution. A brief outline of this law has been given by Kakwani (1980) as follows:

Let an individual's initial income be x_0 and subsequently encounter a series of random, independent, proportional changes $m_1, m_2, \ldots, m_t$ where m_1 can be either negative or positive. After t periods during which these changes have taken place, his income becomes

$$x_t = x_0(1 + m_1)(1 + m_2)\ldots(1 + m_t). \qquad (3.15a)$$

taking a logarithmic transformation yields

$$\log x_t = \log x_0 + \sum_{i=1}^{t} u_i \qquad \text{where } u_i = \log (1 + m_i). \qquad (3.15b)$$

By the central limit theorem, we know that if time t were sufficiently large the distribution of $\log x_t$ will tend toward normality. The distribution of $\log x_t$ can be denoted as

$$\log x_t \approx N(\mu_t, \sigma_t^2) \qquad (3.15c)$$

In other words, the random variable x_t will follow the lognormal distribution defined by Kakwani (1980) as "the distribution of a random variable whose logarithm follows the normal probability law."

Equation (3.15c) shows that the variance of $\log x_t$ increases continuously as the time goes by. The tendency for such an increase, however, is never likely to be observed in practice. A number of solutions have been proposed. For instance, Kalecki (1945) solved this problem by suggesting a constraint be imposed on the final distribution with a constant logarithmic variance. This assumed that the proportionate random increment to x_t, (viz., m_t) was negatively correlated to the size of x_t. Although this modification would prevent the variance of $\log x_t$ from increasing continuously, the assumption is artifical without further evidence or justification.

Since the transformation $Y = \log x$ is a normal distribution having parameters μ (mean) and σ^2 (variance), we can derive the lognormal distribution. The probability density function is written as

$$f(x) = (2\pi\sigma^2 x^2)^{-1/2} \exp(-(\log x - \mu)^2/(2\sigma^2)), \qquad x > 0 \qquad (3.15d)$$
$$= 0 \qquad x \leq 0$$

The corresponding probability distribution function is defined as

$$F(x) = \Lambda(x|\mu, \sigma^2)$$
$$= \int_0^x (2\pi\sigma^2 X^2)^{-1/2}\exp(-(\log X - \mu)^2/(2\sigma^2))dX, \qquad X > 0 \qquad (3.15e\text{-}f)$$
$$= 0 \qquad X \leq 0$$

The lognormal distribution exhibits, a positively skewed income distribution for the observed income data and provides a reasonably close approximation to the normal distribution.

So far we have briefly introduced Pareto and lognormal distributions which have been proposed as models of income distribution. Although the estimated parameters from both distributions can be interpreted in an economically meaningful way (e.g., parameters can be directly related to inequality measures) empirically neither model fits the full range of data very well. As Singh and Maddala (1976) remarked: "The Pareto function fits the data fairly well toward the higher levels but the fit is poor toward the lower income levels. If one considers the entire range of income, perhaps the fit may be better for the lognormal but the fit toward the upper end is far from satisfactory."

Therefore, as an alternative model of income distribution, Salem and Mount (1974) suggested a two-parameter gamma density function (Pearson Type III). This function is

$$f(X;k,\lambda) = \lambda/\Gamma(k) \ X^{k-1} \ e^{-\lambda X}, \quad 0 < X < \infty \qquad (3.16)$$

where $\Gamma(k) = \int_0^\infty e^{-u} u^{k-1} \ du$ is the gamma function, k and λ are positive parameters which are considered as measures of skewness and of scale respectively. Accordingly, these parameters are directly related to standard inequality measures and to Gibrat's law of proportionate effect after the process of transformation of $F(Y;k,\lambda)dY = f(X;k,\lambda)dX$ where $Y = cX$ and c is a constant. Salem and Mount (1974) applied the Gamma distribution to U.S. personal income data for the years 1960 and 1969 to both the gamma and the lognormal distributions and concluded that the gamma distribution gives a better fit than the lognormal distribution. Molina and Slottje (1987) have briefly discussed this functional form.

In 1976, Singh and Maddala derived a distribution function which can be generated from the Pareto and the Weibull distributions. Their functional form incorporates hazard rates or failure rates which are widely used in reliability theory. They applied this model to U.S. family income data for the two years 1960 and 1969. The empirical results showed that the new distribution function fits the data better than the gamma function suggested by Salem and Mount (1974).

In addition, Singh and Maddala proposed an alternative derivation in terms of the rate of decay. This process is as follows:

F(x) is given as a certain mass at point x which is initially equal
to one and will decay to zero as x approaches ∞ ($0 \leq x \leq \infty$). The Pareto
process is an example of what is said to be a "memoryless" process since
the rate of decay depends on only the left-out mass (1-F).

$$\frac{dF}{dx} = a(1 - F)^{(1+1/a)} \qquad (3.17a)$$

But the Weibull process is said to be a "memory" process, because

$$\frac{dF}{dx} = ax^b(1 - F) \qquad (3.17b)$$

Since Singh and Maddala's function is generated from both the Pareto
and Weibull process, the rate of decay for their function is

$$\frac{dF}{dx} = ax^b(1 - F)^c \quad \text{(a, b, and c are constants).} \qquad (3.17c)$$

The integral for this equation is

$$F = 1 - (1 + a_1x^{a_2})^{-a_3}$$

where $a_1 = (c - 1)(a/(b + 1))$,   (3.17d-g)

$$a_2 = b + 1,$$

and $a_3 = 1/(c - 1)$

The above relations also demonstrate the relationships between the
Pareto, Weibull, and Singh and Maddala distributions.

As a special case of this distribution, let $a_3=1$ and take the first-
order derivative of (3.17d) with respect to x. This yields:

$$\frac{dF}{dx} = a_1a_2x^{a_2-1}(1 + a_1x^{a_2})^2 \qquad (3.18a)$$

which can be transformed into

$$\frac{dF}{d\phi} = \frac{e^\phi}{(1+e^\phi)^2}$$

$$(3.18b-c)$$

where $e^{\phi} = (x/x_0)^{\alpha}$

by means of the transformation $a_1 = (1/x_0)^{\alpha}$ and $a_2 = \alpha$.
The distribution function in (3.18a) is the hyperbolic secant square distribution suggested by Fisk (1961).

Thurow (1970) first used the beta density function as a model for the distribution of income. McDonald and Ransom (1979) compared the beta density function to the lognormal, gamma, and Singh-Maddala functions as descriptive models for the distribution of family income for 1960 and 1969 through 1975. McDonald and Ransom noted immediately that the gamma is a limiting case of the beta, thus the beta fits at least as well as the gamma. By deriving the Gini ratio for the four different functional forms they concluded that the beta density and Singh-Maddala density fit better than the lognormal density or gamma density. One frequently encountered problem with these comparisons, however, is that different estimation techniques are used to estimate the parameters of the different functions. Thus, McDonald and Ransom were cautious to conclude that the beta density fit better or vice versa because the performance of the two depended on the estimation technique. In another study, McDonald (1984) has demonstrated that a generalized beta density of the second kind fits income data better than the Singh-Maddala density, a generalized gamma density or the beta density of the first kind. Basmann et al. (1984) have used the beta of the second kind in empirical applications. Slottje (1984, 1987) and Shackett and Slottje (1987) have demonstrated the merits of this functional form for describing several different sets of data. We will discuss this form below in greater detail.

The distribution functions we ju⌐t explored all impose a functional form hence a parametric specification on the observed distribution. We now discuss methods of nonparametric analysis of the observed distributions.

3.5   The Lorenz Curve: A Nonparametric Description of the Observed
       Distribution

The Lorenz curve, suggested by Lorenz in 1905, is most frequently used as a graphical technique to depict and analyze the size distribution of income. In words, the Lorenz curve is the relationship between the

cumulative percentage of the total income of the economy and the
cumulative percentage of income for the receiving units.

The 45 degree line connecting the points (0,0) and (1,1) is called
the "egalitarian" line. If a country had an equal income distribution,
the Lorenz curve would be the "egalitarian" line. That is, any 10% of
income receivers or households would get 10% of income; and 20%, 20% of
income; and so on. Typically actual distributions bulge downward: the
greater the concavity, the greater the degree of inequality. Thus if one
Lorenz curve lies below another then we say that the first distribution
is more unequal than the second. Complete inequality means that only one
household gets the total income available. Below is a Lorenz type chart
in a unit square (Figure 3.1).

Given n families with incomes X_1, $X_2, \ldots X_n$ arranged in a
monotonically nondecreasing order:

$$0 \leq X_1 \leq X_2 \ldots \leq X_n, \tag{3.19a}$$

we can compute the income share q_j by

$$q_j = \frac{x_j}{\sum\limits_{i=1}^{n} x_i} \quad \text{and} \quad \sum\limits_{j=1}^{n} x_j = 1 \tag{3.19b}$$

The empirical Lorenz curve, L(z), is a real-valued function defined on z
(which is equal to 0, 1/n, 2/n, ... n/n) so that

$$L(0) = 0$$
$$\tag{3.19c-d}$$
and $L(z) = x_1 + x_2 + \ldots + x_i \quad (0 \leq z \leq 1).$

A typical Lorenz curve, L(z), usually has the following properties:
    (i) if z = 0, L(z) = 0,
    (ii) if z = 1, L(z) = 1,   (3.19e-h)
    (iii) $L(z) \leq z$,
    (iv) L(z) is twice differentiable and the slope of the curve
          increases monotonically (i.e., $L'(z) \geq 0$, $L''(z) > 0$).

The conventional definition of the Lorenz curve is usually in terms
of two equations by Kendall and Stuart (1977):

(i) the cumulative distribution function, $F(x)$, corresponding to the probability density function, $f(x)$, and random variable x defined as

$$z = F(x) = \int_0^x f(t)dt \tag{3.20}$$

(ii) the equation for Lorenz curve derived from (3.20),

$$L(z) = \Phi(x)\int_0^x tf(t)dt \tag{3.21}$$

$\Phi(x)$ exists only if the mean μ (which is defined below in equation (3.23)) exists.

Gastwirth in 1971 presented an alternative definition of the Lorenz curve in terms of the inverse of the cumulative distribution function and applied to both discrete and continuous variables. The inverse function, $F^{-1}(x)$, is given by

$$F^{-1}(t) = \inf\{x: F(x) \geq t\}. \tag{3.22}$$

This equation implies that the minimum value of x is chosen so that $F(x) \geq t$, and ensures the existence of x for all values of $F(x)$. The mean μ is defined as

$$\mu = \int xf(x)dx = \int xdF(x). \tag{3.23}$$

The Lorenz curve corresponding to μ and $F(x)$ is written as

$$L(z) = \frac{1}{\mu} \int_0^z F^{-1}(t)dt \qquad (0 \leq z \leq 1) \tag{3.24}$$

By using the conventional definition of the Lorenz curve, Kakwani (1980), moreover, gave another interesting and detailed explication of this curve.

Consider the number X to be a sample drawn from $F(x)$ which represents the percentage share of income units with income less than or equal to x, where

$$z = F(x) = \int_0^x f(X)dX \qquad (0 < z < 1) \tag{3.25}$$

which implies

$$\frac{dz}{dx} = f(x) \tag{3.26}$$

The first-moment distribution function of X with the existence of μ is given by

$$L(z) = F_1(x) = \frac{1}{\mu}\int_0^x XdF(X) \tag{3.27}$$

where $0 < L(z) < 1$. This means that the percentage share of total income earned by the units with an income is less than or equal to x. $F_1(x)$ is a monotonically nondecreasing function of x, since

$$\frac{dL(z)}{dx} = \frac{xf(x)}{\mu} \geq 0. \tag{3.28}$$

The Lorenz curve can exhibit the income distribution by establishing the interdependence of the two functions derived from the income density function. z, shown on the abscissa, is plotted against $L(z)$, shown on the ordinate, in a unit square (recall Figure 3.1). The slope of the Lorenz curve is obtained by taking the first derivative of $L(z)$ with respect to z

$$L' = \frac{dL(z)}{dz} = \frac{x}{\mu} \tag{3.29}$$

which is positive. The second derivative of the curve is

$$L'' = \frac{d^2L(z)}{dz^2} = \frac{1}{\mu f(x)} \tag{3.30}$$

which is also positive. The two equations (3.29) and (3.30) indicate that the Lorenz curve is monotone-increasing and convex to the z-axis (i.e., $L(z) < z$). Equations (3.25)-(3.30) satisfy the properties of the Lorenz curve stated in (3.19e-h) above.

Now given our discussion of the Lorenz curve and recalling our description of the positive inequality measures in section 3.2 above, we can derive the Gini measure, Kakwani's measure, the relative mean deviation measure and Theil's measure in terms of the Lorenz curve. As noted above, the Lorenz curve can be generated by defining the income earner units as (say) quantile shares where q_i, $i=1, \ldots, n$ represents the ith income earner share and letting

$$0 \leq q_1 \leq q_2, \ldots, \leq q_n \leq 1. \tag{3.31}$$

From this simple ordering the inequality measures described above can be formulated. We derive them in Chapter 6 below.

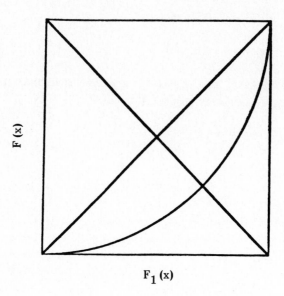

Figure 3.1
Lorenz Curve Diagram

Chapter 4

IDENTIFYING DISTRIBUTIONAL FORMS UTILIZING THE κ - CRITERION

4.1 Introduction

As should be clear from Chapter 3, the choice of an appropriate functional form of hypothetical statistical distribution to approximate the income graduation is fundamental to analyzing income inequality. Recently, Molina and Slottje (1987), Hirschberg, Molina and Slottje (1987) and Hirschberg and Slottje (1988) have all resurrected a technique from classical statistics that allows for the a priori checking of data against various functional forms (classes) of Pearsonian distributions.

As we noted above, beginning with the seminal work of Pareto (1897) the choice of an appropriate statistical distribution to approximate empirical income distributions has been somewhat arbitrary. While many forms have been tested, members of the Pearsonian Family of statistical distributions seem to be most prevalent in the literature. The Pearsonian distributions are utilized because the hypothetical forms are reasonable approximations to the J-shape of usual graduations as we will discuss below. The Pareto distribution, the lognormal distribution, the gamma distribution, the Beta I distribution and the Beta II distribution are all members of this family which have been extensively studied. Aitchison and Brown (1957) explored the lognormal distribution and found it "fit" earnings data well except at the tails. Amoroso (1925) and Salem and Mount (1974) introduced the gamma distribution into the literature. Thurow (1970) discussed the Beta I in macro economic income inequality applications. The Beta II distribution has been analyzed by Basmann, Molina and Slottje (1984a,b), McDonald (1984), and Slottje (1984, 1987).

In this chapter we provide a selection criterion by which one can a priori eliminate certain members of the Pearson Family as candidates for describing actual empirical income distributions. The a priori approach presented here is one that relies primarily on the relationship of the parametric characteristics of the empirical and the hypothetical IDF. Other valid and certainly not contradictory approaches to the method presented here rely more heavily on characteristics of the hypothetical IDF. These type of approaches are well represented by the work of MaCurdy (1984) and Molina (1984). The use of any hypothetical distribution to approximate actual empirical data is only appropriate if

the form "fits" the data well. The "fit" of a functional form to the
data is generally based on the sum of squared error test (SSE), sum of
absolute error test (SAE), the χ^2 test and the Kilmogorov-Smirnov test.
The (SSE), (SAE) and χ^2 tests are based on subtracting predicted
frequencies from observed frequencies. To find the predicted frequencies
entails calculating the parameters of the hypothetical distributions
based on the moments from the empirical distributions. After finding the
parameters these are then substituted into the hypothetical distributions
and integration is performed to find the predicted number of
observations. The purpose of this chapter is to present an **a priori**
discrimination criterion which allows the researcher to reject specific
functional forms without undergoing the tedious fitting procedures
involved in doing the above four tests. We now discuss criteria that a
statistical distribution should satisfy if it is to approximate an income
distribution and then present the κ - criterion. We utilize this
criterion in analyzing income distributions in Chapters 6 and 7 below.

4.2 The Test

The hypothetical income distribution function (IDF) should satisfy
several theoretical and practical requirements, as we noted in Chapter 3.
Given these desirable properties, the members of the Pearsonian Family
discussed above are all strong candidates. We now present the criterion.
The criterion is based on Elderton's (1938) κ - criterion.

Elderton (1938) constructed the criterion κ by noting first that
frequency distributions start usually at zero, rise to a maximum and then
fall, usually at different rates. The ends of the distribution usually
have high contact (low probability). Mathematically, a series of
equations $y = F(x)$, $y = \phi(x)$, etc. must be selected so each equation in
the series satisfies

$$\frac{dy}{dx} = 0 \qquad\qquad\qquad (4.1)$$

for certain values of x, namely at the maximum and the end of the curve
where contact occurs. Elderton then suggested

$$\frac{dy}{dx} = \frac{y \cdot (x \cdot a)}{F(x)} \qquad\qquad\qquad (4.2)$$

so if $y = 0 \Rightarrow \frac{dy}{dx} = 0$. Also, if $x = -a$ then $\frac{dy}{dx} = 0$. If $F(x)$ is general, then $\frac{dy}{dx}$ is general. Elderton (1938) then expanded $F(x)$ by Maclaurin's theorem in ascending powers of x; this produced

$$\frac{dy}{dx} = \frac{y\ (x+a)}{b_0+b_1x+b_2x^2+\ldots} \tag{4.3}$$

Elderton (1938) then considered the hypergeometrical series which is required for (4.3),

$$\frac{1}{y}\frac{dy}{dx} = \frac{a + x}{b_0+b_1x+b_2x^2} \tag{4.4}$$

we can rewrite $\frac{1}{y}\frac{dy}{dx}$ as $\frac{d \log y}{dx}$, therefore the roots of

$$b_0 + b_1x + b_2x^2 = 0 \tag{4.5}$$

will convey much information about the distribution in question. The k - criterion is based on whether the underlying quadratic of the Pearson IDF has real roots of equal or opposite signs or whether it has complex roots. Simply, the κ - criterion utilizes the skewness and kurtosis of the empirical and hypothetical IDFs and maps them each into the real line. Consequently, if the κ - criterion of the empirical and the hypothetical IDFs do not intersect on the real line then in that particular instance the hypothetical IDF under consideration does not properly describe the empirical distribution. On the other hand, should the κ - criterion of the empirical and the hypothetical IDFs intersect on the real line then the hypothetical IDF under consideration cannot be ruled out **a priori**.

Define μ'_j to be the j-th moment of a hypothesized form, i.e., $\mu'_j = E[X^j]$. Thus, the first four moments about the mean (μ_j) are defined as:

$$\mu_1 = \mu'_1 \tag{4.6a-d}$$
$$\mu_2 = \mu'_2 - [\mu'_1]^2$$
$$\mu_3 = \mu'_3 - 3\,\mu'_1\,\mu'_2 + 2[\mu'_1]^3$$
$$\mu_4 = \mu'_4 - 4\,\mu'_1\,\mu'_3 + 6[\mu'_1]^2\,\mu'_2 - 3[\mu'_1]^4$$

Now following Ord (1972, p. 5) define the κ - criterion as

$$\kappa = \frac{\beta_1 \, (\beta_2 + 3)^2}{4(4\beta_2 - 3\beta_1)(2\beta_2 - 3\beta_1 - 6)} \tag{4.7}$$

where

$$\beta_1 = \mu_3^2 \, / \, \mu_2^3$$

$$\beta_2 = \mu_4 \, / \, \mu_2^2 \tag{4.8a-b}$$

For the IDF's discussed above, the values of the κ - criterion and their relevant ranges are presented in Table 4.1 below.

As can be seen from Table 4.1, positive values for the κ - criterion will eliminate the Beta I distribution while negative values eliminate the Beta II, lognormal and Pareto forms. The range for the gamma, unfortunately, is undefined so the test is not very useful for this form,cf. Molina and Slottje (1987). It is instructive, however, in that the gamma distribution is always a candidate and the other forms are not.

Actual use of the κ-criterion generally requires us to use sample data on income. Since we are using sample data we will be estimating the moments of the underlying distribution. Since the moments will be sensitive to the sample size, we should properly put variances on our estimates of the κ's. To construct variances on the estimates of the κ's in order to be more precise about which forms to eliminate **a priori** requires a rather involved procedure. The calculation of the variance for the estimate $\hat{\kappa}$ is computed from estimates of the first four raw moments $(\hat{\mu}_1', \; \hat{\mu}_2', \; \hat{\mu}_3', \; \hat{\mu}_4')$. By substitution of equations (4.6a-d) into (4.8a-b), then into equation (7.7), we can write it as a function of the raw moments. Thus:

$$\kappa = f(\underline{\mu}'), \tag{4.9}$$

where: $\underline{\mu}' = (\mu_1', \; \mu_2', \mu_3', \mu_4')$, and we can approximate κ using a first order Taylor series expansion of $f(\underline{\mu}')$ around the mean values of the raw moments $\bar{\underline{\mu}}'$.

$$\hat{\mu} \approx f(\bar{\underline{\mu}}') + \frac{\partial f(\bar{\underline{\mu}}')}{\partial \bar{\underline{\mu}}'} \, (\underline{\mu}' - \bar{\underline{\mu}}') + Q \tag{4.10}$$

where Q is the residual. Thus we can approximate the variance of κ by:

$$\hat{\text{Var}}\ (\hat{\kappa}) = \frac{\partial f(\bar{\mu}')}{\partial \bar{\mu}'}^{(')} \hat{\text{cov}}\ (\bar{\mu}')\ \frac{\partial f(\bar{\mu}')}{\partial \bar{\mu}'} \qquad (4.11)$$

where the estimated covariance of the vector of first four raw moments is estimated from the application of the Central Limit Theorem (Kendall and Stuart [1977]) to the multivariate case. Thus the covariance of the first four powers of the sample values are divided by 1/n where n is the sample size to compute the estimated covariance for the first four raw moments:

$$\hat{\text{cov}}(\bar{\mu}') = \frac{1}{n}\ \text{cov}(x,\ x^2,\ x^3,\ x^4,) \qquad (4.12)$$

where x is a vector of observations.

   The basic problem encountered in employing this method is the lengthy nature of the derivatives of the κ with respect to the raw moments, $(\partial\ f(\bar{\mu}')\ /\ \partial\ \bar{\mu}')$. It is in the computation of these values that algebraic manipulation programs become very helpful. In one case where we used the criterion, we employed both MACSYMA and REDUCE primarily for comparison of the forms they produce and to verify our numeric results. See Hayes, Hirschberg and Slottje (1987a,b) for a detailed discussion of computer algebra systems in economic applications. The particular derivation employed here is described in Hayes, Hirschberg, and Slottje (1987b).

   Once the estimates of $\hat{\mu}'$ and $\hat{\text{cov}}(\bar{\mu}')$ are known, we estimate the values of the partial derivative of κ with respect to μ'. To perform this computation we used REDUCE to derive the derivatives of κ. The program works in the following manner:

   First, the first four moments and the covariance are estimated from the data. The moment estimates are then used to compute the four derivatives. And last the derivatives and the covariance of the moments are multiplied to compute the variance of κ. We discussed this variance calculation for completeness. In Chapters 6 and 7 we analyze many different income graduations and report their κ values but not their variances. We do not report the variances because we wish only to present a broad description of each income graduation and to attempt to construct each $\hat{\kappa}$ and each variance $(\hat{\kappa})$ would have been too large a task and taken us too far afield from our primary purpose here. That is, we are interested in many graduations primarily to demonstrate that much information is lost by solely concentrating on one attribute. Hirschberg and Slottje (1988) discuss the issue of the efficiency of the $\hat{\kappa}$ at length in their paper.

There have been many functional forms of statistical distributions used to approximate income graduations over the last 90 years, the most prevalent class has been from the Pearsonian family. The purpose of the first part of this chapter has been to make the researcher in this area aware of a technique from classical statistics which helps the income distribution specialist discriminate a priori between these various functional forms.

To aid the researcher who may not be conversant with all of the standard distributions, we now present several flow diagrams which show the relationships between various functional forms in Figures 4.1 and 4.2. We include these diagrams solely as a pedagogical note for the researcher who isn't conversant with all these distributions but would like to know more about them. We include them here because it is a reasonable place to put them. We also note that non-parametric kernel estimation can be done to examine distributions without imposing a functional form, cf. Hirschberg and Slottje (1989). We give examples of these in Figures 4.3 and 4.4. These compare the distributions of Kappa values for the 50-59 age cohort (see chapter 6).

Table 4.1
κ Values and Critical Ranges

IDF	Reference	κ - criterion range
Beta I	L. Thurow (1970)	$\kappa < 0$
Beta II	Basmann, Molina, Slottje (1984a,b)	$\kappa > 1$
Gamma	Salem and Mount (1974)	$\kappa \to \pm \infty^{*}$
Lognormal	Aitchison and Brown (1957)	$\kappa > 0$
Pareto	Pareto (1897)	$\kappa > 0$

*Approximates positive and negative infinity.

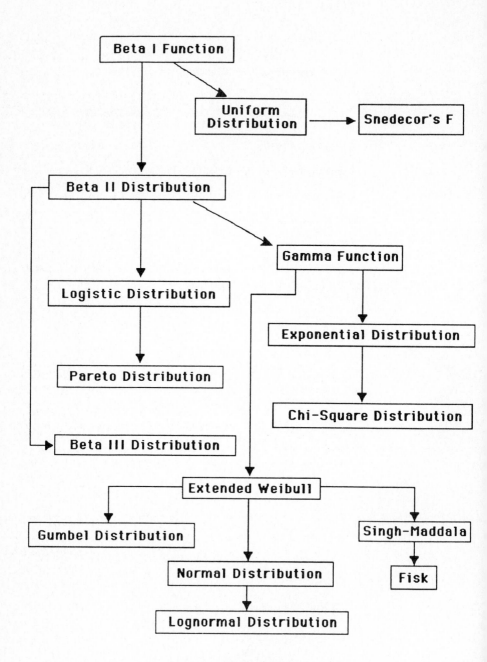

Figure 4.1
Continuous Distributions
Originating from a Beta Distribution

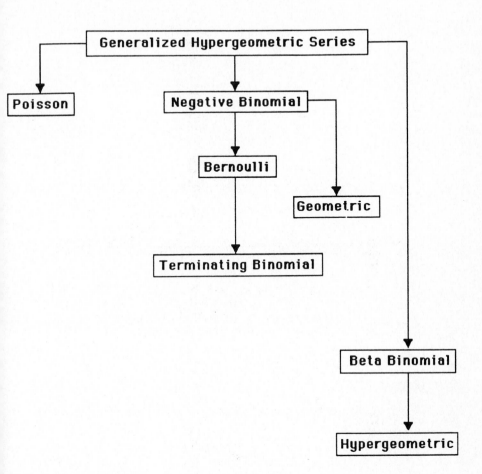

Figure 4.2
Discrete Distributions Originating
from a Hypergeometric Series

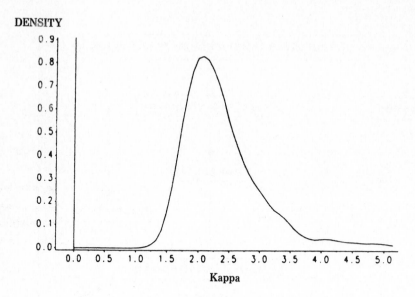

Figure 4.3
Non-parametric Density for the κ-criterion,
Ages 50-59, 1979, Bandwidth = 0.39

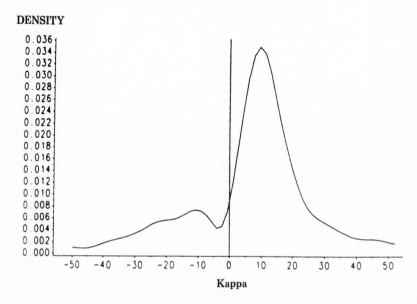

Figure 4.4
Non-parametric Density for the κ-criterion,
Ages 50-59, 1984, Bandwidth = 10.0

Chapter 5

APPROXIMATING INCOME DISTRIBUTIONS: THE BETA
DISTRIBUTION OF THE SECOND KIND

5.1. Introduction

In Chapters 3 and 4 above we discussed the problem of approximating
income graduations with specific forms of hypothetical statistical
distributions. Most of the forms utilized, as we noted, have problems
fitting well over the entire range of the observed graduation or have
inherent properties that make their use problematic. In this chapter we
present a functional form that is a good approximation to actual income
data and also is flexible enough to allow for meaningful comparisons
between attributes (we will demonstrate this below). In addition, the
form utilized here is multidimensional.

As Jorgenson and Slesnick (1984a) pointed out in their study, it was
Dalton who long ago noted that,

> The   economist   is primarily interested, not in the
> distribution of income as such, but in the effects of the
> distribution of income upon the distribution and total
> amount of economic welfare (Dalton, 1920).

Basmann et al. (1984), Jorgenson and Slesnick (1984 a,b) and Slottje
(1984, 1987) have all attempted to measure a multidimensional aspect of
economic   inequality by incorporating other information into their
analysis. As Maasoumi (1986) points out, one approach to doing this is
to take a multivariate distribution of various components of income and
expenditures on various commodities. Basmann et al. (1984) noted that
the selection of initial forms of theoretical models of the multivariate
personal distribution of components of income and expenditures should be
guided by the following criteria:

1.   The first criterion calls for minimization of the number
      of ad hoc parameters in the theoretical multivariate
      personal distribution.

2.   The   second criterion calls for the selection of a
      multivariate form such that derived marginal distributions
      of the sums of one or more components of income and
      expenditures shall have the same form as the multivariate
      personal distribution.

3.   The third criterion is that the form selected should be a
      good approximation to the data in the sense that the

errors from the difference between observed and predicted
frequencies are small.

4.   The last criterion calls for the form selected to satisfy
     the weak Pareto law (see Dagum, 1980).

The first criterion is essentially one of research economy, if the
number of parameters necessary to describe a distribution is large, then
the value of modelling the data is obviously diminished.   The third
criterion simply says that the form should be a reasonable approximation
of the actual data keeping in mind criterion number one.   The fourth
criterion is based on the tail behavior of the empirical distribution
following the Pareto law as the number of observations gets large.   It is
the second criterion that concerns us here.   In order to make meaningful
comparisons between the multivariate distribution and (say) the marginal
distribution of one of the income components, then criterion number two
is desirable.   For example, selection of a lognormal form of multivariate
distribution is ruled out since the sums of lognormal variables are not
lognormally distributed.

This second criterion is particularly important here since we want
to examine the relationship between the marginal distribution of total
income and the marginal distributions of various income components.   As
we noted above, the distribution of income has been extensively analyzed
since Pareto first broached the subject a hundred years ago.   Our aim is
to compare the marginal distributions of various income components to the
marginal distribution of total income so that we can get closer to
Dalton's notion, but still keep the analysis in a positive framework.   In
the next section we present the multivariate distribution of expenditures
and income that satisfies the criteria discussed above and allows us to
make meaningful comparisons between these various marginal distributions.

5.2 The Model

Accepted economic theory implies that amounts of income consumers
receive and the expenditures consumers make on commodities cannot, in
principal, be statistically independent.   Therefore a more efficient
method of examining inequality in the size distribution of income is to
utilize a joint distribution of components of income and various
commodity group expenditures.   The model of inequality is composed of two
main parts.   The cross-section model is a specified multivariate personal
distribution of annual expenditures on different groups of commodities,

and receipts of income from various sources. Inequalities in the personal marginal distribution of expenditures and components of income depend on parameters of the joint distribution. The parameters are presumed to change from year to year. In broad terms, the parameters of the cross-section model characterize the wants and want-satisfying skills of individuals in relation to their opportunities to satisfy wants. For each year the parameters of the joint distribution reflect the relation among individuals' wants, their abilities to satisfy those wants directly by economic activities that do not show up in the social accounts, and their abilities to satisfy wants indirectly by purchases of commodities and sales of labor and services that do show up in the social accounts. The model of intertemporal change, called the intertemporal model (of the parameters of the cross-section model) relates to year-to-year changes in the personal joint distribution to exogenous variables. Among the latter are changes in socio-economic variables. Consequently, the intertemporal model predicts year-to-year changes in various measures of inequality in the various marginal income distributions under the impact of such exogenous variables. In selecting a hypothetical joint distribution function of commodity expenditures and components of income we chose a functional form with a view to the feasibility and economy of intended subsequent application. We now define the cross-section model of the joint density of annual expenditures on commodities and components of income as follows:

$$f(m_1, \cdots, m_n; w_1, \cdots, w_q)$$

$$= \frac{K^{b*} \, m_1^{a_1-1} \cdots m_n^{a_n-1} \, w_1^{c_1-1} \cdots w_q^{c_q-1}}{B(a_1, \cdots, a_n; c_1, \cdots, c_q; b*) \, [K + m + w]^b} \tag{5.1a}$$

$$m_i > 0; \quad w_k > 0 \tag{5.1b}$$

$$= 0 \text{ otherwise,}$$

where all of the parameters $a_i (i = 1, 2, \cdots, n)$, c_k $(k = 1, 2, \cdots, q)$, b^*, b, and k are positive, and where expenditure on commodity group i is m_i, i = 1, $\cdots$, n. Total expenditure on all commodities is m,

$$m = m_1 + \cdots + m_n. \tag{5.1c}$$

We define w_k as income of the kth income source $k = 1, \cdots, q$. Total income W is defined as

$$W = w_1 + \cdots + w_q. \tag{5.1d}$$

$$b^* = b - \sum_{i=1}^{n} a_i - \sum_{k=1}^{n} c_k. \tag{5.1e}$$

Parameters a_i, c_k, b^*, K, and b are population parameters. They should bear time-period subscripts t, which are suppressed here for convenience. In Basmann et al. (1984) we studied the intertemporal dependence of parameters a_i on commodity prices and various measures of economic development in Mexico and the United States over the years 1947-1978. Slottje (1984, 1987) has studied the intertemporal dependence of income component parameters c_k on commodity prices and several economic growth variables in the United States for the period 1952-1981. We mention this empirical work here only to emphasize that the parameters of the personal multivariate distribution of components of income and expenditures on commodities are not fixed constants.

Let y designate the sum of one or more of the expenditures $m_1, \ldots, m_n$ and components of income $w_1, \ldots, w_q$ and let α designate the sum of the corresponding exponents in (5.1a). The marginal distribution function of y derived from (5.1a-d) is

$$H(y; \alpha, b^*, K) = 0 \qquad\qquad (y < 0) \qquad\qquad (5.2a)$$

$$= 1 - \frac{K}{K + y}^{b^*} \quad b^* B(\alpha, b^*) \quad {}_2F_1 \left[b^*; 1 - \alpha; b^* + 1; \frac{K}{K + y} \right]$$

$$(y \geq 0) \qquad\qquad (5.2b)$$

where the symbol ${}_2F_1$ (A; B; C; Z) stands for the ordinary hypergeometric function. Notice that for $\alpha = 1$, Eq. (5.1a-b) becomes the ordinary Pareto distribution function with parameter b^* and lower terminal K. As $y \to \infty$, the hypergeometric function in (5.2a-b) converges to unity; consequently for any α the marginal distribution function (5.2a-b) satisfies the weak Pareto law. For this reason we call b^* the generalized Pareto parameter. In the special case for which y is the sum of income components we have $\alpha = c$, where c is the sum of $c_1, \ldots, c_q$, so that the marginal personal distribution of total income $H(w; c, b^*, K)$ that is deductively implied by (5.1a-d) satisfies the weak Pareto law as required.

Inequality in the empirical multivariate distribution of components of income and expenditures on commodities described above and inequality in its theoretical counterpart (5.1a-d) have many diverse aspects for which there are a number of different inequality measures. For purposes of this chapter we can make do with only one aspect of economic inequality and its corresponding inequality measure based on (5.1a-d). Referring to the marginal distribution function (5.2a-b), we note that the Gini concentration ratio for the sum y is

$$g(\alpha, b^*) = \frac{\Gamma(\alpha + b^*)\Gamma(\alpha + 1/2)\Gamma(b^* + 1/2)}{\Gamma(1/2)\Gamma(\alpha + 1)\Gamma(b^*)\Gamma(\alpha + b^* + 1/2)}$$

$$x \quad 1 + \frac{2a}{2b^* - 1} \quad , \quad b^* > 1. \qquad (5.3)$$

As $\alpha \to 0$, $g(\alpha, b^*) \to 1$; as $b^* \to 0$, $g(\alpha, b^*) \to 1$. Formula (5.3) holds for all sums y of one or more components of income and expenditures on commodities.

The estimates $g(\alpha, b^*)$ in (5.3) can then be specified to look at any income component w_j with parameter $\alpha = c_j$. The estimate of $g(\alpha, b^*)$ is based on the generalized variance method of moments. This simply means that the estimates of $g(\alpha, b^*)$ are computed from the joint statistical estimates of parameters of (5.1a-d) and are functions of survey components of both income and commodity expenditures. If we estimated the inequality measure $g(\alpha, b^*)$ for (say) total income from the marginal distribution of total income alone, ignoring the interdependence of income and expenditures, we would be using the single variance method of moments (SVMM). The generalized variance method of moments is used because it incorporates more sample information into estimation of $g(\alpha, b^*)$. It is in this sense that our analysis is multidimensional. We now report some empirical results.

5.3 The Beta Distribution of the Second Kind and Income Inequality Across States for Various Population Subgroups

One example of the flexibility of the Beta distribution of the second kind in examining income inequality is for subgroups of the population across states over time.

Using Bureau of the Census data, measures of inequality will be derived for the entire population of each state. In addition, this section analyzes income inequality across segments of the population within each state. The distribution of income in each state will be analyzed by rural and urban classification as well as by racial mix.

While many researchers have analyzed these subgroups individually, little work has been done on comparing various subgroups and attributes simultaneously. To do so requires a flexible functional form of statistical distribution that allows the marginal distributions and their attendant parameters to maintain the same form as the joint distribution. Otherwise, meaningful comparisons can not be made. As noted above, a major feature of utilizing this comprehensive model is that the marginal distributions of income by states and for the various attributes are all derived from the same joint distribution allowing for meaningful comparisons between states by the various attributes.

Again, it must be emphasized that this is not a trivial point. To analyze and measure inequality by subgroups of the population necessarily implies strong assumptions about the aggregation and/or decomposition going on in the population among these subgroups. As a simple example, it is well known that the sum of lognormally distributed random variables are not lognormally distributed. Thus, if we constructed inequality measures for each state under the assumption of lognormally distributed income by state and compared these measures to an aggregate inequality measure of national income that was also assumed lognormally distributed we would be committing a grave error. If the lognormally derived state inequality measures were compared to a total income inequality measure based on another underlying functional form then we could not make meaningful comparisons between them. We utilize the functional form of statistical distribution, the Beta of the second kind, where the disaggregated (or decomposed) variables are flexible and do maintain the same form as their sum or vice versa as described above. By providing measures of income inequality across states and disaggregating within states by race and region, a policy maker is given timely and relevant information to use in formulating policies designed to deal with diverse segments of the population across the country.

The Beta distribution of the second kind is a three parameter distribution that allows for exact aggregation of the marginal distribution of total national income form the joint distribution of income for all fifty states. A unique feature of the Beta distribution of the second kind is that summation of the parameters (of the joint distribution) yields a marginal distribution that retains the same form as the joint distribution. The joint distribution of income for all the states is hypothesized to be distributed as a Beta of the second kind. Thus, the marginal distribution of total national income is hypothesized to be distributed as a Beta of the second kind. By deriving a measure of inequality (in this case, the Gini measure) assuming this particular functional form, the framework allows us to analyze income inequality for the entire nation as well as to make comparisons between states and, of course, within states. The same framework allows for comparison of marginal distributions of income based on demographic characteristics, as will be seen below. Recalling (5.1), we respecify it so that:

$$g(s_1, \ldots, s_{51}; c_1, \ldots, c_{51}, b^*, k)_{t,z} =$$

$$\frac{k^{b^*} s_1^{c_1-1} \ldots s_{51}^{c_{51}-1}}{B(c_1, \ldots, c_{51}, b^*) [k + s]^{b* + c}} \tag{5.4}$$

$= 0$ otherwise

$t = 1960, 1970, 1980$

$z =$ total state population, race by state, urban-rural classification by state

where $c = c_1 + \ldots + c_{51}$ $s = s_1 + \ldots + s_{51}$

$c_j > 0$ $j = 1, \ldots, 51$

s_i is defined as income in the ith state. Again, the k is called the lower terminal k and b^* the Pareto parameter because under certain restrictions on the c_is and b^*, equation (5.4) becomes the well-known Pareto distribution. The c_i's are called interincome inequality parameters for reasons that will be clear shortly. Z is a vector of the characteristics region, race and total state population. By summing over the s_i's we find the marginal density of total national income which takes the form:

$$g(s) = \frac{k^{b^*} s^{c-1}}{B(c, b^*) [k + s]^{b* + c}} \qquad s = s_1 + \ldots + s_{51} \tag{5.5}$$

Similarly, the marginal distribution of income for the ith state takes
the form:

$$g(s_i) = \frac{k^{b*} \; s_i^{c_i-1}}{B(c_i,b^*)[k + s_i]^{b* + c_i}} \tag{5.6}$$

$$= 0 \text{ otherwise} \qquad\qquad c_i > 0$$

Now from equation (5.5) and equation (5.6) Gini measures of inequality
are derived which (for total income) take the form:

$$G(c,b^*) = \frac{\Gamma(c + 1/2) \; \Gamma(b^* + 1/2) \; \Gamma(b^* + c)}{\Gamma(1/2) \; \Gamma(b^* + c + 1/2) \; \Gamma(c + 1) \; \Gamma(b^*)} \; x \; 1 + \frac{2c}{2b^* - 1} \tag{5.7}$$

To derive the Gini measure for the marginal distributions of income
by individual state, simply change the c to c_i in (5.7). From equation
(5.7) it can be seen that inequality in the various marginal
distributions is solely a function of the interincome inequality
parameters $c(c_i$'s) and the b^*. The b^* and $c(c_i$'s) are estimated from
actual empirical data by the method of moments, cf. Elderton (1938). The
lower terminal k is found by locating the individual in the survey with
the lowest income level. This income figure is the k.

The actual data utilized is from the Bureau of the Census. The
census is done every ten years. Thus, we report results for 1960, 1970,
and 1980. The income data is reported in frequency form for all fifty
states and the District of Columbia. Within each state, income data is
given based upon race and urban-rural mix, as well as upon total income.
By using equations (5.4) - (5.7) the marginal distribution of the
demographic characteristic in question can be derived. The joint
distribution (5.4) contains the marginal distributions of the various
attributes. To analyze the marginal distribution of (say) non-whites in
Hawaii in 1960, simply integrate out everything else in (5.4). By
utilizing the Beta of the second kind as the appropriate functional form,
meaningful comparisons can be made between states for various attributes
over time. The empirical results are now reported in section three.

5.4 Empirical Results

The empirical data used is from the 1960, 1970, and 1980 Census of the Population. In defining each term of data, definitions and explanations of subject characteristics from each volume of the Census of the Population are followed. The date of enumeration for each Census (1960, 1970, and 1980) was April 1st of each year in accordance with the requirements of the Act of Congress of August 31, 1954, which codified Title 13 of the United States Code. Therefore, although the income statistics cover the calendar year 1959, 1969, and 1979, the characteristics of persons and the composition of families refer to the time of enumeration.

In analyzing income inequality across states, the distribution of income should be examined from all sources among consuming units, for a concern with the distribution of current income implies a concern for the distribution of potential consumption. If income is pooled within a household for the purpose of consumption, then the household is an appropriate unit. However, families may share consumption, but not all households do. Because income is typically not shared among unrelated cohabiting individuals and the proportion of unrelated individuals in the population is growing, the family unit (the families and unrelated individuals) is a more appropriate focus. From the 1960 and 1970 Censuses of the Population, data is easily obtained about the income of the family unit. But, unfortunately, the same data is not available from the 1980 Census of the Population. Accordingly, household income data is used instead of the family unit income data in 1980. Given this condition, the results for empirical data in 1960, 1970, and 1980 are presented.

Table 5.1 shows the national summary statistics of mean income and Gini coefficients for the nation, region and race in 1960, 1970, and 1980. The first part of this section discusses trends in 1960. As indicated in the table, the mean income for the nation was $5,767; the mean income for urban residents was $6,216; and the mean income for rural dwellers was $4,624. The rural regions had, on average, roughly 74 percent of the mean income of the urban areas. Moreover, the Gini coefficient of the rural region shows that the income distribution in rural residences had more inequality than in urban residences. The mean income in the nonwhite group was $3,274 which was about 54 percent of the mean income in the white group. Similar to the regional case, the Gini coefficient for the nonwhites was greater than for whites. The mean incomes for the urban and the white cohorts were both above the national average.

Table 5.1 also shows the national statistics for 1970. The mean income of the nation was $9.579. The mean income in the urban regions and for the white population were all above the mean income of the nation. Also, the mean income of the rural regions was $8,431 which was about 85 pecent of the urban areas mean income. The mean income of the nonwhites ($6,334) was about 63 percent of the white population mean income. Although the Gini coefficient in the rural areas was less than in the urban areas, the Gini coefficient for the nonwhites was greater than for the whites. Therefore, it is clear that the income distribution for whites and in urban regions was more equal (as measured by the Gini coefficient) than for nonwhites in rural regions in 1970.

Table 5.1 also shows the national statistics for 1980. Because data in 1980 was collected from the household instead of the family unit it is not precisely comparable to data for 1960 and 1970. Urban area mean income was greater than mean income in the rural areas but the income distribution was more equal in the rural regions than in the urban regions. Rural area mean income ($19,102) was about 91 percent of that of the urban areas. White cohort mean income was greater than for the nonwhite cohort with the nonwhite population having mean income ($15,351) that was about 72 percent of mean income for the white population. The Gini coefficient for the nonwhites was greater than for the whites, meaning less inequality for the white cohort.

Tables 5.2-5.4 provide relative comparisons of trends in inequality for various states (for different attributes) over time, with the qualification that 1980 is not precisely comparable to 1960 and 1970. From Table 5.2 several interesting results appear. Alaska, for example, went from 12th in 1960 to 1st in 1980 in mean income and went from having a low amount of relative inequality in 1960 and 1970 to the 13th highest level of inequality in the nation in 1980. Table 5.3 reveals that Alaska's urban and rural populations followed the same trend over time. Examination of Alaska's white and non-white population over time, however, reveals a different picture in Table 5.4. The mean income ranking of the non-white group increased over time but the inequality ranking in the marginal distribution of income for the nonwhites was relatively unchanged from 1960 to 1980.

Several states such as Connecticut, Illinois, Maryland, Michigan, New York, and Nevada all demonstrated consistently high mean income rankings and low levels of relative inequality over time with the same patterns holding for all of the attributes analyzed. On the other hand, Alabama, Arkansas, Florida, Georgia, Kentucky, Mississippi, Oklahoma, Louisiana, and North Carolina all had consistently low mean income rankings and high levels of relative inequality over time, with the same trends generally holding across different attributes. There are many interesting cases such as Maine that demonstrated a low mean income ranking and relatively low levels of inequality over time with the same pattern holding for the various attributes. Washington, D.C. is interesting in that low levels of inequality over time with the same pattern holding for the various attributes. Washington, D.C. is interesting when analyzing trends in the entire district population, and then disaggregating so trends across attributes are examined. In Table 5.2, Washington D.C. demonstrates a trend of a high mean income ranking and a relatively high inequality ranking over time. From Table 5.4 it can be observed, however, that the District of Columbia had a high relative ranking of mean income for whites over time and a sudden change in the mean income ranking for nonwhites from 1970 to 1980. The Gini coefficients are equally interesting with the white cohorts having consistently high levels of relative inequality and the nonwhite groups going from low relative inequality in 1970 to a very high ranking in inequality in 1980. This last example illustrates that much information is lost when aggregate measures (such as an entire country or state) of inequality are used, and the distribution of income of subgroups within the population are ignored. Several policy implications of this chapter are discussed now in section 5.5.

5.5 Policy Implications

There are a number of ways that the results reported above can be utilized by the policymaker. There has been growing interest of late in the use of unemployment statistics as an indicator of economic need in terms of allocating federal funds. Many economists argue that unemployment statistics may not be an accurate indicator of labor market performance thus, other information should be utilized as well in allocating federal funds earmarked for relieving problems in needy areas, cf. Stephenson (1979), Nilsen (1979) and Ashenfelter and Solon (1982).

This chapter provides relevant information that can be used in addition to unemployment statistics in assessing economic need.

The policymaker whose stated goal is to achieve economic growth and promote lower levels of income inequality can analyze past policy actions in states such as Maryland and Michigan and contrast these with policy actions in states such as Alabama and Arkansas. This must be done in conjunction with a general analysis of economic conditions in states with high mean income levels and relatively low inequality levels vis a' vis the economic conditions existing in states with low mean income levels and high inequality measures. Along this same vein, this chapter affords the policymaker the opportunity to look at special cases (such as Washington D.C.) and examine why significant changes occur in (say) the inequality ranking of a particular attribute in a given state from one census to the next. This could be very revealing to the policymaker in deciding on instituting a new policy or continuing on the present course with current policy.

Finally, this research provides the policymaker many avenues to explore with future research and analysis. It may be the case that racial composition changes due to immigration have impacted inequality and income levels in particular regions. Changes in labor force composition and participation rates by sex also may have had significant impact on the trends observed. This multidimensional approach, then, provides a natural framework for future research and analysis with significant implications for the concerned policymaker.

5.6 Another Example: The Size Distribution of Labor and Nonlabor Income

The model explicated in (5.1) - (5.3) is also useful in examining the size distributions of labor and nonlabor income simultaneously. As we indicated in Chapter 1, the distribution of labor and nonlabor income has class conflict implications but also is important if the stated goal of the policymaker is to redistribute income. Clearly if (say) nonlabor income is highly unequal in its distribution then the policymaker may be committing an error in targeting labor income as the means to redistribute total income. Following Black, Hayes and Slottje (1987), we present a simple overlapping generations model where each generation lives three periods. In periods one and two the consumers provide labor services, but in the third period, the consumers retire. In return for their labor services the consumers receive wage earnings $w(1)$ and $w(2)$ respectively. As older workers accumulate seniority and training we assume that $w(1) < w(2)$. Each consumer selects levels of consumption $[c(i)]$ that maximize lifetime utility V, given by

$$V = u[c(1)] + u[c(2)]/(1+r) + u[c(3)]/(1+r)^2, \qquad (5.8)$$

where r is the individual's discount rate, and $u(\cdot)$ is a monotonic, strictly concave function of consumption. The budget set of the consumer is

$$w(1) + w(2)/(1+r) = c(1) + c(2)/(1+r) + c(3)/(1+r)^2, \qquad (5.9)$$

where we have assumed that the market rate of interest is equal to the consumer's discount rate.

Let the consumer's savings in periods one and two be given by

$$s(1) = w(1) - c(1)$$
$$ \qquad (5.10)$$
$$s(2) = w(2) + (1+r) s(1) - c(2).$$

The consumer's maximization problem reduces to the selection of savings in periods one and two to maximize

$$V = u[w(1) - s(1)] + u[w(2) + s(1)(1+r) - s(2)]/(1+r)$$
$$ + u[s(2)(1+r)]/(1+r)^2. \qquad (5.11)$$

In a stationary economy where each generation faces the same wages and the same discount rate, each generation will choose the same savings schedule, and each generation will achieve the same level of utility. In fact, consumption is constant in each period. Nevertheless, the distribution of labor income (W) and nonlabor income (Y) are disperse. The total labor and nonlabor income for the economy are given by

$$\Sigma W = w(1)(1+g)^2 N^0 + w(2)(1+g)N^0 \qquad (5.12a\text{-}b)$$

$$\Sigma Y = r\, s(1)(1+g)\, N^0 + r\, s(2)\, N^0$$

where N^0 is the number of retired consumers and g is the growth rate of the population. The distributions of these incomes are

$$f(W) = 1/(3+3g+g^2) \qquad\qquad W = 0$$
$$= (1+g)^2/(3+3g+g^2) \qquad W = w(1)$$
$$= (1+g)/(3+3g+g^2) \qquad W = w(2) \qquad\qquad (5.13a\text{-}f)$$
$$g(Y) = (1+g)^2/(3+3g+g^2) \qquad Y = 0$$
$$= (1+g)/(3+3g+g^2) \qquad Y = r\ s(1)$$
$$= 1/(3+3g+g^2) \qquad\qquad Y = r\ s(2).$$

The generational rankings of these distributions are inconsistent: the oldest generation has the least labor income, but the greatest nonlabor income. The increase in the population increases the measure of inequality in nonlabor income because the young and assetless outnumber the old.

The distribution of total income (I) is given by

$$h(I) = 1/(3+3g+g^2) \qquad\qquad I = r\ s(2)$$
$$= (1+g)^2/(3+3g+g^2) \qquad I = w(1) \qquad\qquad (5.14a\text{-}c)$$
$$= (1+g)/(3+3g+g^2) \qquad I = w(2) + r\ s(1).$$

Notice that the use of the distribution of income rather than the distribution of wages leads to a reduction in the measure of inequality between the third and first generations, but leads to an increase in the measure of inequality between the first and second generations. The utility level is the same in each period, but both the distribution of total income and labor income suggests that the third generation is worse off. None of the distributions capture the fact that the utilities of the first and second generations are equal.

This simple life cycle model has demonstrated several of the problems that arise in inferring welfare judgments from cross-sectional measures of the distribution of income. By construction, the agents in this economy had the same lifetime utility level, but the distribution of income is nondegenerate. The individual has the highest utility level in the third period, but two of the three distributions suggest that welfare is the lowest in the third period. It should be obvious, therefore, that the relationships between respective size distributions of labor and nonlabor income remain an empirical question.

The estimates $g(\alpha, b^*)$ in (5.3) can be specified to look at only labor income $(w_1 = w_\ell)$ with parameter c_ℓ or non labor income $(w_{n\ell} = w_2 + \cdots + w_q)$ with parameter $c_{n\ell}$. To find the marginal distribution of labor income, we simply integrate out all other components in the joint distribution. The same procedure is of course followed to find the marginal distribution of nonlabor income. The marginal distributions of labor and nonlabor income have the same form as (5.2a-b) and the same inequality measure as (5.3). The estimate of $g(\alpha, b^*)$ is again based on the generalized variance method of moments. This simply means that the estimates of $g(\alpha, b^*)$ are computed from the joint statistical estimates of parameters of (5.1a-d) and are functions of survey components of both income and commodity expenditures. If we estimated the inequality measure $g(\alpha, b^*)$ for (say) total income from the marginal distribution of total income alone, ignoring the interdependence of income and expenditures, we would be using the single variance method of moments (SVMM). The generalized variance method of moments is used because it incorporates more sample information into estimation of $g(\alpha, b^*)$. It is in this sense that our analysis is multidimensional.

Use of the model described in section 5.1 requires cross-section data on consumer expenditures as well as data on various income components in frequency form. The Bureau of the Census collects expenditure data every few years at tremendous cost on behalf of the Bureau of Labor Statistics. The data is collected in survey form. The survey we used is the Consumer Expenditure Survey, 1972-1973. This survey provides comprehensive expenditure and income data for the year specified. We describe this data in the appendix at the end of the book. As noted above one of the primary features of analyzing the distribution of total income utilizing the multivariate distribution (5.1a-b) is that expenditure as well as income data is incorporated into the estimates of income inequality by using the Beta II multivariate distribution. The expenditure information is incorporated into the analysis through the lower terminal k. The actual empirical data in frequency form for labor and nonlabor income is from the Internal Revenue Service: Statistics of Income. We discuss and describe the IRS data in the appendix at the back of the book. Now utilizing (5.3), we report the Gini coefficients for the years 1952-1981 in Table 5.5.

Utilizing the IRS data and CES survey, we estimated (5.3) for total income, for nonlabor income and for labor income. We report these estimates in Table 5.5 below. Labor income is the IRS's definition of labor income, i.e., wage and salary income. Nonlabor income includes dividend income, interest income, rents and all other reported non-wage and salary income. As can be seen from Table 5.5, inequality in the marginal distribution of labor income is less than inequality in the marginal distribution of nonlabor income. This result is not unexpected since as Ehrenberg and Smith (1987) point out, the owners of financial capital (stocks, bonds, real estate) probably are people whose assets grow over time, thus becoming more concentrated. Ehrenberg and Smith also predict that the distribution of total income will be less equal than the distribution of labor earnings since people with many financial assets also generally have high earnings. As Table 5.5 indicates, the empirical evidence does not bear this out. This result is not surprising if it is recalled that many individuals (such as retirees) may have low labor earnings, but high incomes. Thus, when the marginal distribution of total income is analyzed, inequality is not as great. Another explanation, of course, is that much income at the upper tail is not reported so the observed distribution is actually truncated.

This section demonstrates then, that the marginal distribution of total income may have less inequality than the marginal distribution of labor income, a result in apparent disagreement with many labor economists. We do find, however, that the marginal distribution of nonlabor income has more inequality than the marginal distribution of labor income, a result consistent with accepted theory.

In Chapters 6 and 7 below, we explore in depth the socio-economic and occupational choice factors that, in part, account for the observed distributions taking the form that they do.

5.7 Summary and Conclusions

This chapter utilized a recently developed model of comprehensive economic inequality to analyze the size distribution of income in the United States for the fifty states and for various attributes within the states for the years 1960, 1970, and 1980. With a view to the flexibility and subsequent application of the form chosen, this study used a Beta distribution of the second kind to approximate the joint distribution of income across states and by attributes. This functional form is attractive since it allows for exact aggregation and decomposition of various marginal distributions of income across states and attributes and also provides a good approximation of the actual empirical data. The empirical results show interesting trends in inequality for various states and for various attributes within states over time, thereby providing timely and relevant information to the policymaker that can be utilized in a number of applications. One important application of this approach lies in the area of allocating federal funds to regions based on employment statistics. The results of this chapter could be used as further information in ascertaining economic need for allocating federal funds.

We also demonstrated in Chapter 5 that our joint distribution approach provides a very fruitful way to analyze the distribution of labor and nonlabor income. The relationship between the marginal total income distribution and the marginal labor/nonlabor income distribution appeared to be one of more inequality in the marginal distribution of nonlabor income vis a' vis the other two distributions. This is not an unexpected result and further serves to remind us that the policymaker and economist concerned with redistributive welfare questions should search beyond the total pie's distribution in really gauging how to redistribute resources.

Table 5.1

NATIONAL STATISTICS OF MEAN INCOME, AND GINI COEFFICIENTS IN THE NATION, AND BY REGION AND RACE FOR THE YEARS 1960, 1970 AND 1980

	Nation	Urban	Rural	White	Nonwhite
1960					
Mean	$5.767	6.216	4.624	6.053	3.274
Gini	0.387038	0.384792	0.394926	0.382103	0.393727
1970					
Mean	$9.579	9.942	8.431	9.987	6.334
Gini	0.388727	0.388681	0.383864	0.385025	0.400684
1980					
Mean	$20.561	21.058	19.102	21.441	15.351
Gini	0.34738	0.347821	0.34568	0.342968	0.355349

*in thousands of dollars

Source of Data: U.S. Bureau of the Census, 1960 Census of Population: Characteristics of the Population, Vol.I, Washington, Government Printing Office, 1963.

————, 1970 Census of Population: Characteristics of the Population, Vol.I, Washington, Government Printing Office, 1973.

————, 1980 Census of Population: Characteristics of the Population, Vol.I, Washington, Government Printing Office, 1983.

Table 5.2

BANK ORDERING OF STATES BY MEAN INCOME AND GINI COEFFICIENTS FOR 1960, 1970 AND 1980

State	Mean Income			Gini Coefficent		
	1960	1970	1980	1960	1970	1980
Alabama	4.36 (46)	7.56 (45)	17.02 (47)	.409 (11)	.406 (8)	.357 (6)
Alaska	6.28 (12)	11.35 (3)	33.7 (1)	.369 (42)	.368 (47)	.353 (13)
Arizona	5.74 (22)	9.24 (20)	30.85 (25)	.401 (15)	.389 (25)	.342 (26)
Arkansas	3.68 (50)	6.38 (50)	15.65 (51)	.428 (2)	.416 (3)	.368 (3)
California	6.60 (3)	10.34 (11)	22.78 (8)	.376 (30)	.382 (35)	349 (16)
Colorado	5.74 (23)	9.11 (24)	21.76 (12)	.381 (27)	.387 (26)	.338 (35)
Connecticut	7.27 (1)	12.22 (1)	24.33 (3)	.376 (32)	.377 (39)	.341 (30)
Deleware	6.52 (7)	10.19 (12)	21.58 (14)	.385 (22)	.377 (38)	.342 (27)
Florida	5.05 (35)	8.78 (29)	18.92 (34)	.418 (4)	.413 (3)	.365 (4)
Georgia	4.60 (42)	8.40 (33)	18.64 (35)	.408 (12)	.399 (14)	.356 (8)
Hawaii	6.09 (13)	10.86 (7)	25.29 (2)	.383 (24)	.375 (42)	.338 (36)
Idaho	5.26 (29)	8.27 (36)	18.23 (39)	.362 (42)	.385 (29)	.339 (34)
Illinois	6.60 (2)	10.76 (8)	22.85 (7)	.372 (36)	.373 (40)	.338 (37)
Indiana	5.80 (21)	9.60 (15)	20.34 (23)	.365 (46)	.364 (51)	.326 (49)
Iowa	5.87 (34)	8.68 (31)	19.84 (28)	.390 (19)	.385 (28)	.337 (38)
Kansas	5.23 (28)	8.50 (32)	19.80 (29)	.392 (17)	.396 (16)	.345 (22)
Kentucky	4.39 (45)	7.51 (46)	17.20 (46)	.416 (6)	.403 (10)	.353 (13)
Louisiana	4.70 (38)	7.81 (40)	19.07 (32)	.416 (7)	.418 (2)	.363 (5)
Maine	4.67 (41)	7.69 (43)	16.25 (49)	.372 (37)	.373 (44)	.330 (45)

Maryland	6.46 (8)	11.21 (4)	24.29 (4)	.369 (39)	.368 (46)	.334 (42)
Massachussetts	6.23 (10)	10.41 (10)	21.07 (16)	.373 (34)	.378 (37)	.341 (28)
Michigan	6.33 (9)	10.87 (5)	22.40 (10)	.362 (48)	.366 (49)	.332 (44)
Minnesota	5.49 (25)	9.48 (18)	21.01 (17)	.381 (28)	.382 (33)	.337 (39)
Mississippi	3.44 (51)	6.43 (51)	15.74 (50)	.432 (1)	.425 (1)	.371 (2)
Missouri	5.17 (32)	8.78 (28)	18.94 (33)	.403 (13)	.401 (12)	.348 (17)
Montana	5.23 (30)	8.22 (38)	18.41 (36)	.369 (40)	.392 (22)	.342 (25)
Nebraska	4.96 (36)	8.21 (34)	19.08 (30)	.388 (21)	392 (21)	.344 (23)
Nevada	6.56 (6)	10.44 (9)	22.16 (11)	.367 (44)	.367 (48)	.336 (41)
New Hampshire	5.40 (26)	9.10 (25)	19.88 (27)	.371 (38)	.382 (34)	.328 (48)
New Jersey	7.02 (2)	11.72 (2)	23.80 (5)	.357 (50)	.366 (49)	.339 (33)
New Mexico	5.62 (24)	8.25 (37)	18.22 (40)	.381 (26)	.366 (49)	.352 (14)
New York	6.60 (5)	10.87 (6)	20.84 (18)	.382 (25)	.391 (23)	.356 (7)
North Carolina	4.30 (47)	7.78 (41)	17.47 (44)	.418 (5)	.402 (11)	.347 (18)
North Dakota	4.54 (43)	7.67 (44)	18.35 (37)	.373 (33)	.396 (18)	.347 (18)
Ohio	6.22 (11)	10.14 (13)	20.53 (22)	.368 (43)	.382 (45)	.329 (47)
Oklahoma	4.80 (37)	7.87 (39)	18.21 (38)	.413 (9)	.416 (4)	.356 (9)
Oregon	5.80 (20)	9.15 (22)	20.06 (24)	.376 (31)	.389 (24)	.339 (32)
Pennsylvania	5.85 (19)	9.48 (17)	19.88 (26)	.372 (35)	.382 (32)	.336 (40)
Rhode Island	5.37 (27)	9.18 (21)	19.07 (31)	.378 (29)	.397 (15)	.341 (29)
South Carolina	4.07 (49)	7.49 (47)	17.67 (42)	.412 (8)	.396 (17)	.347 (19)
South Dakota	4.26 (48)	7.34 (48)	16.30 (48)	.390 (20)	.408 (7)	.356 (10)

Tennessee	4.39 (44)	7.71 (42)	17.46 (45)	.420 (3)	.404 (9)	.356 (11)
Texas	5.21 (31)	8.77 (30)	20.67 (19)	.411 (10)	.399 (13)	.351 (15)
Utah	5.89 (17)	9.01 (26)	20.57 (20)	.357 (51)	.381 (36)	.323 (50)
Vermont	4.70 (39)	8.28 (35)	17.69 (41)	.384 (23)	.384 (30)	.339 (31)
Virginia	5.14 (33)	9.14 (23)	21.52 (15)	.394 (16)	.386 (27)	.345 (21)
Washington	5.99 (14)	9.75 (14)	21.59 (13)	.365 (45)	.374 (43)	.333 (43)
West Virginia	4.68 (40)	7.20 (49)	17.49 (43)	.392 (18)	.394 (20)	.346 (20)
Wisconsin	5.87 (18)	9.57 (16)	20.55 (21)	.369 (41)	.373 (41)	.330 (46)
Wyoming	5.93 (16)	8.91 (27)	22.67 (9)	.360 (49)	.383 (31)	.332 (50)
Washington D.C.	5.96 (15)	9.37 (19)	23.11 (6)	.401 (14)	.411 (11)	.387 (1)

---

*Income figures are in thousands of dollars

Note:The number in parentheses represents the states relative ranking from highest to lowest for the year listed. Gini coeffcient rankings are from highest level of inequality to lowest level. Thus, Alabama in 1960 had a Gini coefficient designation .409. This means in 1960 Alabama had the 11th highest level of inequality.   (11)

Table 5.3a

RANK ORDERING OF STATES BY MEAN INCOME FOR
URBAN AND RURAL RESIDENCES IN 1960, 1970, AND 1980

State	Mean Income (Urban)			Mean Income (Rural)		
	1960	1970	1980	1960	1970	1980
Alabama	5.07	8.27	17.95	3.33	6.42	15.55
	(44)	(39)	(46)	(48)	(48)	(47)
Alaska	8.34	11.38	35.57	5.06	11.32	30.19
	(1)	(4)	(1)	(20)	(4)	(1)
Arizona	6.04	9.47	20.34	4.85	8.16	18.07
	(20)	(22)	(24)	(25)	(28)	(30)
Arkansas	4.39	7.28	16.29	3.03	5.80	14.63
	(50)	(50)	(51)	(49)	(49)	(49)
California	6.76	10.51	22.83	5.55	9.08	22.49
	(8)	(10)	(9)	(7)	(17)	(9)
Colorado	5.99	9.19	21.75	4.95	8.78	21.83
	(23)	(25)	(14)	(21)	(21)	(11)
Connecticut	7.08	11.60	23.03	8.05	14.65	29.66
	(3)	(2)	(7)	(1)	(1)	(2)
Deleware	7.04	10.55	22.53	5.55	9.28	19.33
	(5)	(9)	(11)	(6)	(14)	(27)
Florida	5.27	9.04	19.21	4.34	7.59	17.21
	(40)	(28)	(34)	(28)	(34)	(35)
Georgia	5.24	8.88	19.43	3.70	7.56	17.24
	(4)	(31)	(33)	(42)	(35)	(34)
Hawaii	5.76	11.17	25.84	4.23	9.18	21.90
	(9)	(5)	(2)	(32)	(16)	(10)
Idaho	5.60	8.22	18.44	4.90	8.36	15.69
	(32)	(42)	(41)	(22)	(24)	(46)
Illinois	6.88	10.99	20.96	5.27	9.51	21.82
	(6)	(8)	(18)	(17)	(13)	(12)
Indiana	5.99	9.56	19.92	5.43	9.70	21.17
	(23)	(19)	(27)	(10)	(11)	(14)
Iowa	5.65	8.77	20.14	4.32	8.54	19.38
	(30)	(34)	(25)	(30)	(23)	(22)
Kansas	5.88	8.92	20.41	4.44	7.69	18.50
	(26)	(30)	(22)	(27)	(33)	(26)
Kentucky	5.28	8.31	18.28	3.55	6.48	16.00
	(39)	(38)	(45)	(45)	(47)	(44)
Louisiana	5.20	8.23	19.51	.368	6.83	18.03
	(42)	(40)	(32)	(43)	(43)	(31)
Maine	4.96	7.55	16.44	4.33	7.86	16.33
	(48)	(48)	(50)	(29)	(30)	(42)

Maryland	6.81	11.40	24.48	5.49	10.53	23.40
	(7)	(3)	(3)	(9)	(5)	(5)
Massachusetts	6.17	10.16	20.62	6.57	11.96	23.58
	(18)	(13)	(21)	(2)	(2)	(4)
Michigan	6.59	11.14	22.88	5.52	10.03	21.17
	(11)	(6)	(8)	(8)	(8)	(15)
Minnesota	6.17	10.10	22.24	4.17	8.06	18.23
	(17)	(14)	(12)	(34)	(29)	(28)
Mississippi	4.31	7.17	16.88	2.78	5.73	14.57
	(51)	(51)	(49)	(50)	(50)	(50)
Missouri	5.83	9.35	19.97	3.78	7.32	16.62
	(27)	(22)	(26)	(39)	(38)	(41)
Montana	5.56	8.21	18.57	4.87	8.24	18.22
	(33)	(43)	(40)	(23)	(26)	(29)
Nebraska	5.68	8.82	19.84	4.02	7.41	17.77
	(29)	(32)	(30)	(36)	(34)	(32)
Nevada	7317	10.50	22.15	5.41	10.18	22.27
	(4)	(11)	(13)	(13)	(6)	(8)
New Hampshire	5.31	8.78	18.63	5.94	9.57	21.08
	(35)	(33)	(38)	(19)	(12)	(17)
New Jersey	7.09	11.72	23.62	6.46	11.74	25.41
	(2)	(1)	(4)	(3)	(3)	(3)
New Mexico	6.27	8.67	18.86	4.26	7.06	16.31
	(15)	(35)	(36)	(31)	(42)	(43)
New York	6.70	11.01	20.97	5.91	10.11	20.18
	(10)	(7)	(17)	(4)	(7)	(19)
North Carolina	5.07	8.12	18.32	3.71	7.44	16.68
	(44)	(44)	(44)	(41)	(36)	(39)
North Dakota	5.35	7.62	19.58	4.03	7.71	17.12
	(38)	(47)	(31)	(35)	(32)	(36)
Ohio	6.43	10.25	20.36	5.56	9.76	21.06
	(12)	(12)	(23)	(5)	(9)	(16)
Oklahoma	5.38	8.41	18.93	3.74	6.59	16.92
	(36)	(36)	(35)	(40)	(46)	(37)
Oregon	6.00	9.24	19.92	5.42	8.93	20.43
	(21)	(24)	(28)	(12)	(19)	(18)
Pennsylvania	6.00	9.58	19.87	5.40	9.22	19.92
	(22)	(18)	(29)	(14)	(15)	(21)
Rhode Island	5.38	9.26	18.63	5.32	8.72	22.38
	(37)	(23)	(39)	(16)	(22)	(7)
South Carolina	4.72	7.77	18.39	3.53	7.17	16.76
	(49)	(46)	(42)	(47)	(41)	(38)
South Dakota	5.09	7.49	17.67	3.65	7.20	15.02
	(43)	(49)	(48)	(44)	(40)	(48)

Tennessee	5.06 (46)	8.33 (37)	18.37 (43)	3.54 (46)	6.72 (44)	15.99 (45)
Texas	5.60 (31)	9.12 (27)	21.07 (16)	3.97 (38)	7.31 (39)	19.14 (24)
Utah	6.07 (19)	9.18 (26)	20.83 (19)	5.26 (18)	8.22 (27)	19.08 (25)
Vermont	5.03 (47)	8.23 (41)	17.74 (47)	4.47 (26)	8.31 (25)	17.68 (33)
Virginia	5.75 (28)	9.83 (15)	23.05 (6)	4.21 (32)	7.75 (31)	18.35 (27)
Washington	6.25 (16)	9.77 (17)	21.55 (15)	5.37 (15)	9.71 (10)	21.72 (13)
West Virginia	5.56 (33)	7.91 (45)	18.83 (37)	4.02 (36)	6.64 (45)	16.63 (40)
Wisconsin	6.37 (13)	9.83 (15)	20.80 (20)	4.85 (24)	9.00 (18)	20.05 (20)
Wyoming	6.29 (14)	8.97 (29)	22.79 (10)	5.43 (11)	8.80 (20)	22.45 (6)
Washington D.C.	5.96 (24)	9.37 (21)	23.11 (5)	N/A N/A	N/A N/A	N/A N/A

---

*Income figures are in thousands of dollars.

Note: See table II for explanation of numbers.

Table 5.3b

RANK ORDERING OF STATES BY MEAN INCOME AND GINI COEFFICIENTS
FOR URBAN AND RURAL RESIDENCES IN 1960, 1970, AND 1980

State	Gini Coefficient (Urban)			Gini Coefficient (Rural)		
	1960	1970	1980	1960	1970	1980
Alabama	.401	.407	.358	.405	.392	.351
	(12)	(8)	(8)	(12)	(15)	(19)
Alaska	.330	.373	.347	.381	.362	.364
	(51)	(45)	(19)	(30)	(43)	(5)
Arizona	.385	.386	.357	.455	.387	.355
	(18)	(29)	(10)	(1)	(21)	(13)
Arkansas	.415	.419	.340	.425	.404	.365
	(4)	(2)	(33)	(2)	(8)	(4)
California	.373	.381	.348	.402	.389	.358
	(32)	(34)	(17)	(16)	(17)	(8)
Colorado	.378	.387	.336	.389	.385	.347
	(25)	(27)	(36)	(25)	(22)	(23)
Connecticut	.374	.373	.342	.381	.382	.331
	(30)	(43)	(26)	(38)	(30)	(36)
Deleware	.372	.370	.336	.409	.401	.356
	(33)	(47)	(37)	(10)	(9)	(11)
Florida	.419	.414	.365	.405	.399	.361
	(2)	(5)	(4)	(13)	(10)	(7)
Georgia	.403	.403	.359	.401	.382	.349
	(10)	(12)	(7)	(17)	(28)	(21)
Hawaii	.374	.373	.335	.390	.383	.355
	(28)	(44)	(40)	(22)	(24)	(14)
Idaho	.363	.390	.339	.358	.377	.352
	(43)	(25)	(34)	(48)	(36)	(17)
Illinois	.369	.376	.372	.382	.365	.328
	(37)	(42)	(2)	(29)	(42)	(41)
Indiana	.364	.372	.332	.364	.347	.313
	(42)	(46)	(48)	(44)	(50)	(49)
Iowa	.387	.387	.333	.387	.381	.343
	(17)	(28)	(45)	(26)	(32)	(28)
Kansas	.388	.397	.343	.390	.388	.346
	(16)	(17)	(23)	(23)	(18)	(24)
Kentucky	.397	.398	.349	.432	.404	.357
	(13)	(16)	(15)	(4)	(7)	(10)
Louisiana	.413	.419	.362	.411	.408	.362
	(6)	(1)	(5)	(9)	(4)	(6)
Maine	.369	.376	.341	.373	.369	.336

	(35)	(41)	(29)	(37)	(38)	(34)
Maryland	.359	.364	.335	.398	.382	.328
	(46)	(51)	(41)	(19)	(29)	(40)
Massachusetts	.373	.381	.345	.371	.357	.321
	(31)	(35)	(21)	(38)	(47)	(44)
Michigan	.361	.369	.335	.361	.351	.320
	(44)	(48)	(38)	(46)	(48)	(46)
Minnesota	.374	.380	.332	.380	.382	.344
	(27)	(37)	(47)	(32)	(26)	(26)
Mississippi	.416	.415	.368	.435	.397	.372
	(3)	(4)	(3)	(3)	(11)	(1)
Missouri	.395	.399	.343	.408	.436	.353
	(14)	(14)	(24)	(11)	(1)	(16)
Montana	.360	.393	.340	.380	.389	.345
	(45)	(22)	(31)	(33)	(16)	(25)
Nebraska	.380	.393	.336	.390	.387	.357
	(23)	(23)	(35)	(24)	(20)	(9)
Nevada	.355	.365	.335	.394	.379	.341
	(49)	(50)	(39)	(21)	(35)	(29)
New Hampshire	.369	.385	.333	.374	.381	.329
	(35)	(31)	(44)	(36)	(31)	(38)
New Jersey	.356	.366	.340	.375	.366	.328
	(48)	(49)	(32)	(35)	(41)	(39)
New Mexico	.365	.390	.347	.415	.407	.367
	(41)	(24)	(18)	(7)	(5)	(2)
New York	.383	.396	.361	.365	.368	.326
	(20)	(19)	(6)	(42)	(39)	(42)
North Carolina	.423	.416	.354	.399	.380	.339
	(1)	(3)	(12)	(18)	(33)	(30)
North Dakota	.368	.396	.333	.370	.395	.351
	(38)	(18)	(46)	(40)	(12)	(18)
Ohio	.370	.378	.334	.355	.349	.312
	(34)	(40)	(43)	(49)	(49)	(50)
Oklahoma	.409	.414	.355	.405	.412	.356
	(8)	(6)	(11)	(14)	(2)	(12)
Oregon	.381	.393	.341	.363	.376	.336
	(22)	(21)	(30)	(45)	(37)	(33)
Pennsylvania	.374	.388	.343	.365	.361	.319
	(29)	(26)	(25)	(45)	(45)	(47)
Rhode Island	.379	.396	.344	.369	.406	.316
	(24)	(20)	(22)	(41)	(6)	(48)
South Carolina	.410	.404	.348	.405	.382	.344
	(7)	(11)	(16)	(15)	(27)	(27)
South Dakota	.375	.405	.345	.398	.411	.365

	(26)	(10)	(20)	(20)	(3)	(3)
Tennessee	.414	.407	.357	.419	.387	.350
	(5)	(9)	(9)	(5)	(19)	(20)
Texas	.407	.398	.350	.418	.394	.354
	(9)	(15)	(14)	(6)	(13)	(15)
Utah	.357	.383	.324	.348	.361	.320
	(47)	(32)	(50)	(50)	(44)	(45)
Vermont	.385	.385	.341	.382	.384	.338
	(19)	(31)	(27)	(28)	(23)	(31)
Virginia	.381	.381	.341	.413	.394	.348
	(21)	(36)	(28)	(8)	(14)	(22)
Washington	.365	.378	.335	.361	.359	.338
	(39)	(38)	(42)	(47)	(46)	(37)
West Virginia	.388	.402	.354	.383	.379	.338
	(15)	(13)	(13)	(27)	(34)	(32)
Wisconsin	.365	.379	.328	.370	.367	.333
	(40)	(39)	(49)	(39)	(40)	(35)
Wyoming	.350	.383	.322	.377	.382	.321
	(50)	(33)	(51)	(34)	(25)	(44)
Washington D.C.	.401	.411	.387	N/A	N/A	N/A
	(11)	(7)	(1)			

---

*Income figures are in thousands of dollars.

Note: See table II for explanation of numbers.

Table 5.4a

RANK ORDERING OF STATES BY MEAN INCOME FOR
WHITE AND NON-WHITE GROUPS FOR 1960,1970, AND 1980

State	Mean Income (Whites)			Mean Income (Non-Whites)		
	1960	1970	1980	1960	1970	1980
Alabama	5.13	8.53	20.17	2.24	4.32	14.43
	(38)	(35)	(29)	(47)	(48)	(44)
Alaska	6.75	12.21	35.58	3.50	6.62	29.38
	(9)	(3)	(2)	(24)	(18)	(1)
Arizona	5.99	9.55	20.91	2.80	5.08	17.08
	(16)	(20)	(22)	(33)	(35)	(20)
Arkansas	4.12	7.12	17.90	1.79	4.17	13.93
	(51)	(51)	(47)	(50)	(50)	(45)
California	6.77	10.68	23.94	4.55	7.77	19.56
	(8)	(11)	(9)	(3)	(5)	(10)
Colorado	5.79	9.23	22.28	4.13	6.46	16.41
	(23)	(27)	(16)	(7)	(20)	(22)
Connecticut	7.42	12.53	25.13	4.08	7.51	15.84
	(1)	(1)	(5)	(8)	(7)	(29)
Deleware	7.05	10.86	22.78	3.22	6.07	15.21
	(4)	(9)	(12)	(28)	(24)	(33)
Florida	5.52	9.35	19.78	2.59	5.00	12.95
	(29)	(23)	(35)	(38)	(37)	(48)
Georgia	5.35	9.43	20.60	2.33	4.88	12.56
	(34)	(22)	(26)	(45)	(41)	(49)
Hawaii	5.78	9.65	25.18	6.32	11.92	25.40
	(24)	(19)	(4)	(1)	(1)	(2)
Idaho	5.28	8.31	18.61	3.63	5.93	17.78
	(37)	(41)	(43)	(23)	(25)	(15)
Illinois	6.86	11.20	24.49	4.25	7.61	19.42
	(6)	(8)	(7)	(4)	(6)	(11)
Indiana	5.90	9.76	20.31	4.03	7.32	20.39
	(20)	(16)	(28)	(12)	(11)	(5)
Iowa	5.08	8.71	19.92	3.96	6.36	15.90
	(39)	(33)	(32)	(14)	(21)	(28)
Kansas	5.42	8.66	20.15	3.36	5.61	14.99
	(32)	(34)	(30)	(25)	(28)	(36)
Kentucky	5.61	7.73	18.99	2.49	4.86	15.62
	(27)	(47)	(40)	(41)	(42)	(32)
Louisiana	5.64	9.01	22.43	2.39	4.58	15.81
	(26)	(31)	(14)	(43)	(46)	(30)
Maine	4.68	7.71	16.42	2.66	4.27	16.33
	(47)	(48)	(51)	(37)	(49)	(23)

Maryland	6.97	11.96	26.63	3.71	7.48	21.08
	(5)	(4)	(3)	(20)	(8)	(4)
Massachusetts	6.29	10.55	21.03	3.91	6.54	21.22
	(13)	(12)	(21)	(15)	(19)	(3)
Michigan	6.55	11.22	24.04	4.05	8.06	20.06
	(11)	(7)	(8)	(10)	(2)	(7)
Minnesota	5.51	9.53	21.14	3.78	6.81	16.11
	(30)	(21)	(20)	(19)	(16)	(26)
Mississippi	4.46	7.74	18.10	1.65	3.52	10.23
	(49)	(45)	(46)	(51)	(51)	(51)
Missouri	5.35	9.04	19.40	3.27	6.32	14.97
	(35)	(30)	(37)	(27)	(22)	(37)
Montana	5.28	8.32	18.61	3.21	5.30	13.49
	(36)	(40)	(44)	(29)	(33)	(47)
Nebraska	4.99	8.38	19.28	3.67	5.83	14.55
	(41)	(39)	(39)	(21)	(26)	(40)
Nevada	6.74	10.70	22.69	4.08	7.06	20.38
	(10)	(10)	(13)	(9)	(14)	(6)
New Hampshire	5.41	9.12	19.89	3.19	5.78	18.61
	(33)	(28)	(33)	(30)	(27)	(13)
New Jersey	7.29	12.24	25.01	3.66	7.43	16.87
	(2)	(2)	(6)	(22)	(9)	(21)
New Mexico	5.80	8.50	19.35	2.90	4.93	13.61
	(22)	(36)	(38)	(32)	(40)	(46)
New York	6.86	11.39	22.30	3.99	7.25	14.52
	(6)	(6)	(15)	(13)	(12)	(42)
North Carolina	4.87	8.48	18.79	2.19	4.98	12.46
	(43)	(37)	(42)	(48)	(38)	(50)
North Dakota	4.56	7.73	18.46	2.76	4.72	14.48
	(48)	(46)	(45)	(35)	(44)	(42)
Ohio	6.41	10.43	21.16	4.03	7.18	19.35
	(12)	(13)	(19)	(11)	(13)	(12)
Oklahoma	5.00	8.17	19.67	2.59	4.95	16.26
	(40)	(44)	(36)	(38)	(39)	(25)
Oregon	5.84	9.23	20.12	3.89	6.30	19.96
	(21)	(26)	(31)	(16)	(23)	(9)
Pennsylvania	6.02	9.75	20.68	3.78	6.72	18.58
	(15)	(17)	(25)	(18)	(17)	(14)
Rhode Island	5.43	9.32	18.90	3.13	5.40	19.96
	(31)	(24)	(41)	(31)	(32)	(8)
South Carolina	4.93	8.47	20.44	1.91	4.52	15.70
	(42)	(38)	(27)	(49)	(47)	(31)
South Dakota	4.31	7.42	17.85	2.47	5.01	14.94
	(50)	(49)	(48)	(42)	(36)	(38)

Tennessee	4.76 (45)	8.18 (43)	19.82 (34)	2.35 (44)	4.85 (43)	15.17 (34)
Texas	5.56 (28)	9.26 (25)	21.96 (17)	2.59 (40)	5.22 (34)	14.77 (39)
Utah	5.92 (18)	9.10 (29)	20.77 (24)	3.89 (17)	5.42 (31)	16.32 (24)
Vermont	4.70 (46)	8.28 (42)	17.69 (49)	2.26 (46)	7.77 (4)	17.72 (17)
Virginia	5.66 (25)	9.85 (15)	22.96 (10)	2.79 (34)	5.55 (29)	15.10 (35)
Washington	6.05 (14)	9.86 (14)	21.86 (18)	4.15 (6)	7.39 (10)	17.75 (16)
West Virginia	4.78 (44)	7.30 (50)	17.60 (50)	2.76 (36)	4.64 (45)	14.45 (43)
Wisconsin	5.91 (19)	9.65 (18)	20.77 (23)	4.22 (5)	7.06 (15)	16.06 (27)
Wyoming	5.98 (17)	8.48 (32)	22.88 (11)	3.34 (26)	5.44 (30)	17.70 (19)
Washington D.C.	7.09 (3)	11.50 (5)	38.81 (1)	4.56 (2)	8.00 (3)	17.72 (18)

*Income is in thousands of dollars.

Note:Please see Table II for an explanation of numbers in parentheses.

Table 5.4b

RANK ORDERING OF STATES BY GINI COEFFICIENT FOR WHITE AND NON-WHITE GROUPS FOR 1960,1970, AND 1980

State	Mean Income (Whites)			Mean Income (Non-Whites)		
	1960	**1970**	**1980**	**1960**	**1970**	**1980**
Alabama	.391 (14)	.393 (16)	.344 (16)	.406 (15)	.457 (9)	.360 (16)
Alaska	.356 (49)	.358 (51)	.331 (43)	.409 (14)	.404 (27)	.366 (9)
Arizona	.396 (12)	.384 (27)	.338 (33)	.426 (8)	.437 (13)	.351 (30)
Arkansas	.415 (1)	.406 (4)	.360 (3)	.440 (2)	.559 (1)	.369 (8)
California	.385 (31)	.380 (35)	.346 (11)	.364 (38)	.382 (39)	.351 (31)
Colorado	.381 (25)	.386 (25)	.336 (36)	.409 (13)	.382 (38)	.341 (36)
Connecticut	.374 (32)	.375 (39)	.338 (32)	.349 (49)	.366 (49)	.357 (25)
Deleware	.376 (29)	.371 (44)	.336 (37)	.380 (31)	.386 (35)	.357 (24)
Florida	.411 (3)	.408 (3)	.360 (2)	.375 (32)	.436 (15)	.380 (4)
Georgia	.391 (13)	.388 (23)	.345 (14)	.396 (21)	.405 (26)	.375 (5)
Hawaii	.408 (5)	.396 (12)	.351 (6)	.364 (39)	.356 (51)	.332 (46)
Idaho	.361 (46)	.383 (29)	.339 (29)	.449 (1)	.465 (7)	.338 (40)
Illinois	.369 (38)	.373 (42)	.332 (42)	.360 (40)	.374 (45)	.345 (33)
Indiana	.363 (43)	.363 (48)	.329 (45)	.355 (45)	.373 (46)	.320 (51)
Iowa	.390 (14)	.384 (26)	.337 (34)	.425 (9)	.429 (17)	.360 (15)
Kansas	.391 (15)	.394 (14)	.343 (19)	.370 (34)	.428 (20)	.361 (12)
Kentucky	.390 (16)	.400 (8)	.344 (17)	.396 (22)	.428 (19)	.359 (19)
Louisiana	.398 (11)	.402 (6)	.346 (12)	.394 (24)	.502 (2)	.373 (6)
Maine	.371 (35)	.382 (43)	.339 (26)	.390 (26)	.384 (36)	.336 (42)

Maryland	.361	.362	.329	.370	.380	.336
	(45)	(50)	(44)	(35)	(41)	(43)
Massachusetts	.372	.377	.342	.366	.380	.337
	(34)	(28)	(21)	(37)	(42)	(41)
Michigan	.359	.364	.329	.359	.368	.332
	(48)	(46)	(46)	(41)	(47)	(45)
Minnesota	.381	.382	.336	.372	.412	.361
	(24)	(33)	(35)	(33)	(23)	(13)
Mississippi	.401	.401	.354	.426	.478	.389
	(10)	(7)	(4)	(7)	(4)	(2)
Missouri	.401	.399	.346	.394	.409	.360
	(9)	(10)	(13)	(23)	(24)	(18)
Montana	.368	.389	.341	.403	.466	.359
	(40)	(21)	(24)	(17)	(6)	(21)
Nebraska	.388	.392	.343	.354	.380	.361
	(19)	(19)	(20)	(37)	(43)	(14)
Nevada	.363	.364	.334	.388	.452	.339
	(44)	(47)	(39)	(30)	(10)	(37)
New Hampshire	.371	.382	.328	.358	.389	.329
	(36)	(31)	(49)	(42)	(34)	(48)
New Jersey	.354	.362	.333	.398	.366	.359
	(51)	(49)	(40)	(20)	(50)	(20)
New Mexico	.377	.391	.347	.425	.437	.356
	(28)	(20)	(9)	(11)	(14)	(26)
New York	.379	.388	.350	.357	.382	.372
	(26)	(22)	(7)	(43)	(40)	(7)
North Carolina	.405	.393	.340	.404	.476	.360
	(7)	(17)	(25)	(16)	(5)	(17)
North Dakota	.373	.395	.341	.425	.392	.393
	(33)	(15)	(23)	(10)	(33)	(1)
Ohio	.365	.370	.329	.354	.379	.328
	(41)	(45)	(47)	(46)	(44)	(49)
Oklahoma	.408	.412	.353	.435	.433	.358
	(4)	(2)	(5)	(4)	(16)	(22)
Oregon	.372	.387	.339	.388	.443	.338
	(30)	(24)	(27)	(29)	(12)	(39)
Pennsylvania	.370	.381	.378	.356	.384	.331
	(37)	(34)	(31)	(44)	(37)	(47)
Rhode Island	.377	.396	.342	.369	.402	.335
	(27)	(11)	(22)	(36)	(30)	(44)
South Carolina	.388	.382	.325	.416	.427	.351
	(20)	(30)	(38)	(12)	(21)	(32)
South Dakota	.388	.404	.344	.427	.492	.366
	(21)	(5)	(18)	(6)	(3)	(10)

Tennessee	.413 (2)	.399 (9)	.349 (8)	.403 (18)	.406 (25)	.356 (27)
Texas	.405 (8)	.394 (15)	.347 (10)	.399 (19)	.416 (22)	.352 (29)
Utah	.356 (50)	.379 (36)	.322 (50)	.427 (5)	.446 (11)	.339 (38)
Vermont	.384 (22)	.384 (28)	.339 (38)	.438 (3)	.457 (8)	.344 (35)
Virginia	.384 (23)	.379 (37)	.338 (30)	.388 (28)	.396 (31)	.358 (23)
Washington	.364 (42)	.373 (41)	.332 (41)	.389 (27)	.394 (32)	.345 (34)
West Virginia	.390 (18)	.392 (18)	.344 (15)	.392 (25)	.404 (28)	.384 (3)
Wisconsin	.369 (39)	.374 (40)	.329 (48)	.342 (50)	.403 (29)	.355 (28)
Wyoming	.360 (47)	.382 (32)	.321 (51)	.335 (51)	.428 (18)	.325 (50)
Washington D.C.	.405 (6)	.425 (1)	.397 (1)	.351 (48)	.368 (48)	.361 (11)

*Income is in thousands of dollars.

Note:Please see Table II for an explanation of numbers in parentheses.

Table 5.5

GINI COEFFICIENTS OF INEQUALITY FOR THE MARGINAL DISTRIBUTIONS OF LABOR EARNINGS, NON-LABOR INCOME AND TOTAL INCOME

Year	Labor Earnings	Non-Labor Income	Total Income
1952	0.315984	0.417585	0.308228
1953	0.308689	0.415573	0.301865
1954	0.314139	0.414786	0.306825
1955	0.292814	0.383159	0.286143
1956	0.309093	0.400836	0.302263
1957	0.304369	0.399035	0.297942
1958	0.328202	0.426538	0.321043
1959	0.328636	0.425430	0.321852
1960	0.324847	0.424995	0.318466
1961	0.327761	0.422926	0.321165
1962	0.327357	0.421785	0.320973
1963	0.331319	0.422219	0.324817
1964	0.334521	0.422931	0.328128
1965	0.336319	0.420617	0.329817
1966	0.354057	0.442451	0.347503
1967	0.357665	0.445950	0.351236
1968	0.359180	0.445534	0.352791
1969	0.350569	0.447051	0.345054
1970	0.352415	0.447873	0.347007
1971	0.349765	0.444327	0.344480
1972	0.347857	0.437317	0.342563
1973	0.346091	0.433483	0.340735
1974	0.345076	0.429350	0.339255
1975	0.343290	0.437048	0.337841
1976	0.339111	0.429775	0.333742
1977	0.355421	0.446047	0.349723
1978	0.319399	0.402100	0.314278
1979	0.351257	0.435840	0.345278
1980	0.341018	0.438637	0.336195
1981	0.338273	0.443703	0.333119

ENDNOTES

[1]Fei et al. (1978), Pyatt et al. (1980), Blackorby et al. (1980), Shorrocks (1983) and Maasoumi (1984) have reported some empirical results, but all have been primarily concerned with theoretical questions and none have analyzed regional and attribute distributions as this current work does.

[2]Standard tests of the goodness-of-fit of a distribution include the sum of squares of errors (SSE) and sum of absolute errors (SAE) as well as the chi square test. All of these tests are computed by finding predicted frequencies (based on the assumption that the data is of a particular functional form) and subtracting the predicted values from observed values.

[3]The analysis is only meaningful if the Beta of the second kind provides a good approximation to the actual empirical data over time. The SSE ranged from .004 in 1960 to .007 in 1980 for the marginal distributions of total income. For the various marginal distributions whose Gini measures are reported in Tables 5.2-5.4 the SSE ranged from .002 to .009, all indicating a good fit, cf. McDonald (1984).

[4]Cowell (1977) discusses the issues involved in comparing data collected in different units.

[5]Illinois and New York both broke with these trends interestingly, with respect to their Gini coefficients for urban residents in 1980, see Table 5.3.

Chapter 6

INEQUALITY ACROSS DEMOGRAPHIC GROUPS

As we discussed in Chapter 1, one of the data sets we utilize in this book is the <u>Current Population Survey March File</u> (CPS) for selected years. The CPS data allows us to examine inequality for various subgroups of the population where the disaggregation is done by age, education, race and sex as well as by income-recipient unit and depending on the definition of income. We discuss this below. As the debate continues over whether income inequality has worsened, improved or remained constant in the last few years, some important questions need to be further examined by policymakers and academics concerned with these issues. For example, what has happened to the distribution of income for various subgroups of the population over time? Does the income receiving unit matter and how about the time interval in which income is measured?

The discussion in Chapter 5 provided some insight into what has happened across states from decade to decade and to the labor/nonlabor composition, using census data and I.R.S. data and the joint distribution approach. That analysis was predicated on a specified form of hypothetical statistical distribution. Another approach is to use the Lorenz curve as a basis for constructing several well-known measures of inequality as we discussed in Chapter 3. We will follow that strategy here and construct measures of inequality for various subgroups without imposing an underlying hypothetical form of inequality on the data.

By undergoing the systematic disaggregation of income-earner units by the demographic and employment attributes and measuring their respective levels of inequality we hope to provide timely new information. It will become readily apparent that discrepancies across groups by (say) education may provide more relevant information to the Congress than simply running a regression on the log of earnings where education is an explanatory variable. We will say more about this below.

We do not attempt to make comparisons of inequality levels by using specified measures which allow for within and across income types à la Lerman and Yitzaki (1984, 1986), Pyatt (1980) and others because, as Shorrocks (1982) has noted, such measures are problematic. Dagum (1980) has introduced ingenious ways to analyze distance between distributions but all this research presupposes a parametric specification of the underlying distributions. Blackburn (1988a,b,c) and Blackburn and Bloom

(1987a,b) have discussed many of the issues we discuss here but with specified decomposition measures and with a human capital regression model.

In the present chapter we seek only to use the March CPS sample to pull out income receiving units in the particular subgroup in question and measure the level of inequality for that group based on our several measures. Blackburn (1988c) has discussed possible bias in using the March survey vis-a-vis the May survey. We can say that a subgroup X has a Gini coefficient of .43 and another subgroup Y has a Gini coefficient of .35 but we can't say that group X is Q percent more unequal than Y because the comparison is vacuous. We can only say that inequality in the size distribution of income for group X as measured by the Gini coefficient is higher than for group Y. At the same time we remind ourselves that the Gini coefficient is a mathematical description of <u>one</u> aspect of the actual income graduation.

As we noted above, the literature on income distribution has proliferated over the past hundred years with most of the emphasis on generation, description and measurement of the observed distribution. Unfortunately, a consensus has not been reached on many of the fundamental issues that underlie this body of research. For example, the choice of the appropriate income-recipient unit to analyze has divided researchers in this field.

Kuznets (1976) pointed out that an ideal income-recipient unit must satisfy three criteria: identifiability, inclusiveness, and distinct independence. Since the income from family owned assets can not always be identified as belonging to specific individuals within each family, considering the total number of persons as income-recipient units will not meet Kuznet's criteria. Families include both "economically active" and inactive members of the population, so limiting the analysis to only the "economically active" would eliminate a segment of population that is of great importance for analyzing long term economic trends, viz., the young. However, inclusion of the economically dependent deviates from Kuznets' criterion of independence. Therefore, "...in a meaningful distribution of income by size the recipient unit has to be a family or household and cannot be a person..." (Kuznets, 1976, p. 1).

Another issue concerns the definition of income and time. As Cowell points out, what we really desire is a comprehensive concept of income....an index that will serve to represent generally a person's well-being in society, cf. Cowell (1977, p 41). Obvious candidates are wealth, lifetime income, labor earnings in a given time period and Cowell's measure, the increase in a person's command over resources during a given time period (Cowell, 1977, p. 5). Theoretically, the latter would seem to be much preferred to the first three; however, practicability is another matter. Among the criteria that a definition of income should meet, measurability, comparability among individuals and accessability for analytical purposes should all be considered. Wealth may include not only assets that are difficult to value in a market sense but also includes human capital attributes which may have important implications for future earnings that is impossible to measure. Lifetime earnings necessarily require a termination point and expectations about future earnings to be useful so isn't very practical. Labor earnings are one aspect of an individual's ability to control resources but ignores other nonlabor income. The fourth concept is simply impossible to measure. Below we examine earnings both annually and weekly to attempt to get at least some idea of how time and the income unit affect levels of inequality.

We have seen then, that two major issues are the appropriate specification of income-recipient unit and a reasonable definition of income. To demonstrate that a divergence arises when we specify one income-recipient unit vis-a-vis another, below we analyze inequality among families, households and individuals. We do not adjust for household equivalence scaling because we want to observe the difference across the various units without adjustments. We also distinguish between earnings and total income. Labor earnings in the United States have accounted for about two thirds to three fourths of total income as we noted in Chapter 5. As also noted in Chapter 5, however, the proportion of labor income to total income varies significantly by age and occupation.

To distinguish between earnings and total income inequality simultaneously by household, family and individuals and also adjust for age, race, sex and education over time, necessarily requires a comprehensive data base that provides yearly observations to detect changes over time for these various demographic characteristics. The data we utilize to achieve this aim are from the March File of the Current Population Survey (CPS). We leave the technical description of this data to the appendix.

6.1 Measuring Income Inequality

There are no a priori reasons for selecting one measure of income inequality over another, since any particular income inequality measure captures only one aspect of the observed distribution as we have continually emphasized. For this reason, several measures of inequality are employed in this chapter.

As Chapter 3 made clear, one approach to measuring inequality, without imposing a functional form of statistical distribution on the income graduation, is to use Lorenz-based inequality measures. As Kakwani noted, the Lorenz curve is defined as the relationship between the cumulative proportion of income units and the cumulative proportion of income received when units are arranged in ascending order of their income.

Recall that the Lorenz Curve can be generated by defining the income earner units as (say) quintile shares where q_i, i=1,...,5 represents the ith income earner share and letting

$$0 \leq q_1 \leq q_2, \ldots, \leq q_5 \leq 1. \tag{6.1}$$

From this simple ordering many well-known inequality measures can be formulated. For instance, the Gini (1912) measure is defined as,

$$G = 1 - \frac{1}{n} - \frac{2}{n} [\sum_{k=1}^{n-1} (n-k)q_k]. \tag{6.2}$$

The Gini measure is the average difference of all pairwise comparisons of income. It is most frequently criticized for putting more weight on a transfer between middle income earners than at the tails. This measure is bounded by 0 for perfect equality and one for perfect inequality. The relative mean deviation measure is defined as:

$$R = \frac{1}{2} \cdot \frac{n}{n-1} [\sum_{k=1}^{n-1} | q_k - \frac{1}{n} |]. \tag{6.3}$$

As Kakwani notes, "if the population is divided into two groups, (a) those who receive less than or equal to mean income and (b) those who receive more than mean income, the relative mean deviation represents the percentage of total income that should be transferred from the second group to the first so that both groups have exactly the same mean income." It also is a zero-one measure. The R measure doesn't satisfy transfer properties but does have some economic intuition, which is why it is included here. Theil's normalized entropy measure is defined as:

$$T = 1 + \frac{1}{\ln(n)} \left[\sum_{k=1}^{n-1} q_k \ln q_k \right]. \tag{6.4}$$

Theil formulated his measure based on whether a given physical system was more or less orderly. He reinterpreted this "order" as income levels. The measure has a lower bound of zero and no upper bound.

Kakwani's measure takes the form:

$$K = \frac{\bar{\ell} - \sqrt{2}}{2 - \sqrt{2}} \quad \text{with } \bar{\ell}_k = \sqrt{q_k^2 + \frac{1}{n^2}} \tag{6.5}$$

$$\bar{\ell} = \sum_{k=1}^{n} \bar{\ell}_k.$$

Kakwani's measure looks at inequality between the classes and the weighted sum of inequality within each class. This measure is not bounded by zero or one. This form is more sensitive to redistribution in the middle quintiles.

These alternative inequality measures are all frequently used in the literature. Each measures a different aspect of economic inequality. It is for completeness that we analyze each of them in this chapter. Before proceeding to discuss the levels of inequality across demographic groups based on the CPS data we first look at total income data.

The inequality measures above were estimated from consumer income data from the <u>Current Population Reports</u> for the period 1947-84. The data are for families (defined as two-or-more related individuals <u>living</u> together), and some authors (e.g. Blackburn and Bloom (1987a,b)) argue the family should include dependent relations not living at home as well. We will stick with the CPR data as that is what is available. The definition of income in the survey is quite comprehensive in that it includes cash transfers; however, it does not include transfers in kind and taxes paid.

Since the data are reported in quintiles only, the measures above have been specified in quintiles. The use of quintiles will bias the inequality measures as a description of the underlying distribution to the extent each quintile diverges from a uniform distribution. Basmann, Hayes and Slottje (1988) discuss this problem rigorously. In an examination of the sensitivity of inequality measures to data grouping. Blinder and Esaki (1978) and several others (including the authors) have actually used the quintiles as measures of inequality and since it is the only data disaggregated by demographic attributes we will follow that practice here. This allows us to examine different portions of the income graduation over time. The data are reported in Table 6.1. Table 6.2 contains the Gini, Kakwani, Relative Mean Deviation and Theil indices. We will use both the quintiles and the explicit measures as indicators of income inequality. Thus, the results will be robust if they are consistent across these inequality measures.

We give the results in Tables 6.1 and 6.2 before we analyze the disaggregate inequality measures from the CPS. We want to emphasize the information content that is missed by only looking at summary statistics of inequality for the whole population. Table 6.1 indicates that the percentage of income in each quintile's share has been relatively stable from 1947 to 1984. A linear regression against a trend variable found no statistically significant time trend. The inequality measures (based on this information from Table 6.1) given in Table 6.2 reflect the same thing, i.e., relatively stable distributions. We will contrast these results with our results for income and earnings distribution for various disaggregated cohorts below.

6.2 Empirical Results For Various Demographic Groups

As can be seen from Table 6.3, the level of earnings inequality (as indicated by our measures) for males under thirty years of age varies considerably by education level. There appears to be a higher level of earnings inequality for males under thirty without high school diplomas than for high school and college graduates. The results appear robust across inequality measures. The results are not surprising in light of the fact that most males in this group have flat earnings profiles in relatively low wage occupations. However some individuals will "violate" this expected flat age/earnings scenario and do very well. This contrast might lead to measures indicating relatively high levels of earnings inequality. Interestingly, when we compare these results to those for males aged 30-59 in Table 6.4, we see the differences by educational cohort dissipate somewhat. The group with less education has higher inequality measures, but the magnitudes of variation with the other group are smaller. Again, the results for the older males are robust across measures. Clearly, the most extreme measured levels of earnings inequality for males falls upon those males in the sixty and over age group. The results shown in Table 6.5 indicate higher measured levels of inequality somewhat more clearly segmented by educational level than the results for the other age classes. Over all age classes, earnings inequality measures for males vary inversely with educational attainment. As might be expected, measured earnings inequality is lowest among those males in peak earning years. The measured inequality levels then rise sharply for males age 60 and over.

These results may be very misleading since men over 60 may have relatively high nonlabor income (from pension benefits, etc.) and, if we observed total income levels, we might find that the income distribution for this group flip-flops. That is, men with high earnings might have low nonlabor earnings and vice versa. Therefore, the observed distributions of earnings and income might indicate the same level of inequality, but the same individuals will be at opposite ends of the earnings distribution. However, to the extent that labor income and assets are correlated, the results are indicative of the actual distribution. The earnings levels given in Table 6.5 indicate that the high earners are still working.

From Table 6.6, we see that overall inequality measures for male earnings exhibited an increasing trend over the period. The results are higher than those for males age 30 to 59, indicating the peak earners suffer the least earnings inequality among males, regardless of education cohort. In contrast, measured earnings inequality is higher at all education levels for the males 60 and over than for males overall. Blackburn (1988b) observes similar patterns and suggests that the increase in inequality may be due to the shift in the age composition of the population and to a sectoral shift to services production. As baby boomers enter the labor force, there is a lag before they get a substantial return on their educational investment and, relative to peak earners, inequality should rise. If Lydall's (1968) hierarchy model is a reasonable hypothesis, then as the service sector enlarges we won't observe gradual pay increases. Rather a dichotomy exists with only high-skill wage workers and low-wage skill workers. This results in an increase in inequality. Both hypotheses are consistent with our findings. For males under thirty, measured earnings inequality is near or slightly above the overall measured levels for those without high school diplomas, then declines with the increase in educational attainment. In each case, the results are robust across measures. This may be due to the fact that many of the low education workers are not full-time workers, so they will probably have higher inequality levels.[1]

For females under thirty, each of the measures in Table 6.7 shows that measured earnings inequality varies strongly and inversely by level of education. The magnitudes of the measures appear strongly segmented by education level, with the greatest inequality variation within a class falling on those without high school diplomas. Comparing these results to those for females age 30-59 in Table 6.8, we see that measured earnings inequality for the older age group similarly decreases with education level. However, the variation of measured earnings inequality among education levels narrows significantly for the older women, possibly reflecting in part on the pronounced differences in the education and career patterns of the two groups. Specifically, the group under age thirty during the years 1976-86 was comprised of increasing numbers of females entering nontraditional educational and career tracks. Chapter 2 noted the trend toward increased labor force participation and higher educational attainment by this group might be expected to lead to increased variety in the earning activities pursued by these women and, hence, in their earnings levels. Conversely, the older women could expect lower returns from investing in education during their younger years when they were more likely to do so, and so on average probably invested less in their human capital. Thus, when compared to 30 to 59-year-olds, who are more likely to be engaged in more traditional earning activities, we would expect greater measured earnings variation for the younger group, and that is what is observed.

The Table 6.9 results for females age 60 and older display a marked difference from those for the other two age classes. Specifically, while measured earnings inequality for the two younger age groups was lowest among college graduates, this result is not borne out by the results for females age 60 and over. For this group, average measured earnings inequality over the period was either higher than that for high school graduates (Theil and Kakwani) or equal to that for those with high school diplomas (Gini). Thus, higher educational attainment among women 60 and over did not serve to decrease their measured earnings inequality. This interesting result might be explained by a pension/asset effect. Since these individuals tend to be employed in low paying jobs, we observe that they continue to work and not retire as men in this age group/income category tend to do. A comparison of the earnings levels for these groups supports this. Among the three age classes, each of the inequality measures indicates the greatest inequality among females 60 and over, regardless of education cohort. Interestingly, while measured inequality among those without high school diplomas appears lowest for females in the peak earning years (30-59), females under thirty suffer the least inequality among the two higher educational levels. This may be related to the infiltration of the nontraditional educational and career areas by the youngest age group as mentioned above.

Comparison of measured earnings inequality by age with the Table 6.10 results for females overall reveals some relationships similar to the equivalent comparison for males above. For example, as with males, females 60 and over at every education level suffered greater measured earnings inequality than did females overall. For the under-thirty age group, measured earnings inequality was lower than overall levels for all but those without high school diplomas. While these results were robust across measures, the results for females age 30 to 59 without high school diplomas indicate a mixed signal. Specifically, the Gini and Kakwani measures indicate less inequality compared to the levels for females overall, while the Theil measures are slightly higher for this group than those in the summary table.

A comparison of Tables 6.6 and 6.10 clearly reveals overall lower measured earnings inequality for males than for females, which is not surprising given that women are more likely to have interrupted working cycles and therefore less likely to invest in as much education. Comparisons between earnings inequality measures for males and females by age, however, reveal some interesting relationships. Across all of the measures, males in any particular age and education class suffered less measured earnings inequality than did females in the counterpart class-- that is, measures were lower on average for males under thirty without high school diplomas than for similarly classified females, and so on. Further, on average, the "gap" or magnitude by which females' measured earnings inequality exceeded that for males appears to be fairly constant among the education levels for all groups except one. Interestingly, for males and females under thirty, the average "gap" among the measures narrows appreciably at the college graduate level of education. Again, this seems to support the notion suggested above that some women in this age group are engaging in nontraditional education and earning activities which will steepen their earnings profiles.

Against the overall levels of measured earnings inequality in Table 6.11, measures for males overall compare appreciably lower, while measures for females on average exceed the overall levels. More specifically, an examination of Tables 6.12-6.14 reveals that white males appear to suffer the least measured earnings inequality. While the measures for black males are lower than those for individuals overall, on average, the inequality measures for white males are lower than those for every other sex and ethnic classification, and for individuals overall. This implies white males in the sample are equally able to achieve about the same level of income. In contrast, while measured inequality among white females appeared lower than for black females, all measures except the Theil measure indicate greater earnings inequality among white females than among females in other ethnic groups. Thus, some white females appear to have a larger relative advantage over their ethnic counterparts that the white males exhibit. Females from other ethnic groups in general suffered lower measured earnings inequality than did black females and white females, although the average of the Theil measures for other ethnic females exceeded that for white females. We conclude that white females and females in general have been most successful in breaking out of the norm and thus leading to greater inequality in this group.

Turning the analysis to family earnings, the results in Tables 6.15 to 6.17 indicate that black families suffered greater measured earnings inequality than did white families and families overall. This result, which was robust across measures, may be due to an observed prevalence of females as heads of households and primary wage earners in black families. As mentioned before, earnings inequality measures for these females was higher than those for black males and for white males and females.

The same hypothesis could apply to the Tables 6.18-6.20 results, which show that, except for measures in the "individuals" and "others" classes, earnings inequality measures for black single parent female families were higher than those for all other ethnic classes and family types. In contrast, family types suffering the least measured earnings inequality were married two-earner couple families, with the measures slightly higher for that class of blacks than for the class overall. Among the family types, measures are highest for "others" class, with the overall measures on average slightly above those for the same class of blacks except for the Theil.

The Table 6.18 measures of income inequality again indicate the least amount of inequality among married two-earner couples as compared with all other family types. This result is robust across all measures. Compared to Tables 6.19 and 6.20 (earnings inequality), the measures of income inequality are generally lower across comparable family types, suggesting the importance of the effects of nonlabor income on the income distribution. Interestingly, female individuals enjoy slightly lower measured income inequality than do males (a robust result) in contrast to the comparison of earnings inequality measures. Also in contrast to those measures, the highest measured income inequality falls upon the "separated" group, rather than on the "others" class.

Just as families with multiple earners suffered lower measured income inequality, the results in Tables 6.21 and 6.22 suggest that households also benefitted from the likelihood of multiple earners. Specifically, measured income inequality generally was lowest for households with more than one family, although the Theil measure for this class did exceed that for one-family households and for households overall. In contrast, although the first few years of observations are deceptively low, the "others" household group suffered the highest measured income inequality, followed by the households of individuals.

Among individual income earners (Tables 6.23-6.26), not surprisingly, measured income inequality is lower for white males than for any other sex or ethnic class and for individuals overall.[2] Interestingly, while the measures for white females are slightly less than the overall measures, they slightly exceed those for black females in general suggesting that white women are better able to succeed. Only the Theil measure contradicts these two comparisons. Of all groups, white and other ethnic females appear to suffer the highest measured income inequality. The measures for these two groups fall very near those for individuals overall, although there is no consistent dominance by any group in this comparison.

Finally, we also look at differences in weekly earnings distributions. While the previous discussion has highlighted differences in inequality in the various income receiving units and their respective distributions, we have not discussed one last aspect, that of course being time. The unit of time in which income is measured is probably the least discussed aspect of the inequality literature. It is, however, very critical in discussions of inequality of income and earnings. We see from comparing Table 6.27 to Table 6.6 that there is a great deal more inequality in the distribution of annual earnings than in the distribution of weekly earnings irregardless of which inequality measure is chosen for all males. As Kin Blackburn pointed out to us, this has to be the case since if Earnings, E, equals hours worked, H, times the wage rate, w, then Var (lnE) = Var (lnH) + Var (ln) + 2Cov (lnH,ln) so inequality will be higher unless hours and wages are strongly negatively correlated as we go from weekly to annual series. The extent to which our results are due to economic behavior versus this statistical artifact is difficult to appraise. We observe from Tables 6.28-6.30 when compared with Tables 6.3-6.6 that this relationship holds across all age and educational cohorts. Tables 6.31 and 6.10 show the same result for women as do 6.32-6.34 and 6.11-6.14 when we examine age/education cohorts. The results are consistent in all cases, that is, there is significantly more inequality in the various distributions of annual earnings than in the distributions of weekly earnings. This result suggests (keeping in mind the "Blackburn caveat") that unemployment rates (recall Table 2.12 for duration rates) may have a large impact on the distribution of earnings when annualized. Since those that are unemployed in any given week no longer are in the observed distributions, it might be expected that their absence will be reflected in lower inequality levels for weekly data. This result also suggests that those that fall in and out of the employed ranks may also be low skill, low wage workers. At any given point in time, when they are out of the employed portion of the labor force, the inequality measure may indicate less inequality.

We conclude this chapter by noting that virtually every Kappa value for every cohort reported in Tables 6.3-6.34 is positive and large (most are greater than one). Recalling Table 4.1, the lognormal, Pareto, gamma and Beta II distributions are all candidates for describing these observed income/earnings graduations. It appears, however, that the magnitudes of the Kappa values suggest the gamma and Beta II distributions are the most appropriate candidates. As we noted in Chapter 4, these results are only meaningful if we can put bounds

(confidence intervals) on the K values. This is a future research
project and was not attempted in this study. We now discuss occupation
earnings distributions in Chapter 7.

Table 6.1

QUINTILE DATA FROM THE CURRENT POPULATION SURVEY SERIES

YEAR	Q1	Q2	Q3	Q4	Q5
1947	0.050	0.119	0.170	0.231	0.430
1948	0.049	0.121	0.173	0.232	0.424
1949	0.045	0.119	0.173	0.235	0.427
1950	0.045	0.120	0.174	0.234	0.427
1951	0.050	0.124	0.176	0.234	0.416
1952	0.049	0.123	0.174	0.234	0.419
1953	0.047	0.125	0.180	0.239	0.409
1954	0.045	0.121	0.177	0.239	0.418
1955	0.048	0.123	0.178	0.237	0.413
1956	0.050	0.125	0.179	0.237	0.410
1957	0.051	0.127	0.181	0.238	0.404
1958	0.050	0.125	0.180	0.239	0.407
1959	0.049	0.123	0.179	0.238	0.411
1960	0.048	0.122	0.178	0.240	0.413
1961	0.047	0.119	0.175	0.238	0.422
1962	0.050	0.121	0.176	0.240	0.413
1963	0.050	0.121	0.177	0.240	0.412
1964	0.051	0.120	0.177	0.240	0.412
1965	0.052	0.122	0.178	0.239	0.409
1966	0.056	0.124	0.178	0.238	0.405
1967	0.055	0.124	0.179	0.239	0.404
1968	0.056	0.124	0.177	0.237	0.405
1969	0.056	0.124	0.177	0.237	0.406
1970	0.054	0.122	0.176	0.238	0.409
1971	0.055	0.120	0.176	0.238	0.411
1972	0.054	0.119	0.175	0.239	0.414
1973	0.055	0.119	0.175	0.240	0.411
1974	0.055	0.120	0.175	0.240	0.410
1975	0.054	0.118	0.176	0.241	0.411
1976	0.054	0.118	0.176	0.241	0.411
1977	0.052	0.116	0.175	0.242	0.415
1978	0.052	0.116	0.175	0.241	0.415
1979	0.052	0.116	0.175	0.241	0.417
1980	0.051	0.116	0.175	0.243	0.416
1981	0.050	0.113	0.174	0.244	0.419
1982	0.047	0.112	0.170	0.243	0.427
1983	0.047	0.111	0.171	0.243	0.428
1984	0.047	0.110	0.170	0.244	0.429

Table 6.2

INCOME INEQUALITY MEASURES FOR THE U.S. 1947-1984

YEAR	G	K	R	T
1947	0.436	0.114	0.326	0.127
1948	0.432	0.111	0.321	0.124
1949	0.441	0.116	0.328	0.130
1950	0.439	0.117	0.326	0.129
1951	0.421	0.108	0.313	0.118
1952	0.427	0.109	0.317	0.121
1953	0.419	0.108	0.310	0.118
1954	0.432	0.114	0.321	0.125
1955	0.423	0.108	0.313	0.119
1956	0.415	0.107	0.308	0.115
1957	0.408	0.103	0.302	0.111
1958	0.413	0.106	0.307	0.114
1959	0.420	0.107	0.311	0.117
1960	0.423	0.111	0.316	0.119
1961	0.434	0.115	0.324	0.125
1962	0.423	0.108	0.316	0.118
1963	0.422	0.108	0.315	0.118
1964	0.421	0.107	0.315	0.117
1965	0.416	0.105	0.310	0.114
1966	0.405	0.101	0.303	0.108
1967	0.406	0.101	0.303	0.109
1968	0.407	0.098	0.303	0.109
1969	0.407	0.100	0.304	0.109
1970	0.414	0.102	0.309	0.113
1971	0.415	0.104	0.311	0.113
1972	0.419	0.107	0.316	0.116
1973	0.417	0.104	0.314	0.114
1974	0.415	0.104	0.313	0.113
1975	0.419	0.106	0.315	0.115
1976	0.419	0.106	0.315	0.115
1977	0.426	0.109	0.321	0.120
1978	0.427	0.108	0.321	0.120
1979	0.427	0.111	0.322	0.120
1980	0.428	0.112	0.323	0.121
1981	0.435	0.114	0.329	0.124
1982	0.447	0.118	0.338	0.132
1983	0.447	0.120	0.339	0.132
1984	0.449	0.121	0.341	0.133

Table 6.3
Inequality Measures for the Earnings of Males under 30 by Education Cohort
1976 - 1985

	YEAR	GINI	RMD	THEIL	KAKAWANI	FRACTION	CV	MEAN	OBSERVS	KAPPA
No High School Degree	1976	0.501	0.374	0.056	0.223	0.056	97.01	7543.5	2250	9.98479
	1977	0.508	0.378	0.056	0.228	0.057	96.28	7661.5	2786	4.05007
	1978	0.499	0.368	0.054	0.220	0.055	93.61	7928.3	2655	3.06510
	1979	0.481	0.352	0.050	0.205	0.053	90.67	8381.8	2528	3.46360
	1980	0.469	0.341	0.047	0.195	0.053	87.78	8816.1	2971	2.93037
	1981	0.479	0.351	0.049	0.204	0.053	89.87	8070.0	3001	3.05012
	1982	0.494	0.365	0.053	0.215	0.051	93.99	8031.7	2595	4.05292
	1983	0.504	0.373	0.056	0.223	0.046	96.60	7167.8	2368	4.67818
	1984	0.497	0.367	0.055	0.220	0.046	92.98	7023.6	2319	2.77161
	1985	0.505	0.372	0.058	0.222	0.043	96.67	7199.9	1728	4.22571
High School Graduate	1976	0.356	0.254	0.024	0.119	0.183	65.05	13013.6	7348	1.72518
	1977	0.368	0.262	0.025	0.126	0.193	69.14	13332.1	9381	3.84673
	1978	0.357	0.254	0.023	0.118	0.195	65.83	13582.3	9256	1.91440
	1979	0.352	0.250	0.023	0.115	0.197	64.31	14090.5	9332	1.47290
	1980	0.354	0.251	0.022	0.116	0.200	65.10	14117.0	11203	1.79698
	1981	0.367	0.262	0.024	0.124	0.201	67.34	13311.2	11324	1.68393
	1982	0.382	0.273	0.027	0.134	0.195	71.56	12807.9	9874	3.47221
	1983	0.397	0.284	0.029	0.144	0.191	73.58	12085.9	9651	2.48103
	1984	0.397	0.285	0.029	0.144	0.191	72.69	11964.3	9567	1.77984
	1985	0.390	0.279	0.029	0.139	0.183	72.98	12327.1	7282	3.30023
College Graduate	1976	0.347	0.243	0.027	0.115	0.055	64.64	17291.5	2229	2.07096
	1977	0.354	0.249	0.027	0.118	0.057	67.00	17584.1	2799	3.43694
	1978	0.356	0.245	0.028	0.120	0.055	66.67	17632.1	2615	2.60450
	1979	0.349	0.245	0.027	0.115	0.055	64.84	17641.2	2623	1.88940
	1980	0.352	0.246	0.026	0.116	0.053	65.31	17832.2	3000	1.97560
	1981	0.347	0.254	0.026	0.115	0.051	63.09	17043.0	2904	1.01361
	1982	0.359	0.254	0.029	0.121	0.049	66.95	17349.3	2478	2.36799
	1983	0.373	0.262	0.031	0.131	0.050	69.78	17084.1	2573	2.50428
	1984	0.380	0.271	0.032	0.134	0.050	69.46	17025.2	2510	1.46597
	1985	0.371	0.261	0.032	0.129	0.050	70.08	17832.0	1989	3.52884

RMD = Relative Mean Deviation
CV = Coefficient of Variation
Observs = Number of observations

Table 6.4

Inequality Measures for the Earnings of Males 30-59 by Education Cohort

1976 - 1985

	YEAR	GINI	RMD	THEIL	KAKAWANI	FRACTION	CV	MEAN	OBSERVS	KAPPA
No High School Degree	1976	0.386	0.274	0.032	0.146	0.151	71.13	14313.7	6077	1.61934
	1977	0.391	0.277	0.032	0.148	0.145	71.86	14735.9	7024	1.63589
	1978	0.387	0.274	0.031	0.145	0.136	71.01	15140.2	6468	1.39803
	1979	0.391	0.276	0.032	0.147	0.128	71.84	15203.2	6064	1.48059
	1980	0.403	0.286	0.033	0.155	0.121	73.58	14835.8	6775	1.28784
	1981	0.411	0.293	0.035	0.160	0.117	74.38	13982.4	6571	1.00142
	1982	0.419	0.299	0.037	0.165	0.112	77.70	13648.3	5684	2.33721
	1983	0.448	0.322	0.042	0.187	0.108	82.98	12404.5	5458	2.27685
	1984	0.452	0.324	0.043	0.189	0.101	84.02	12861.6	5054	2.40559
	1985	0.448	0.319	0.044	0.185	0.099	85.04	13041.0	3964	4.64097
High School Graduate	1976	0.301	0.205	0.018	0.091	0.252	58.03	21707.8	10102	3.42541
	1977	0.306	0.209	0.018	0.094	0.249	58.48	21921.1	11894	2.74455
	1978	0.306	0.209	0.018	0.093	0.251	57.73	22295.5	11816	1.81138
	1979	0.312	0.215	0.019	0.097	0.255	57.50	22288.5	11919	1.22886
	1980	0.307	0.212	0.018	0.093	0.257	56.56	22136.0	14282	0.88543
	1981	0.314	0.218	0.018	0.097	0.257	56.82	21210.2	14482	0.48762
	1982	0.328	0.228	0.024	0.105	0.261	61.04	20844.8	13168	1.68277
	1983	0.354	0.248	0.024	0.122	0.263	65.17	19699.9	13301	1.28352
	1984	0.354	0.248	0.024	0.121	0.267	65.40	19810.3	13337	1.46566
	1985	0.348	0.244	0.024	0.118	0.276	64.91	19982.0	10981	2.03531
College Graduate	1976	0.311	0.214	0.020	0.092	0.101	57.91	33483.8	4082	1.54427
	1977	0.306	0.212	0.019	0.088	0.104	56.56	33072.1	5034	1.36165
	1978	0.307	0.215	0.018	0.089	0.110	55.92	32962.8	5226	0.96557
	1979	0.301	0.216	0.018	0.089	0.115	55.90	32514.2	5454	0.94832
	1980	0.300	0.213	0.017	0.086	0.121	53.90	31270.5	6760	0.48200
	1981	0.300	0.214	0.017	0.087	0.124	53.29	29996.4	7004	0.24520
	1982	0.325	0.227	0.020	0.099	0.131	59.64	30663.4	6637	1.28290
	1983	0.340	0.239	0.022	0.108	0.137	61.90	30540.8	6962	1.04050
	1984	0.329	0.232	0.021	0.101	0.142	59.23	30675.9	7105	0.76860
	1985	0.340	0.237	0.023	0.107	0.137	63.14	32429.7	5459	1.78230

RMD = Relative Mean Deviation
CV = Coefficient of Variation
Observs = Number of observations.

Table 6.5

Inequality Measures for the Earnings of Males 60 and Over by Education Cohort

1976 - 1985

	YEAR	GINI	RMD	THEIL	KAKWANI	FRACTION	CV	MEAN	OBSERVS	KAPPA
No High School Degree	1976	0.801	0.683	0.159	0.567	0.117	201.14	3971.7	4722	32.3825
	1977	0.806	0.684	0.158	0.570	0.112	205.57	4048.7	5459	33.5151
	1978	0.814	0.696	0.164	0.585	0.113	210.66	3753.8	5402	33.1553
	1979	0.817	0.703	0.166	0.592	0.110	210.98	3764.1	5217	29.4165
	1980	0.823	0.708	0.168	0.600	0.104	215.01	3587.9	5846	28.8188
	1981	0.831	0.715	0.169	0.605	0.101	212.19	3288.8	5678	23.5090
	1982	0.831	0.725	0.176	0.619	0.100	217.71	3085.5	5055	23.9780
	1983	0.843	0.745	0.186	0.642	0.099	229.26	2845.5	5000	29.2146
	1984	0.851	0.753	0.193	0.651	0.094	239.34	2741.4	4702	40.2000
	1985	0.854	0.757	0.200	0.657	0.099	245.34	2851.0	3952	55.3423
High School Graduate	1976	0.680	0.559	0.115	0.418	0.060	141.18	9328.0	2434	7.5016
	1977	0.698	0.573	0.118	0.434	0.063	148.99	9156.9	3048	10.4222
	1978	0.705	0.579	0.120	0.442	0.064	150.78	9319.6	3062	9.9259
	1979	0.709	0.585	0.121	0.448	0.067	151.19	9396.2	3198	8.7955
	1980	0.705	0.581	0.116	0.442	0.067	147.21	8885.3	3781	6.8963
	1981	0.723	0.602	0.124	0.467	0.068	153.98	7935.6	3868	7.7593
	1982	0.744	0.625	0.134	0.494	0.073	165.61	7920.7	3706	11.5320
	1983	0.752	0.632	0.137	0.503	0.075	168.68	7678.6	3811	11.6828
	1984	0.767	0.648	0.143	0.522	0.079	176.01	6963.1	3984	13.3053
	1985	0.763	0.642	0.145	0.515	0.082	176.29	7077.7	3278	16.6096
College Graduate	1976	0.666	0.541	0.125	0.401	0.020	131.56	16491.1	827	4.4842
	1977	0.700	0.571	0.137	0.436	0.019	143.69	15226.6	933	6.1322
	1978	0.692	0.564	0.133	0.427	0.019	139.90	15680.0	843	6.2171
	1979	0.673	0.549	0.125	0.408	0.020	134.04	16317.5	993	4.5101
	1980	0.664	0.546	0.119	0.404	0.021	129.60	15675.0	1219	4.0428
	1981	0.678	0.559	0.122	0.417	0.023	134.22	14053.6	1313	5.2071
	1982	0.696	0.570	0.130	0.430	0.024	142.18	14955.2	1254	6.1380
	1983	0.692	0.566	0.127	0.428	0.026	139.88	15300.4	1349	5.4690
	1984	0.678	0.552	0.122	0.412	0.026	135.21	15803.7	1314	5.1240
	1985	0.704	0.581	0.137	0.441	0.026	114.93	16215.2	1049	6.4166

RMD = Relative Mean Deviation
CV = Coefficient of Variation
Observs = Number of observations.

Table 6.6
Inequality Measures for Male Earnings by Year
1976 - 1985

YEAR	GINI	RMD	THEIL	KAKWANI	CV	MEAN	OBSERVS	KAPPA
1976	0.468	0.334	0.038	0.201	89.47	16201.1	40071	4.21831
1977	0.470	0.336	0.037	0.202	89.32	16348.3	48358	3.76510
1978	0.469	0.336	0.037	0.201	88.31	16653.9	47443	3.03996
1979	0.465	0.333	0.036	0.199	87.07	16903.8	48328	2.65913
1980	0.460	0.330	0.035	0.194	84.82	16827.0	55837	1.95240
1981	0.466	0.338	0.036	0.200	85.45	16055.0	56145	1.68680
1982	0.484	0.349	0.039	0.212	91.42	16046.8	50451	3.37706
1983	0.504	0.366	0.042	0.228	95.68	15534.2	50473	3.61743
1984	0.503	0.366	0.042	0.226	94.78	15674.8	49892	3.18745
1985	0.506	0.367	0.043	0.229	97.62	16060.3	39682	4.95143

RMD = Relative Mean Deviation
CV = Coefficient of Variation
Observs = Number of observations.

Table 6.7
Inequality Measures for the Earnings of Females under Thirty by Education Cohort
1976 - 1986

	YEAR	GINI	RMD	THEIL	KAKAWANI	FRACTION	CV	MEAN	OBSERVS	KAPPA
No High School Degree	1976	0.601	0.468	0.085	0.311	0.053	117.71	3121.0	1627	4.7148
	1977	0.609	0.466	0.086	0.315	0.054	124.49	3396.8	2010	10.9296
	1978	0.611	0.475	0.087	0.320	0.053	124.02	3458.6	1978	9.2016
	1979	0.594	0.451	0.082	0.299	0.052	125.90	3522.8	1981	41.5295
	1980	0.584	0.444	0.078	0.292	0.048	118.55	3826.3	2219	15.9724
	1981	0.605	0.465	0.083	0.312	0.046	121.04	3308.5	2172	6.3777
	1982	0.594	0.458	0.083	0.306	0.045	117.38	3556.0	1918	6.6848
	1983	0.628	0.489	0.094	0.339	0.043	127.98	3319.3	1808	8.1056
	1984	0.613	0.476	0.089	0.323	0.041	121.70	3265.5	1726	5.7058
	1985	0.637	0.494	0.101	0.344	0.039	134.38	3346.8	1370	17.3098
High School Degree	1976	0.420	0.309	0.034	0.163	0.218	75.96	7256.3	6610	1.2905
	1977	0.427	0.313	0.035	0.168	0.224	79.10	7313.5	8246	4.2689
	1978	0.430	0.315	0.035	0.170	0.226	77.82	7344.6	8314	1.2718
	1979	0.421	0.306	0.034	0.164	0.229	78.14	7634.3	8660	3.3618
	1980	0.416	0.300	0.032	0.160	0.226	77.10	7701.6	10324	3.0652
	1981	0.422	0.308	0.033	0.164	0.228	77.68	7615.0	10612	2.1539
	1982	0.432	0.316	0.035	0.171	0.220	80.13	7534.5	9241	3.3022
	1983	0.441	0.323	0.037	0.177	0.218	82.09	7461.7	9160	3.7116
	1984	0.441	0.322	0.036	0.176	0.212	80.96	7539.0	8948	1.9532
	1985	0.439	0.320	0.037	0.176	0.202	80.92	7643.7	7023	2.4054
College Graduate	1976	0.353	0.256	0.030	0.123	0.052	63.59	11304.4	1598	0.8843
	1977	0.354	0.259	0.029	0.123	0.053	63.43	11097.9	1977	0.6754
	1978	0.351	0.252	0.029	0.120	0.052	66.37	11635.2	1937	11.1958
	1979	0.357	0.253	0.029	0.122	0.055	66.99	11508.3	2082	3.8352
	1980	0.351	0.248	0.027	0.118	0.055	64.02	11929.2	2508	1.0716
	1981	0.364	0.259	0.029	0.126	0.053	66.21	11707.1	2486	1.0996
	1982	0.373	0.265	0.030	0.131	0.054	69.45	11834.4	2277	1.1658
	1983	0.371	0.265	0.030	0.129	0.055	67.25	12025.0	2339	1.1660
	1984	0.374	0.266	0.031	0.132	0.053	68.20	12145.6	2267	1.2634
	1985	0.352	0.250	0.028	0.118	0.053	64.25	12673.7	1853	1.3219

RMD = Relative Mean Deviation
CV = Coefficient of Variation
Observs = Number of observations.

Table 6.8
Inequality Measures for the Earnings of Females 30-59 by Education Cohort
1976 - 1985

	YEAR	GINI	RMD	THEIL	KAKAWANI	FRACTION	MEAN	OBSERVS	KAPPA
No High School Degree	1976	0.528	0.396	0.061	0.253	0.139	102.50	5347.0	4215
	1977	0.509	0.397	0.060	0.252	0.129	101.86	5463.0	4760
	1978	0.521	0.391	0.058	0.247	0.125	97.74	5580.7	4596
	1979	0.523	0.390	0.059	0.248	0.113	99.04	5739.5	4294
	1980	0.523	0.392	0.059	0.250	0.106	98.31	5717.3	4836
	1981	0.524	0.389	0.059	0.250	0.102	98.33	5723.5	4771
	1982	0.534	0.401	0.062	0.259	0.101	99.56	5449.0	4252
	1983	0.539	0.404	0.065	0.265	0.091	102.97	5398.2	3857
	1984	0.538	0.404	0.064	0.263	0.085	100.90	5616.0	3606
	1985	0.541	0.407	0.067	0.268	0.085	102.29	5650.9	2974
High School Graduate	1976	0.440	0.321	0.038	0.180	0.277	80.36	8739.7	8379
	1977	0.459	0.334	0.040	0.193	0.279	85.58	8622.3	10271
	1978	0.452	0.330	0.039	0.189	0.282	83.56	8903.1	10381
	1979	0.442	0.321	0.037	0.181	0.286	81.87	9185.9	10803
	1980	0.437	0.315	0.035	0.177	0.294	80.41	9168.4	13420
	1981	0.443	0.319	0.036	0.180	0.298	81.99	9155.1	13841
	1982	0.437	0.316	0.036	0.177	0.302	80.02	9212.9	12672
	1983	0.404	0.320	0.037	0.182	0.304	82.94	9400.9	12751
	1984	0.443	0.319	0.036	0.180	0.312	82.23	9646.8	13156
	1985	0.435	0.313	0.036	0.174	0.314	80.65	9585.4	10889
College Graduate	1976	0.405	0.293	0.040	0.159	0.059	73.93	14407.9	1797
	1977	0.412	0.299	0.039	0.163	0.063	75.02	14153.3	2332
	1978	0.415	0.301	0.040	0.165	0.065	76.37	14170.0	2415
	1979	0.419	0.305	0.040	0.166	0.070	77.20	14176.3	2658
	1980	0.408	0.293	0.037	0.160	0.077	74.62	14405.2	3511
	1981	0.404	0.288	0.035	0.155	0.079	73.85	14326.2	3705
	1982	0.404	0.289	0.035	0.154	0.083	75.05	14020.2	3514
	1983	0.405	0.290	0.036	0.156	0.091	74.93	14770.9	3822
	1984	0.398	0.281	0.034	0.150	0.099	73.55	15597.4	4181
	1985	0.399	0.282	0.035	0.151	0.098	75.35	15912.6	3399

RMD = Relative Mean Deviation
CV = Coefficient of Variation
Observs = Number of observations.

Table 6.9

Inequality Measures for the Earnings of Females 60 and Over by Education Cohort

1976 - 1985

	YEAR	GINI	RMD	THEIL	KAKAWANI	FRACTION	CV	MEAN	OBSERVS	KAPPA
No High School Degree	1976	0.839	0.740	0.192	0.633	0.112	231.04	1425.1	3394	32.232
	1977	0.845	0.749	0.194	0.643	0.107	240.26	1409.7	3958	42.152
	1978	0.840	0.740	0.191	0.633	0.105	240.36	1474.6	3894	165.884
	1979	0.848	0.753	0.198	0.649	0.099	248.26	1461.8	3764	109.066
	1980	0.861	0.780	0.207	0.680	0.100	268.00	1284.9	4568	178.281
	1981	0.866	0.785	0.212	0.686	0.097	274.84	1261.7	4509	147.200
	1982	0.868	0.789	0.218	0.691	0.094	281.90	1179.4	3970	349.643
	1983	0.864	0.785	0.214	0.685	0.093	269.55	1138.4	3913	138.641
	1984	0.864	0.785	0.214	0.686	0.090	261.37	1180.1	3814	50.062
	1985	0.873	0.796	0.227	0.701	0.101	289.50	1080.1	3500	273.470
High School Graduate	1976	0.756	0.638	0.149	0.510	0.069	169.23	3451.0	2097	9.792
	1977	0.752	0.625	0.143	0.499	0.072	173.85	3753.5	2660	24.685
	1978	0.750	0.614	0.141	0.489	0.073	174.99	3738.0	2688	28.478
	1979	0.753	0.625	0.142	0.500	0.074	171.70	3843.6	2815	15.430
	1980	0.760	0.639	0.143	0.513	0.074	175.18	3574.8	3391	17.408
	1981	0.761	0.638	0.143	0.514	0.076	176.62	3582.7	3546	19.002
	1982	0.769	0.653	0.147	0.529	0.080	175.79	3442.2	3365	11.228
	1983	0.782	0.664	0.154	0.543	0.083	187.84	3472.5	3520	21.896
	1984	0.788	0.669	0.156	0.549	0.086	189.99	3353.5	3646	18.923
	1985	0.779	0.666	0.154	0.544	0.087	180.51	3306.3	3040	12.103
College Graduate	1976	0.743	0.637	0.176	0.501	0.017	161.08	6658.2	527	7.603
	1977	0.751	0.651	0.178	0.514	0.015	166.49	6133.0	583	9.043
	1978	0.765	0.656	0.187	0.527	0.014	170.34	5288.2	545	9.255
	1979	0.778	0.668	0.192	0.543	0.016	180.60	5274.8	628	12.672
	1980	0.764	0.653	0.177	0.525	0.016	172.99	5248.4	774	10.773
	1981	0.751	0.641	0.172	0.511	0.015	165.34	5691.1	728	8.522
	1982	0.762	0.662	0.181	0.531	0.016	169.89	5374.2	680	8.707
	1983	0.778	0.666	0.187	0.540	0.018	183.99	5578.3	757	17.629
	1984	0.775	0.671	0.187	0.544	0.017	179.78	6295.3	748	13.431
	1985	0.781	0.669	0.198	0.544	0.016	188.85	6020.4	585	26.632

RMD = Relative Mean Deviation
CV = Coefficient of Variation
Observs = Number of observations.

Table 6.10
Inequality Measures for Female Earnings by Year
1976 - 1985

YEAR	GINI	RMD	THEIL	KAKAWANI	CV	MEAN	OBSERVS	KAPPA
1976	0.545	0.410	0.051	0.265	103.56	6888.88	30244	4.16152
1977	0.548	0.413	0.051	0.268	105.21	6951.23	36797	5.17373
1978	0.544	0.409	0.050	0.265	104.07	7113.45	36748	4.93340
1979	0.537	0.402	0.049	0.258	102.84	7383.51	37685	4.81169
1980	0.534	0.398	0.048	0.256	101.37	7491.37	45551	3.87040
1981	0.537	0.401	0.048	0.258	102.08	7477.61	46370	3.81349
1982	0.539	0.403	0.049	0.260	102.40	7460.08	41889	4.02908
1983	0.548	0.409	0.051	0.267	105.36	7644.79	41927	5.09987
1984	0.547	0.408	0.050	0.266	104.91	7945.56	42092	4.59688
1985	0.548	0.410	0.052	0.268	105.95	7922.28	34633	6.04805

Table 6.11
Measures of Inequality for Individual Earnings
1976 - 1985

YEAR	GINI	RMD	THEIL	KAKAWANI	CV	MEAN	OBSERVS	KAPPA
1976	0.532	0.390	0.045	0.249	104.65	12195.7	70315	7.27985
1977	0.535	0.392	0.045	0.251	104.82	12287.6	85155	6.71405
1978	0.533	0.391	0.045	0.250	103.83	12489.6	84191	5.74578
1979	0.529	0.387	0.044	0.246	102.35	12683.6	85013	5.18360
1980	0.523	0.382	0.042	0.244	100.02	12632.7	101388	4.06133
1981	0.526	0.385	0.042	0.244	99.80	12175.2	102515	3.57747
1982	0.536	0.393	0.045	0.252	104.85	12151.5	92340	6.15531
1983	0.548	0.402	0.047	0.262	107.62	11954.3	92400	6.40737
1984	0.545	0.400	0.046	0.259	106.26	12137.9	91984	5.58732
1985	0.549	0.403	0.048	0.263	109.54	12267.7	74315	8.49726

RMD = Relative Mean Deviation
CV = Coefficient of Variation
Observs = Number of observations.

Table 6.12

Measures of Inequality for the Individual Earnings for White Males and White Females

1976 - 1985

	YEAR	GINI	RMD	THEIL	KAKWANI	FRACTION	CV	MEAN	OBSERVS	KAPPA
M A L E S	1976	0.464	0.330	0.037	0.198	0.517	88.47	16687.9	36357	4.0250
	1977	0.465	0.332	0.037	0.199	0.513	88.28	16830.0	43739	3.5948
	1978	0.465	0.332	0.037	0.198	0.510	87.31	17113.3	42977	2.8763
	1979	0.461	0.330	0.036	0.196	0.502	86.18	17352.8	42700	2.5559
	1980	0.455	0.326	0.034	0.191	0.496	83.70	17291.8	50358	1.8266
	1981	0.461	0.333	0.035	0.196	0.492	84.27	16488.1	50476	1.5723
	1982	0.480	0.346	0.039	0.209	0.490	90.50	16501.4	45334	3.2100
	1983	0.500	0.363	0.042	0.255	0.491	94.58	15961.8	45417	3.3874
	1984	0.498	0.361	0.041	0.223	0.487	93.63	16109.7	44806	3.0383
	1985	0.501	0.362	0.043	0.225	0.480	96.37	16563.5	35674	4.7119
F E M A L E S	1976	0.541	0.407	0.051	0.262	0.375	102.99	6972.5	26417	4.2901
	1977	0.546	0.411	0.051	0.266	0.378	105.01	7001.2	32213	5.4683
	1978	0.542	0.406	0.051	0.262	0.381	103.68	7156.4	32109	5.2167
	1979	0.535	0.400	0.049	0.256	0.384	102.43	7431.7	32717	4.8690
	1980	0.531	0.395	0.048	0.253	0.391	100.77	7534.2	39679	3.9094
	1981	0.534	0.398	0.048	0.255	0.393	101.65	7532.6	40311	3.8901
	1982	0.536	0.400	0.049	0.257	0.393	101.98	7539.0	36358	4.2679
	1983	0.546	0.407	0.051	0.265	0.392	105.15	7708.5	36277	5.3245
	1984	0.543	0.405	0.050	0.262	0.397	104.41	8011.8	36519	4.7632
	1985	0.545	0.406	0.052	0.264	0.401	105.21	7990.9	29802	6.1790

RMD = Relative Mean Deviation
CV = Coefficient of Variation
Observs = Number of observations.

Table 6.13
Measures of Inequality for Individual Earnings for Black Males and Black Females
1976 - 1985

	YEAR	GINI	RMD	THEIL	KAKWANI	FRACTION	CV	MEAN	OBSERVS	KAPPA
M A L E S	1976	0.481	0.357	0.052	0.217	0.044	87.32	10702.8	3154	1.2565
	1977	0.487	0.357	0.053	0.219	0.042	90.26	11014.1	3635	2.3150
	1978	0.487	0.356	0.053	0.218	0.041	90.68	11343.4	3526	2.4918
	1979	0.486	0.359	0.052	0.217	0.041	89.43	11789.9	3503	1.8676
	1980	0.486	0.355	0.052	0.218	0.039	89.67	11604.0	4052	1.9631
	1981	0.496	0.363	0.054	0.226	0.039	91.44	11075.9	4061	1.9329
	1982	0.492	0.362	0.053	0.223	0.039	90.06	11093.3	3692	1.6415
	1983	0.516	0.379	0.059	0.242	0.038	98.11	10508.9	3601	4.3081
	1984	0.529	0.391	0.061	0.251	0.040	99.12	10648.5	3680	2.8053
	1985	0.527	0.387	0.061	0.248	0.046	99.67	10716.6	3432	3.4554
F E M A L E S	1976	0.576	0.444	0.074	0.298	0.048	108.02	6002.5	3416	2.5850
	1977	0.573	0.438	0.072	0.294	0.045	108.23	6375.4	3837	2.8830
	1978	0.573	0.438	0.072	0.293	0.046	109.04	6514.6	3940	3.3121
	1979	0.564	0.430	0.069	0.286	0.047	106.13	6681.6	4060	2.7183
	1980	0.570	0.434	0.070	0.292	0.045	107.78	6826.9	4657	2.8989
	1981	0.569	0.432	0.070	0.291	0.046	108.59	6762.1	4727	3.4966
	1982	0.578	0.443	0.073	0.302	0.046	109.57	6533.7	4330	2.9112
	1983	0.576	0.441	0.073	0.300	0.047	110.35	6766.6	4392	3.8965
	1984	0.585	0.447	0.075	0.308	0.047	111.94	7019.8	4351	3.4031
	1985	0.576	0.437	0.072	0.298	0.058	110.18	7345.0	4322	3.7719

RMD = Relative Mean Deviation
CV = Coefficient of Variation
Observs = Number of observations.

Table 6.14

Measures of Inequality for Individual Earnings for Other Ethnic Groups
1976 - 1985

MALES

YEAR	GINI	RMD	THEIL	KAKAWANI	FRACTION	CV	MEAN	OBSERVS	KAPPA
1976	0.471	0.332	0.062	0.198	0.007	91.88	15564.8	560	6.0033
1977	0.486	0.352	0.061	0.211	0.011	92.59	14640.0	984	4.0705
1978	0.471	0.339	0.057	0.199	0.011	89.66	15567.3	940	4.1775
1979	0.469	0.340	0.055	0.198	0.013	86.97	15784.6	1125	2.3750
1980	0.474	0.343	0.054	0.201	0.014	88.80	15254.1	1427	2.9331
1981	0.486	0.356	0.056	0.213	0.015	89.81	15035.6	1608	2.2464
1982	0.500	0.364	0.062	0.223	0.015	96.32	14418.6	1425	4.9808
1983	0.520	0.377	0.066	0.239	0.015	100.67	14623.9	1455	5.0417
1984	0.521	0.384	0.067	0.241	0.015	98.65	14968.8	1406	3.5059
1985	0.522	0.377	0.075	0.236	0.007	101.50	16731.3	576	5.3044

FEMALES

YEAR	GINI	RMD	THEIL	KAKAWANI	FRACTION	CV	MEAN	OBSERVS	KAPPA
1976	0.489	0.359	0.070	0.214	0.005	94.43	8878.0	411	10.8721
1977	0.504	0.371	0.068	0.227	0.008	97.49	7754.1	747	9.3509
1978	0.499	0.368	0.067	0.223	0.008	94.00	8516.2	699	3.4166
1979	0.499	0.360	0.065	0.220	0.010	99.12	8784.9	908	11.1666
1980	0.495	0.357	0.061	0.217	0.011	96.26	8640.3	1215	6.8745
1981	0.496	0.363	0.061	0.221	0.012	92.67	8352.3	1332	6.8379
1982	0.485	0.356	0.059	0.215	0.013	89.83	8411.2	1201	2.2837
1983	0.499	0.367	0.062	0.224	0.013	93.36	8873.9	1258	2.8167
1984	0.502	0.367	0.063	0.227	0.013	95.11	9263.8	1222	3.8507
1985	0.539	0.392	0.084	0.252	0.006	110.92	8808.1	509	19.5586

RMD = Relative Mean Deviation
CV = Coefficient of Variation
Observs = Number of observations.

Table 6.15
Measures of Inequality for Family Earnings
1975 - 1984

YEAR	GINI	RMD	THEIL	KAKAWANI	CV	MEAN	OBSERVS	KAPPA
1975	0.396	0.285	0.024	0.139	76.01	21867.3	48090	4.57275
1976	0.399	0.287	0.024	0.140	76.40	22205.6	57749	4.50316
1977	0.401	0.289	0.024	0.141	76.62	22570.6	57083	4.27631
1978	0.402	0.290	0.024	0.142	76.30	22935.7	57591	3.83491
1979	0.401	0.290	0.023	0.141	75.85	23063.7	68582	3.54908
1980	0.401	0.291	0.023	0.142	75.58	22419.8	69325	3.25896
1981	0.410	0.297	0.025	0.147	78.38	22547.7	62596	4.30758
1982	0.415	0.300	0.025	0.151	79.82	22506.6	62623	4.57818
1983	0.416	0.301	0.025	0.151	79.70	22681.3	62685	4.35693
1984	0.421	0.305	0.027	0.154	81.78	23334.6	50168	5.38118

RMD = Relative Mean Deviation
CV = Coefficient of Variation
Observs = Number of observations.

Table 6.16
Measures of Inequality for Family Earnings
1976 - 1985

YEAR	GINI	RMD	THEIL	KAKAWANI	CV	MEAN	OBSERVS	KAPPA
1975	0.499	0.363	0.042	0.226	93.35	18149.0	48090	2.71350
1976	0.499	0.364	0.041	0.226	93.38	18457.2	57749	2.72161
1977	0.499	0.365	0.041	0.226	92.90	18750.5	57083	2.43158
1978	0.500	0.365	0.041	0.226	92.82	19085.5	57591	2.37473
1979	0.498	0.364	0.040	0.225	91.85	19046.0	68582	2.06447
1980	0.503	0.370	0.041	0.229	92.48	18303.9	69325	1.96373
1981	0.515	0.378	0.043	0.238	96.41	18227.0	62596	2.78622
1982	0.526	0.386	0.045	0.247	99.14	17923.6	62623	3.16247
1983	0.528	0.389	0.045	0.249	99.55	18086.2	62685	3.09823
1984	0.535	0.394	0.047	0.254	101.75	18439.5	50168	3.69881

Table 6.17
Measures of Inequality for Black Family Earnings
1976 - 1985

YEAR	GINI	RMD	THEIL	KAKAWANI	CV	MEAN	OBSERVS	KAPPA
1975	0.557	0.419	0.066	0.277	105.19	11972.9	4689	3.00821
1976	0.556	0.417	0.065	0.275	105.24	12453.2	5365	3.18384
1977	0.554	0.411	0.064	0.271	106.06	12636.9	5376	3.90649
1978	0.555	0.414	0.064	0.272	105.32	13060.8	5406	3.35067
1979	0.557	0.413	0.064	0.273	106.17	13015.2	6240	3.67920
1980	0.564	0.420	0.065	0.280	107.83	12546.0	6351	3.77636
1981	0.572	0.428	0.068	0.288	109.81	12277.3	5044	3.86948
1982	0.570	0.426	0.068	0.287	110.20	11952.8	5850	4.53785
1983	0.583	0.437	0.071	0.298	112.59	12255.8	5872	4.21600
1984	0.582	0.434	0.071	0.295	113.46	12588.1	5629	4.98932

RMD = Relative Mean Deviation
CV = Coefficient of Variation
Observs = Number of observations.

Table 6.18
Measures of Inequality for Family Income by Type of Family
1975 - 1984

	YEAR	GINI	RMD	THEIL	KAKAWANI	CV	MEAN	KAPPA
One earner married couple	1975	0.333	0.233	0.020	0.099	67.10	23755.0	8.8757
	1976	0.333	0.233	0.020	0.100	66.40	23814.7	7.8637
	1977	0.334	0.235	0.020	0.100	65.74	24466.8	6.3494
	1978	0.332	0.234	0.020	0.099	64.72	24662.2	5.2635
	1979	0.335	0.236	0.020	0.100	64.87	24291.9	5.0877
	1980	0.335	0.237	0.019	0.100	63.95	24109.1	3.8707
	1981	0.349	0.246	0.022	0.108	69.12	24330.9	6.7465
	1982	0.362	0.256	0.024	0.116	71.21	24318.3	6.0559
	1983	0.354	0.251	0.022	0.111	68.86	24252.9	5.2337
	1984	0.367	0.259	0.025	0.119	73.04	25337.1	7.4297
Two earner married couple	1975	0.275	0.192	0.012	0.069	52.14	31758.3	3.1685
	1976	0.279	0.195	0.013	0.071	52.98	32336.0	3.2467
	1977	0.278	0.195	0.012	0.070	52.50	33173.6	2.9428
	1978	0.280	0.197	0.012	0.071	52.52	33818.5	2.6005
	1979	0.277	0.195	0.012	0.070	51.76	34166.3	2.2174
	1980	0.278	0.196	0.012	0.071	51.44	34400.7	1.8733
	1981	0.288	0.203	0.013	0.076	53.92	33673.6	2.4237
	1982	0.299	0.211	0.014	0.081	56.04	33619.3	2.5096
	1983	0.301	0.213	0.014	0.082	56.26	34067.3	2.3947
	1984	0.301	0.212	0.015	0.082	57.06	35043.4	3.1481
Separated	1975	0.466	0.336	0.065	0.185	94.28	12905.2	9.8733
	1976	0.503	0.372	0.075	0.214	100.25	14515.2	7.3375
	1977	0.479	0.347	0.067	0.197	93.86	13575.3	6.3161
	1978	0.491	0.353	0.073	0.206	95.25	13970.4	5.1174
	1979	0.476	0.339	0.069	0.193	97.76	15753.8	11.7653
	1980	0.465	0.333	0.066	0.186	96.88	14945.7	17.4545
	1981	0.488	0.356	0.074	0.202	99.42	15540.7	11.1958
	1982	0.479	0.345	0.072	0.196	96.80	14061.1	11.9754
	1983	0.498	0.367	0.076	0.210	98.81	14079.0	6.9470
	1984	0.487	0.361	0.076	0.203	92.23	14706.3	3.6984
Single parent male	1975	0.372	0.263	0.033	0.123	72.98	22088.6	6.3956
	1976	0.384	0.272	0.035	0.131	76.16	21081.3	8.0877
	1977	0.383	0.276	0.034	0.131	72.39	21901.6	3.6329
	1978	0.387	0.278	0.034	0.131	74.88	22825.4	5.3166
	1979	0.396	0.276	0.033	0.131	74.99	22261.0	5.3494
	1980	0.383	0.275	0.034	0.129	73.69	21104.1	4.6344
	1981	0.392	0.281	0.034	0.136	76.58	20859.0	6.5240
	1982	0.403	0.288	0.036	0.143	77.88	20384.5	6.5081
	1983	0.410	0.294	0.037	0.148	79.05	20584.7	5.0256
	1984	0.417	0.300	0.040	0.152	81.67	21626.7	6.2107

Table 6.18 (Continued)
Measures of Inequality for Family Income by Type of Family
1975 - 1984

	YEAR	GINI	RMD	THEIL	KAKAWAI	CV	MEAN	KAPPA
Single parent female	1975	0.399	0.288	0.031	0.139	79.79	13792.2	10.6891
	1976	0.401	0.290	0.031	0.140	80.59	13991.6	10.3512
	1977	0.405	0.293	0.032	0.142	82.60	14266.4	13.4468
	1978	0.405	0.293	0.031	0.142	79.41	14487.6	6.8464
	1979	0.404	0.291	0.030	0.143	79.47	14831.4	7.9681
	1980	0.415	0.301	0.032	0.150	81.90	14344.0	7.4905
	1981	0.422	0.306	0.033	0.154	84.11	13996.0	9.2286
	1982	0.431	0.313	0.035	0.160	85.38	13892.1	8.3474
	1983	0.433	0.315	0.035	0.162	85.36	13901.4	7.7269
	1984	0.442	0.322	0.037	0.168	89.59	14385.1	11.9927
Male individual	1975	0.415	0.300	0.035	0.150	84.90	14462.5	14.2632
	1976	0.413	0.297	0.033	0.149	83.54	14816.6	12.0302
	1977	0.412	0.296	0.033	0.148	84.30	15267.6	15.0492
	1978	0.409	0.294	0.032	0.146	82.14	15861.0	9.8655
	1979	0.396	0.284	0.029	0.138	77.51	15958.2	6.9641
	1980	0.397	0.286	0.029	0.139	77.36	15894.7	6.1509
	1981	0.414	0.297	0.032	0.150	83.27	16394.3	10.3613
	1982	0.416	0.299	0.032	0.151	82.69	16166.2	8.3774
	1983	0.424	0.304	0.034	0.156	84.92	16352.3	9.4165
	1984	0.422	0.302	0.035	0.155	86.29	16478.1	13.0301
Female individual	1975	0.405	0.299	0.031	0.142	81.41	9332.4	9.6666
	1976	0.410	0.303	0.031	0.146	84.39	9508.0	16.8519
	1977	0.402	0.296	0.030	0.140	84.38	9851.1	29.3072
	1978	0.403	0.295	0.030	0.141	82.95	10128.4	17.8375
	1979	0.403	0.293	0.029	0.140	82.05	10249.3	13.9491
	1980	0.403	0.295	0.029	0.141	82.00	10348.2	14.3929
	1981	0.411	0.300	0.031	0.146	84.76	10517.9	18.1484
	1982	0.414	0.301	0.031	0.148	84.74	11053.8	17.0628
	1983	0.414	0.301	0.031	0.148	84.74	11442.1	14.9180
	1984	0.415	0.303	0.032	0.149	87.89	11496.6	26.4103
Others	1975	0.350	0.247	0.028	0.110	80.91	12200.5	77.4385
	1976	0.360	0.257	0.028	0.115	81.06	12921.9	53.7253
	1977	0.360	0.254	0.029	0.115	82.61	13049.4	56.3853
	1978	0.361	0.254	0.028	0.116	80.07	13317.2	30.4077
	1979	0.368	0.259	0.028	0.120	79.29	13511.0	22.5047
	1980	0.376	0.266	0.029	0.125	81.47	14238.9	24.7150
	1981	0.382	0.273	0.030	0.128	81.73	15069.5	19.1671
	1982	0.385	0.275	0.031	0.131	83.33	15354.7	28.6669
	1983	0.379	0.270	0.029	0.126	78.49	15793.0	14.2047
	1984	0.391	0.278	0.033	0.133	85.27	16544.6	25.6666

Table 6.19

Measures of Inequality for Family Earnings by Type of Family

1975 - 1984

	YEAR	GINI	RMD	THEIL	KAKAWANI	CV	MEAN	KAPPA
One earner married couple	1975	0.392	0.274	0.028	0.139	76.10	20239.7	5.2596
	1976	0.394	0.276	0.028	0.141	75.53	20165.7	4.3025
	1977	0.399	0.281	0.029	0.144	75.29	20585.3	3.1265
	1978	0.399	0.282	0.029	0.144	74.98	20578.2	2.8501
	1979	0.400	0.285	0.029	0.145	73.71	20499.2	1.9602
	1980	0.402	0.289	0.029	0.146	73.47	19484.5	1.7110
	1981	0.416	0.296	0.032	0.154	79.34	19518.7	3.8471
	1982	0.433	0.309	0.034	0.166	82.84	19212.3	4.1278
	1983	0.428	0.307	0.033	0.163	80.79	19114.7	3.2674
	1984	0.446	0.320	0.038	0.174	86.46	19775.2	5.3019
Two earner married couple	1975	0.288	0.201	0.014	0.077	53.95	29571.3	2.2807
	1976	0.291	0.203	0.014	0.079	54.70	30162.2	2.4077
	1977	0.288	0.202	0.014	0.077	53.75	30942.3	2.0089
	1978	0.289	0.203	0.014	0.077	53.67	31556.6	1.8899
	1979	0.286	0.201	0.013	0.076	52.61	31658.5	1.4228
	1980	0.288	0.203	0.013	0.077	52.53	30869.9	1.1357
	1981	0.300	0.211	0.015	0.083	55.53	31059.2	1.7990
	1982	0.313	0.220	0.016	0.090	58.09	30760.9	1.8969
	1983	0.315	0.222	0.016	0.091	58.30	31344.1	1.8935
	1984	0.312	0.219	0.016	0.089	58.57	32179.2	2.5667
Separated	1975	0.607	0.457	0.116	0.313	124.75	9424.0	11.1425
	1976	0.616	0.461	0.119	0.319	127.37	10921.5	11.1548
	1977	0.589	0.445	0.107	0.303	113.42	9825.2	4.1455
	1978	0.595	0.444	0.114	0.307	115.82	10444.9	4.8104
	1979	0.567	0.410	0.102	0.274	116.69	12588.6	11.4515
	1980	0.555	0.403	0.097	0.262	116.60	12065.2	18.3476
	1981	0.571	0.419	0.106	0.277	118.51	11620.5	12.1028
	1982	0.556	0.408	0.101	0.265	112.49	11044.7	6.6126
	1983	0.584	0.431	0.110	0.290	116.12	10343.3	6.6166
	1984	0.551	0.410	0.103	0.264	104.17	11406.9	3.4496
Single parent male	1975	0.462	0.329	0.055	0.192	89.24	17692.3	5.1610
	1976	0.469	0.336	0.055	0.198	90.93	16682.6	5.6877
	1977	0.451	0.325	0.049	0.184	83.61	18071.6	2.3401
	1978	0.458	0.330	0.050	0.186	86.38	19126.6	3.4691
	1979	0.457	0.327	0.049	0.186	85.64	18479.7	2.8880
	1980	0.456	0.328	0.048	0.186	85.60	17464.5	2.9764
	1981	0.464	0.335	0.052	0.192	89.06	17351.1	4.9448
	1982	0.470	0.337	0.052	0.196	90.33	16701.2	5.0737
	1983	0.478	0.346	0.053	0.203	90.13	17103.8	3.4108
	1984	0.487	0.352	0.057	0.209	92.31	17599.8	3.6432

Table 6.19 (Continued)

Measures of Inequality for Family Earnigs by Type of Family
1975 - 1984

	YEAR	GINI	RMD	THEIL	KAKAWANI	CV	MEAN	KAPPA
Single parent female	1975	0.584	0.439	0.073	0.299	115.47	8978.7	7.1697
	1976	0.582	0.436	0.071	0.297	115.98	9051.3	8.1569
	1977	0.567	0.422	0.067	0.283	110.71	9474.8	5.6131
	1978	0.560	0.415	0.065	0.276	109.18	9919.4	5.6174
	1979	0.545	0.402	0.060	0.264	105.33	10253.6	5.1108
	1980	0.557	0.413	0.063	0.273	108.05	9859.8	5.1760
	1981	0.560	0.416	0.064	0.276	108.34	9612.3	4.8036
	1982	0.572	0.426	0.067	0.288	112.08	9545.4	5.9971
	1983	0.573	0.427	0.067	0.289	111.10	9677.0	4.7892
	1984	0.571	0.424	0.068	0.286	112.16	9952.0	6.7218
Male individual	1975	0.546	0.403	0.065	0.266	107.79	11686.1	7.9692
	1976	0.529	0.387	0.059	0.250	102.62	12270.1	5.7514
	1977	0.514	0.376	0.055	0.239	98.57	12667.9	4.51
	1978	0.510	0.371	0.054	0.234	97.82	13336.8	4.55
	1979	0.490	0.356	0.049	0.219	92.11	13478.3	2.96
	1980	0.490	0.357	0.048	0.220	90.76	13326.7	2.16
	1981	0.511	0.372	0.053	0.235	97.47	13584.1	4.08
	1982	0.521	0.381	0.055	0.244	99.58	13103.0	4.09
	1983	0.526	0.386	0.056	0.248	100.25	13478.1	3.80
	1984	0.530	0.387	0.059	0.250	103.06	13245.6	5.95
	1975	0.703	0.581	0.109	0.445	146.55	5295.2	6.38
Female individual	1976	0.695	0.573	0.104	0.436	144.31	5417.7	6.52
	1977	0.682	0.557	0.099	0.419	141.09	5693.0	8.86
	1978	0.677	0.551	0.097	0.414	137.99	5884.8	5.72
	1979	0.669	0.543	0.093	0.407	135.49	6067.1	5.35
	1980	0.670	0.549	0.093	0.406	136.19	6196.9	5.68
	1981	0.674	0.558	0.095	0.412	136.49	6122.2	5.12
	1982	0.683	0.555	0.098	0.422	140.99	6296.6	6.69
	1983	0.683	0.555	0.098	0.420	141.13	6552.4	6.88
	1984	0.697	0.573	0.105	0.438	145.43	6173.8	7.01
Others	1975	0.910	0.895	0.379	0.827	589.74	364.1	1162.13
	1976	0.925	0.908	0.395	0.848	672.97	451.3	4094.70
	1977	0.929	0.910	0.389	0.851	655.99	507.1	3807.28
	1978	0.935	0.915	0.382	0.860	606.84	618.6	1801.75
	1979	0.925	0.903	0.378	0.842	654.58	459.1	3019.63
	1980	0.930	0.908	0.378	0.851	648.85	514.4	2492.66
	1981	0.912	0.898	0.414	0.832	802.55	330.8	6071.15
	1982	0.896	0.886	0.407	0.814	776.53	273.5	3741.60
	1983	0.913	0.902	0.423	0.840	806.86	331.1	3824.39
	1984	0.887	0.876	0.403	0.799	754.46	250.3	4779.44

Table 6.20
Measures of Inequality for Black Family Earnings by Type of Family
1975 - 1984

	YEAR	GINI	RMD	THEIL	KAKAWANI	CV	MEAN	KAPPA
One earner married couple	1975	0.388	0.278	0.040	0.140	70.77	12635.0	1.5500
	1976	0.408	0.294	0.044	0.151	77.28	13410.1	4.2896
	1977	0.409	0.293	0.045	0.151	76.66	12921.4	3.1004
	1978	0.406	0.291	0.044	0.150	75.08	13828.8	2.3249
	1979	0.414	0.300	0.044	0.152	77.22	13008.8	2.8022
	1980	0.427	0.303	0.048	0.161	82.63	12809.2	5.0754
	1981	0.394	0.282	0.041	0.141	71.57	12359.8	1.4146
	1982	0.410	0.290	0.045	0.150	78.94	11910.9	5.7940
	1983	0.447	0.321	0.053	0.176	84.91	12233.7	3.9655
	1984	0.435	0.312	0.053	0.168	85.37	11907.3	8.3121
Two earner married couple	1975	0.296	0.209	0.020	0.082	53.83	24080.2	0.9717
	1976	0.292	0.206	0.019	0.079	53.28	25106.4	1.1670
	1977	0.298	0.212	0.020	0.082	54.82	25955.5	1.5038
	1978	0.292	0.208	0.020	0.079	53.17	26969.4	1.1563
	1979	0.299	0.213	0.020	0.083	54.68	27013.6	1.3089
	1980	0.290	0.206	0.019	0.078	52.94	27009.1	1.2469
	1981	0.295	0.209	0.019	0.080	53.75	26949.0	1.2066
	1982	0.298	0.210	0.020	0.082	55.30	25961.9	2.0693
	1983	0.300	0.214	0.020	0.082	54.85	27305.7	1.4572
	1984	0.305	0.219	0.021	0.084	56.03	28414.5	1.6912
Separated	1975	0.558	0.424	0.132	0.268	103.97	7001.6	2.8693
	1976	0.588	0.431	0.150	0.286	116.02	7852.6	6.5321
	1977	0.514	0.372	0.110	0.232	93.90	8969.6	2.1887
	1978	0.492	0.353	0.111	0.215	95.25	9791.6	5.3865
	1979	0.495	0.348	0.114	0.208	100.21	12102.8	11.8449
	1980	0.504	0.370	0.110	0.227	90.65	11093.1	1.3770
	1981	0.620	0.479	0.184	0.324	116.55	7295.1	3.4294
	1982	0.558	0.433	0.142	0.267	101.17	10826.6	2.2505
	1983	0.562	0.416	0.149	0.257	106.58	13136.2	4.5214
	1984	0.581	0.424	0.154	0.275	112.29	11012.1	5.8495
Single parent male	1975	0.485	0.357	0.080	0.209	88.64	12448.5	1.9628
	1976	0.462	0.338	0.072	0.194	86.23	14183.8	2.7980
	1977	0.468	0.337	0.073	0.197	89.16	13502.9	5.6004
	1978	0.474	0.340	0.074	0.202	87.89	14281.3	2.3640
	1979	0.446	0.319	0.063	0.178	82.37	14891.2	2.2231
	1980	0.456	0.321	0.064	0.183	87.31	14220.6	4.3402
	1981	0.445	0.324	0.062	0.179	80.73	14494.2	1.5051
	1982	0.455	0.336	0.066	0.191	82.16	12362.6	1.1915
	1983	0.510	0.385	0.082	0.236	93.68	12294.0	1.8351
	1984	0.524	0.384	0.086	0.236	102.09	12180.4	5.5016

Table 6.20 (Continued)

Measures of Inequality for Black Family Earnings by Type of Family
1975 - 1984

	YEAR	GINI	RMD	THEIL	KAKAWANI	CV	MEAN	KAPPA
Single parent female	1975	0.638	0.494	0.105	0.353	129.11	6841.3	7.1900
	1976	0.630	0.489	0.100	0.347	125.30	6541.2	5.5681
	1977	0.615	0.471	0.095	0.330	123.14	6902.6	6.9636
	1978	0.610	0.462	0.092	0.323	121.65	7415.5	6.6217
	1979	0.605	0.458	0.087	0.320	120.21	7727.4	6.9369
	1980	0.559	0.454	0.087	0.316	116.90	7128.7	4.7537
	1981	0.621	0.473	0.094	0.336	124.39	7090.4	6.6947
	1982	0.619	0.472	0.096	0.334	123.64	7425.4	6.6596
	1983	0.626	0.481	0.096	0.344	125.36	7629.8	6.4823
	1984	0.614	0.467	0.092	0.328	122.93	7785.0	7.0970
Male individual	1975	0.585	0.450	0.101	0.309	113.03	8537.0	4.4802
	1976	0.566	0.424	0.090	0.286	108.70	8907.1	4.2449
	1977	0.552	0.408	0.086	0.271	108.30	9785.8	6.4081
	1978	0.565	0.426	0.088	0.282	107.72	9917.10	3.57
	1979	0.549	0.412	0.082	0.272	103.72	9889.20	3.03
	1980	0.566	0.431	0.087	0.292	106.63	8783.25	2.69
	1981	0.564	0.424	0.088	0.285	108.48	9099.69	4.22
	1982	0.568	0.424	0.091	0.290	112.86	9630.15	8.42
	1983	0.578	0.434	0.091	0.295	110.91	9553.09	3.89
	1984	0.568	0.425	0.089	0.288	107.81	9763.08	3.25
Female individual	1975	0.697	0.570	0.142	0.433	142.86	4578.41	5.58
	1976	0.714	0.591	0.148	0.454	149.37	4917.47	6.65
	1977	0.674	0.549	0.128	0.408	135.27	5622.14	4.70
	1978	0.674	0.546	0.126	0.407	135.80	5512.67	4.99
	1979	0.672	0.545	0.134	0.406	136.58	6012.42	5.81
	1980	0.693	0.553	0.143	0.420	148.64	5744.25	11.64
	1981	0.709	0.578	0.143	0.446	150.35	5408.86	8.25
	1982	0.682	0.561	0.133	0.423	138.04	5568.92	4.90
	1983	0.708	0.580	0.143	0.446	151.61	5687.03	9.93
	1984	0.680	0.559	0.131	0.420	136.52	6143.87	4.57
Others	1975	0.896	0.890	0.612	0.815	646.34	274.29	786.24
	1976	0.923	0.911	0.586	0.849	559.37	433.75	432.50
	1977	0.928	0.898	0.479	0.828	422.85	1142.93	516.85
	1978	0.921	0.892	0.491	0.820	431.48	621.43	269.08
	1979	0.927	0.894	0.481	0.825	471.12	649.57	479.98
	1980	0.939	0.909	0.584	0.850	697.67	572.59	3610.76
	1981	0.912	0.889	0.523	0.814	561.87	379.84	1086.16
	1982	0.832	0.823	0.460	0.715	546.11	164.24	653.98
	1983	0.942	0.930	0.619	0.877	694.61	579.41	1812.90
	1984	0.845	0.843	0.612	0.745	791.40	168.06	2250.58

Table 6.21
Measures of Inequality for Household Income
1976 - 1985

YEAR	GINI	RMD	THEIL	KAKAWANI	CV	MEAN	OBSERVS	KAPPA
1976	0.389	0.279	0.023	0.134	74.323	22622.3	46238	4.294
1977	0.390	0.280	0.023	0.134	74.452	23049.7	55399	4.235
1978	0.392	0.282	0.023	0.136	74.578	23479.0	54644	3.961
1979	0.392	0.282	0.023	0.136	74.060	23973.1	54850	3.486
1980	0.391	0.281	0.022	0.135	73.488	24190.8	65123	3.153
1981	0.391	0.282	0.022	0.135	73.240	23582.7	65631	2.924
1982	0.399	0.288	0.023	0.140	75.853	23729.8	59165	3.855
1983	0.405	0.292	0.024	0.144	77.370	23741.6	59082	4.124
1984	0.406	0.293	0.024	0.144	77.219	23953.9	59034	3.927
1985	0.411	0.297	0.026	0.148	79.218	24504.7	47531	4.833

RMD = Relative Mean Deviation
CV = Coefficient of Variation
Observs = Number of observations.

Table 6.22
Measures of Inequality for Household Income
1976 - 1985

	YEAR	GINI	RMD	THEIL	KAKAWANI	FRACTION	CV	MEAN	OBSERVS	KAPPA
One family in household	1976	0.348	0.246	0.019	0.108	0.764	66.28	25529.1	35358	3.9051
	1977	0.348	0.246	0.018	0.108	0.755	66.09	26041.5	41878	3.7249
	1978	0.350	0.249	0.019	0.110	0.744	66.19	26652.3	40692	3.3409
	1979	0.350	0.249	0.019	0.110	0.737	65.82	27190.7	40444	2.9470
	1980	0.350	0.249	0.018	0.110	0.731	65.29	27478.8	47606	2.6142
	1981	0.351	0.251	0.018	0.111	0.724	65.12	26737.6	47530	2.3132
	1982	0.361	0.258	0.020	0.116	0.722	67.97	26876.7	42757	3.1306
	1983	0.371	0.264	0.021	0.122	0.722	70.03	26738.4	42679	3.3289
	1984	0.370	0.265	0.021	0.122	0.716	69.73	26998.4	42323	3.1193
	1985	0.375	0.267	0.022	0.125	0.718	71.47	27893.5	34133	3.9157
More than one family in household	1976	0.317	0.233	0.028	0.090	0.008	61.73	29730.9	375	5.6164
	1977	0.366	0.260	0.036	0.117	0.008	72.20	32560.7	480	6.0669
	1978	0.328	0.232	0.028	0.096	0.009	62.59	29946.9	545	4.0397
	1979	0.351	0.234	0.031	0.109	0.011	66.39	30681.8	614	3.4008
	1980	0.327	0.234	0.026	0.095	0.011	61.90	32385.9	759	3.4191
	1981	0.341	0.245	0.028	0.103	0.012	65.22	30689.7	807	4.0129
	1982	0.352	0.252	0.030	0.110	0.013	67.61	30084.1	776	4.4578
	1983	0.372	0.265	0.033	0.122	0.014	70.70	30276.6	828	3.7831
	1984	0.380	0.273	0.035	0.127	0.014	72.27	30165.7	833	3.7874
	1985	0.369	0.265	0.034	0.119	0.013	70.53	29816.1	640	4.0816
Individuals	1976	0.446	0.328	0.036	0.170	0.225	93.29	12586.1	10410	16.5668
	1977	0.446	0.328	0.035	0.170	0.233	92.92	13075.5	12919	15.5837
	1978	0.443	0.325	0.035	0.168	0.243	92.94	13557.5	13285	18.2889
	1979	0.433	0.325	0.034	0.168	0.249	90.85	14183.5	13676	11.6888
	1980	0.441	0.323	0.033	0.166	0.255	89.05	14454.0	16630	9.6932
	1981	0.440	0.322	0.033	0.166	0.261	88.69	14550.2	17164	9.2118
	1982	0.445	0.326	0.034	0.170	0.262	91.46	14790.1	15541	12.5381
	1983	0.447	0.327	0.035	0.171	0.261	91.88	15200.4	15468	12.3871
	1984	0.448	0.327	0.035	0.172	0.237	92.11	15513.0	15781	11.9517
	1985	0.446	0.325	0.035	0.170	0.266	92.94	15186.3	12681	14.9405
Others	1976	0.412	0.305	0.060	0.144	0.022	78.22	12416.8	95	4.0445
	1977	0.474	0.343	0.079	0.191	0.022	93.79	14846.1	122	7.1929
	1978	0.511	0.378	0.093	0.217	0.002	112.05	16541.6	122	22.0431
	1979	0.497	0.369	0.086	0.206	0.002	101.42	20785.7	116	8.7459
	1980	0.497	0.370	0.087	0.205	0.001	107.41	17725.5	128	16.8507
	1981	0.550	0.415	0.109	0.248	0.001	122.71	18569.3	130	17.8824
	1982	0.522	0.391	0.100	0.224	0.001	107.85	17637.9	91	10.6674
	1983	0.475	0.360	0.080	0.190	0.001	95.35	12579.7	107	7.0878
	1984	0.495	0.371	0.087	0.206	0.001	94.94	15479.7	97	4.5396
	1985	0.484	0.340	0.093	0.195	0.001	105.00	12799.9	77	19.4661

Table 6.23
Measures of Inequality for Individual Income Earnings
1976 - 1985

YEAR	GINI	RMD	THEIL	KAKWANI	CV	MEAN	OBSERVS	KAPPA
1976	0.442	0.319	0.030	0.170	89.31	14387.8	70315	11.6672
1977	0.447	0.323	0.030	0.173	89.98	14483.8	85155	10.6860
1978	0.448	0.323	0.030	0.174	89.97	14714.2	84191	10.1077
1979	0.443	0.320	0.029	0.170	88.10	14885.3	85013	8.3789
1980	0.437	0.315	0.028	0.166	85.79	14853.7	101388	6.7724
1981	0.435	0.314	0.027	0.165	84.66	14454.2	102515	5.7747
1982	0.442	0.319	0.029	0.169	88.57	14531.0	92340	9.4820
1983	0.449	0.324	0.030	0.174	90.22	14505.0	92400	9.5774
1984	0.445	0.321	0.029	0.172	88.88	14711.6	91984	8.5941
1985	0.449	0.323	0.030	0.174	92.19	14978.0	74315	13.7153

RMD = Relative Mean Deviation
CV = Coefficient of Variation
Observs = Number of observations.

Table 6.24

Measures of Inequality for White Income Earners by Sex

1976 - 1985

YEAR	GINI	RMD	THEIL	KAKAWANI	FRACTION	CV	MEAN	OBSERVS	KAPPA
1976	0.384	0.271	0.024	0.132	0.517	75.98	19284.5	36357	7.7788
1977	0.387	0.274	0.024	0.134	0.513	76.14	19437.6	43739	7.0470
1978	0.389	0.276	0.024	0.134	0.510	76.00	19763.0	42977	6.2699
1979	0.386	0.275	0.023	0.132	0.502	74.63	19914.0	42700	5.1399
1980	0.381	0.272	0.022	0.130	0.496	72.65	19788.1	50358	3.9464
1981	0.382	0.273	0.022	0.130	0.492	71.92	19065.6	50476	3.2297
1982	0.397	0.283	0.024	0.139	0.490	77.19	19228.3	45334	5.8471
1983	0.410	0.293	0.026	0.148	0.491	79.77	18889.0	45417	5.6158
1984	0.406	0.290	0.025	0.145	0.487	78.67	19065.5	44806	5.2908
1985	0.409	0.292	0.027	0.147	0.480	81.71	19663.1	35674	8.6280
1976	0.427	0.307	0.030	0.162	0.375	82.87	8761.2	26417	9.0163
1977	0.439	0.316	0.032	0.170	0.378	86.61	8803.0	32213	11.7939
1978	0.436	0.313	0.031	0.167	0.381	87.08	9001.7	32109	18.2652
1979	0.430	0.309	0.030	0.163	0.384	85.38	9350.9	32717	12.5672
1980	0.423	0.303	0.029	0.158	0.391	83.47	9603.6	39679	10.8970
1981	0.425	0.306	0.029	0.159	0.393	84.16	9621.6	40311	11.8736
1982	0.424	0.305	0.029	0.159	0.393	83.50	9708.6	36358	10.7382
1983	0.432	0.309	0.030	0.163	0.392	86.56	10031.1	36277	15.2838
1984	0.432	0.311	0.030	0.163	0.397	85.81	10339.6	36519	11.9677
1985	0.431	0.309	0.031	0.162	0.401	87.67	10530.6	29802	20.4405

RMD = Relative Mean Deviation
CV = Coefficient of Variation
Observs = Number of observations.

M A L E S

F E M A L E S

Table 6.25
Measures of Inequality for Black Income Earners by Sex
1976 - 1985

	YEAR	GINI	RMD	THEIL	KAKAWANI	FRACTION	CV	MEAN	OBSERVS	KAPPA
MALES	1976	0.386	0.281	0.030	0.134	0.044	71.18	12298.5	3154	2.2305
	1977	0.400	0.288	0.032	0.143	0.042	76.23	12541.0	3635	5.3244
	1978	0.399	0.289	0.032	0.143	0.041	76.58	12866.8	3526	5.1642
	1979	0.401	0.293	0.032	0.143	0.041	75.13	13347.3	3503	3.4873
	1980	0.398	0.287	0.031	0.141	0.039	74.47	13166.8	4052	2.9245
	1981	0.404	0.291	0.032	0.145	0.039	75.89	12774.3	4061	3.2210
	1982	0.402	0.291	0.032	0.144	0.039	74.63	12611.1	3692	2.5555
	1983	0.417	0.300	0.036	0.154	0.038	81.08	12995.5	3601	8.4042
	1984	0.429	0.310	0.037	0.162	0.040	82.17	12479.1	3680	5.1212
	1985	0.430	0.311	0.038	0.162	0.046	83.28	12497.7	3432	5.6867
FEMALES	1976	0.409	0.299	0.033	0.147	0.048	76.38	7662.1	3416	2.7947
	1977	0.403	0.293	0.032	0.142	0.045	77.11	8124.4	3837	4.3304
	1978	0.414	0.302	0.034	0.150	0.046	79.13	8152.8	3940	4.4706
	1979	0.414	0.305	0.034	0.150	0.047	78.91	8244.6	4060	4.0955
	1980	0.428	0.313	0.036	0.160	0.045	81.84	8403.3	4657	4.1362
	1981	0.426	0.312	0.036	0.159	0.046	82.54	8344.1	4727	5.8723
	1982	0.425	0.311	0.036	0.158	0.046	81.17	8163.9	4330	4.3105
	1983	0.430	0.315	0.037	0.162	0.047	83.26	8367.7	4392	6.6056
	1984	0.436	0.321	0.038	0.166	0.047	84.12	8705.3	4351	5.0836
	1985	0.437	0.321	0.038	0.165	0.058	86.36	9021.3	4322	10.4690

RMD = Relative Mean Deviation
CV = Coefficient of Variation
Observs = Number of observations.

Table 6.26

Measures of Inequality for Other Ethnic Groups by Sex

1976 - 1985

YEAR	GINI	RMD	THEIL	KAKAWANI	FRACTION	CV	MEAN	OBSERVS	KAPPA
1976	0.417	0.295	0.047	0.152	0.007	85.11	17779.6	560	11.0386
1977	0.414	0.297	0.042	0.150	0.011	81.00	16563.1	984	7.0251
1978	0.418	0.298	0.043	0.154	0.011	81.64	17265.6	940	6.6962
1979	0.408	0.295	0.039	0.147	0.013	77.97	17634.0	1125	4.4534
1980	0.413	0.298	0.039	0.150	0.014	80.03	17048.6	1427	5.6280
1981	0.422	0.306	0.040	0.158	0.015	79.47	16942.8	1608	3.1639
1982	0.420	0.302	0.041	0.156	0.015	82.50	16506.6	1425	6.8593
1983	0.437	0.313	0.044	0.166	0.015	85.52	16810.4	1455	6.4081
1984	0.442	0.322	0.045	0.171	0.015	85.32	17365.1	1406	5.1388
1985	0.468	0.338	0.058	0.189	0.007	91.58	18729.9	576	5.8564
1976	0.437	0.315	0.056	0.168	0.005	92.49	10182.5	411	55.7016
1977	0.428	0.307	0.047	0.163	0.008	83.15	8780.9	747	10.5977
1978	0.434	0.314	0.049	0.167	0.008	81.98	9573.9	699	3.8312
1979	0.431	0.306	0.047	0.164	0.010	86.61	10042.4	908	14.6424
1980	0.422	0.300	0.043	0.157	0.011	84.03	9980.2	1215	10.0730
1981	0.416	0.299	0.041	0.155	0.012	78.79	9750.0	1332	3.5417
1982	0.433	0.312	0.044	0.166	0.013	78.97	9719.2	1201	4.8717
1983	0.423	0.302	0.043	0.159	0.013	83.80	10331.1	1258	8.4585
1984	0.423	0.302	0.043	0.159	0.013	81.42	10779.9	1222	5.6326
1985	0.468	0.336	0.061	0.190	0.006	97.53	10079.4	509	25.4047

M A L E S

F E M A L E S

RMD = Relative Mean Deviation
CV = Coefficient of Variation
Observs = Number of observations.

Table 6.27
Measures of Inequality for Male Weekly Earnings
1976 - 1985

YEAR	GINI	RMD	THEIL	KAKWANI	COEFF VAR	MEAN	OBSERVS	KAPPA
1976	0.354	0.245	0.022	0.115	81.75	401.30	33761	5125
1977	0.363	0.252	0.023	0.120	95.36	406.24	40740	107762
1978	0.360	0.250	0.021	0.117	78.51	409.88	40004	1367
1979	0.361	0.251	0.023	0.118	107.24	416.19	39899	532902
1980	0.352	0.247	0.020	0.113	80.02	407.12	47369	54506
1981	0.351	0.248	0.019	0.112	68.42	393.97	47389	35
1982	0.367	0.258	0.022	0.121	76.26	397.08	42236	574
1983	0.381	0.268	0.023	0.130	78.55	392.98	41848	171
1984	0.382	0.270	0.024	0.130	83.53	396.01	41180	4296
1985	0.385	0.272	0.024	0.132	81.25	397.88	32817	743

Table 6.28
Measures of Inequality for Male Weekly Earnings
1976 - 1985

AGE LESS THAN 30

	YEAR	GINI	RMD.	THEIL	KAKAWANI	FRACTION	COEFF.VARIATION	MEAN	OBSERVS	KAPPA
NO HIGH SCHOOL DEGREE	1976	0.431	0.307	0.043	0.168	0.063	87.18	188.02	2159.0	38
	1977	0.453	0.321	0.046	0.182	0.066	95.76	194.10	2695.0	114
	1978	0.434	0.309	0.041	0.171	0.064	81.91	194.08	2588.0	4
	1979	0.423	0.297	0.041	0.160	0.061	90.92	204.14	2463.0	526
	1980	0.410	0.289	0.036	0.150	0.061	81.51	210.57	2905.0	20
	1981	0.407	0.286	0.036	0.149	0.061	80.15	200.70	2907.0	14
	1982	0.421	0.295	0.040	0.158	0.059	92.28	202.73	2520.0	174
	1983	0.416	0.293	0.039	0.154	0.054	86.17	190.34	2265.0	44
	1984	0.415	0.293	0.039	0.154	0.053	84.15	180.90	2214.0	26
	1985	0.446	0.307	0.064	0.175	0.050	229.87	188.25	1673.0	257511
HS GRADUATE	1976	0.323	0.225	0.022	0.098	0.206	79.61	297.86	6964.0	9804
	1977	0.333	0.230	0.021	0.102	0.216	70.81	301.31	8826.0	275
	1978	0.330	0.228	0.021	0.100	0.220	70.17	302.96	8823.0	531
	1979	0.324	0.229	0.021	0.097	0.223	76.86	310.47	8935.0	19427
	1980	0.325	0.229	0.020	0.098	0.226	67.43	308.21	10745.0	145
	1981	0.331	0.233	0.020	0.100	0.228	66.88	298.14	10852.0	63
	1982	0.341	0.241	0.021	0.106	0.223	68.48	287.70	9425.0	45
	1983	0.356	0.252	0.024	0.115	0.218	71.81	277.91	9164.0	39
	1984	0.359	0.254	0.025	0.117	0.220	96.36	270.58	9061.0	212038
	1985	0.350	0.249	0.023	0.111	0.213	70.02	265.89	7016.0	95
COLLEGE GRADUATE	1976	0.315	0.215	0.028	0.094	0.062	109.47	379.23	2124.0	104511
	1977	0.314	0.216	0.022	0.092	0.065	65.34	376.96	2683.0	30
	1978	0.308	0.213	0.021	0.089	0.062	62.68	380.85	2491.0	27
	1979	0.299	0.208	0.019	0.083	0.062	56.51	375.08	2512.0	3
	1980	0.312	0.216	0.021	0.090	0.060	60.93	375.65	2878.0	9
	1981	0.303	0.212	0.020	0.087	0.058	60.96	363.09	2781.0	112
	1982	0.329	0.224	0.023	0.095	0.055	72.48	370.68	2362.0	2565
	1983	0.329	0.229	0.023	0.100	0.058	63.10	362.86	2442.0	4
	1984	0.335	0.235	0.025	0.103	0.057	68.53	366.83	2380.0	148
	1985	0.336	0.234	0.027	0.105	0.058	73.42	377.02	1905.0	594

Table 6.29
Measures of Inequality for Male Weekly Earnings
1976 - 1985

30 <or= AGE < 60

	YEAR	GINI	RMD	THEIL	KAKAWANI	FRACTION	COEFF.VARIATION	MEAN	OBSERVS	KAPPA
NO HS DEGREE	1976	0.292	0.203	0.017	0.081	0.161	60.42	345.29	5449.0	69
	1977	0.305	0.213	0.019	0.087	0.154	65.32	357.27	6279.0	253
	1978	0.305	0.214	0.019	0.087	0.145	66.04	362.79	5818.0	373
	1979	0.309	0.217	0.020	0.089	0.136	71.49	361.18	5429.0	2624
	1980	0.317	0.224	0.020	0.092	0.127	63.04	351.66	6056.0	19
	1981	0.319	0.225	0.021	0.094	0.123	69.71	342.41	5831.0	938
	1982	0.322	0.228	0.021	0.095	0.119	65.03	322.94	5040.0	26
	1983	0.344	0.242	0.025	0.108	0.113	81.61	317.69	4766.0	7107
	1984	0.338	0.238	0.024	0.104	0.105	72.97	331.15	4344.0	108
	1985	0.338	0.240	0.024	0.104	0.105	66.82	320.01	3447.0	10
HS DEGREE	1976	0.260	0.177	0.013	0.066	0.283	56.75	464.69	9560.0	213
	1977	0.271	0.184	0.015	0.071	0.285	71.31	471.56	11221.0	12673
	1978	0.271	0.186	0.014	0.071	0.278	59.06	475.00	11155.2	1979
	1979	0.271	0.187	0.013	0.070	0.285	68.55	467.76	13530.0	278893
	1981	0.286	0.198	0.015	0.077	0.288	52.12	454.67	13654.0	9
	1982	0.299	0.207	0.017	0.086	0.293	58.04	449.00	12397.0	39
	1983	0.301	0.210	0.017	0.085	0.297	62.39	434.25	12449.0	432
	1984	0.300	0.208	0.017	0.085	0.302	60.71	434.40	12455.0	57
	1985					0.315	62.21	431.03	10338.0	156
COLLEGE GRADUATE	1976	0.296	0.205	0.019	0.081	0.115	72.30	684.710	3915.00	6083
	1977	0.294	0.206	0.020	0.080	0.118	91.62	676.520	4826.00	277822
	1978	0.288	0.204	0.016	0.076	0.125	53.65	664.070	5025.00	2
	1979	0.299	0.210	0.021	0.083	0.131	104.17	664.420	5265.00	53
	1980	0.286	0.204	0.015	0.076	0.137	56.84	629.230	6513.00	697
	1981	0.278	0.200	0.014	0.072	0.142	49.79	602.340	6771.00	1
	1982	0.303	0.213	0.017	0.084	0.151	57.54	619.560	6397.00	5
	1983	0.317	0.224	0.019	0.092	0.160	60.20	622.680	6697.00	13
	1984	0.310	0.220	0.019	0.089	0.166	69.56	629.410	6848.00	7835
	1985	0.318	0.224	0.019	0.092	0.160	60.28	651.830	5260.00	3

Table 6.30
Measures of Inequality for Male Weekly Earnings
1976 - 1985

AGE >= 60

	YEAR	GINI	RMD	THEIL	KAKAWANI	FRACTION	COEFF.VARIATION	MEAN	OBSERVS	KAPPA
NO HS DEGREE	1976	0.455	0.322	0.050	0.181	0.052	108.41	262.150	1787.00	657
	1977	0.494	0.349	0.062	0.208	0.050	133.27	287.750	2066.00	819
	1978	0.489	0.348	0.066	0.205	0.048	176.04	273.690	1960.00	28118
	1979	0.460	0.328	0.053	0.184	0.045	118.90	267.130	1804.00	810
	1980	0.485	0.345	0.068	0.201	0.042	225.78	273.420	2036.00	257916
	1981	0.439	0.317	0.043	0.168	0.040	85.42	238.700	1917.00	8
	1982	0.455	0.331	0.048	0.180	0.038	95.36	237.960	1621.00	61
	1983	0.470	0.336	0.054	0.192	0.036	106.84	240.670	1514.00	345
	1984	0.467	0.339	0.051	0.189	0.033	91.09	231.980	1382.00	6
	1985	0.461	0.332	0.053	0.184	0.034	101.16	241.710	1126.00	94
HS DEGREE	1976	0.385	0.265	0.037	0.136	0.038	80.43	386.770	1315.00	25
	1977	0.454	0.309	0.065	0.182	0.040	181.87	409.411	1630.00	17801
	1978	0.434	0.298	0.051	0.167	0.040	125.72	414.880	1611.00	9244
	1979	0.432	0.301	0.045	0.165	0.041	93.05	408.000	1668.00	49
	1980	0.409	0.290	0.037	0.149	0.042	80.99	370.330	2002.00	14
	1981	0.419	0.299	0.039	0.156	0.040	81.61	352.000	59.00	1929
	1982	0.447	0.314	0.053	0.176	0.042	136.19	386.000	0.68	1744
	1983	0.438	0.313	0.044	0.171	0.042	83.55	381.860	1791.00	4
	1984	0.443	0.316	0.047	0.172	0.042	100.92	371.910	1737.00	587
	1985	0.439	0.314	0.046	0.169	0.044	95.49	365.850	1452.00	116
COLLEGE GRADUATE	1976	0.414	0.296	0.047	0.156	0.014	75.72	573.810	488.00	2
	1977	0.432	0.313	0.050	0.166	0.012	79.22	573.770	514.00	2
	1978	0.423	0.310	0.048	0.160	0.013	81.64	604.180	533.00	14
	1979	0.418	0.298	0.045	0.156	0.013	81.33	613.820	571.00	8
	1980	0.409	0.291	0.045	0.153	0.014	84.90	588.150	704.00	82
	1981	0.427	0.308	0.049	0.163	0.015	94.68	562.690	747.00	303
	1982	0.445	0.324	0.050	0.177	0.017	81.98	555.420	730.00	2
	1983	0.447	0.319	0.055	0.177	0.018	103.59	604.400	760.00	334
	1984	0.431	0.311	0.049	0.165	0.018	90.12	604.370	759.00	96

Table 6.31
Measures of Inequality for Female Weekly Earnings
1976 - 1985

YEAR	GINI	RMD	THEIL	KAKAWANI	COEFF.VARIATION	MEAN	OBSERVS	KAPPA
1976	0.382	0.268	0.026	0.132	92.56	195.86	24713	9964
1977	0.392	0.275	0.027	0.139	91.39	197.33	30348	4096
1978	0.387	0.272	0.026	0.136	82.43	197.67	30402	628
1979	0.382	0.268	0.026	0.132	91.40	202.97	31293	8981
1980	0.377	0.264	0.023	0.129	78.66	206.31	37613	133
1981	0.379	0.266	0.024	0.130	90.09	205.62	38133	131291
1982	0.379	0.266	0.024	0.130	80.83	205.17	34174	1304
1983	0.389	0.275	0.025	0.136	85.24	209.34	34023	6451
1984	0.393	0.278	0.026	0.138	91.37	215.81	34199	29947
1985	0.391	0.277	0.026	0.136	81.65	214.55	27848	458

Table 6.32
Measures of Inequality for Female Weekly Earnings
1976 - 1985

AGE LESS THAN 30

	YEAR	GINI	RMD	THEIL	KAKAWANI	FRACTION	COEFF.VARIATION	MEAN	OBSERVS	KAPPA
NO HS DEGREE	1976	0.424	0.298	0.051	0.165	0.056	137.54	118.76	1397	53931
	1977	0.426	0.300	0.044	0.164	0.057	91.36	120.50	1736	134
	1978	0.436	0.309	0.043	0.172	0.056	89.48	121.57	1718	41
	1979	0.419	0.296	0.043	0.159	0.056	99.28	121.76	1755	3295
	1980	0.402	0.281	0.039	0.146	0.051	95.74	131.28	1935	2252
	1981	0.409	0.289	0.039	0.151	0.048	84.63	120.81	1839	109
	1982	0.392	0.275	0.037	0.141	0.046	80.73	125.38	1585	52
	1983	0.437	0.306	0.048	0.169	0.042	99.50	123.21	1460	178
	1984	0.424	0.295	0.052	0.161	0.041	150.63	121.44	1401	46304
	1985	0.418	0.296	0.043	0.155	0.039	84.52	115.09	1100	22
HS DEGREE	1976	0.325	0.228	0.021	0.098	0.259	67.45	178.98	6417	159
	1977	0.336	0.234	0.023	0.106	0.263	77.11	182.21	7996	2427
	1978	0.335	0.235	0.022	0.105	0.265	68.14	180.47	8077	178
	1979	0.333	0.231	0.023	0.103	0.269	87.49	184.31	8428	51695
	1980	0.333	0.230	0.022	0.103	0.266	75.23	185.93	10037	1072
	1981	0.332	0.233	0.020	0.102	0.269	66.15	182.47	10284	34
	1982	0.340	0.238	0.022	0.106	0.260	66.15	181.41	8891	72
	1983	0.353	0.248	0.024	0.114	0.257	74.45	180.24	8755	403
	1984	0.354	0.251	0.023	0.114	0.250	71.12	178.54	8557	126
	1985	0.353	0.250	0.024	0.114	0.241	67.39	177.07	6721	6
COLLEGE GRADUATE	1976	0.297	0.204	0.022	0.088	0.063	61.03	260.71	1577	107
	1977	0.296	0.207	0.020	0.086	0.064	55.18	254.45	1959	3
	1978	0.320	0.204	0.020	0.085	0.062	58.64	261.41	1914	25
	1979	0.306	0.217	0.027	0.099	0.065	82.98	262.74	2064	3346
	1980	0.314	0.220	0.021	0.089	0.065	61.86	266.15	2475	118
	1981	0.318	0.223	0.021	0.094	0.064	58.54	257.66	2451	2
	1982	0.319	0.224	0.022	0.095	0.065	59.84	261.64	2233	4
	1983	0.319	0.224	0.022	0.096	0.067	58.65	263.94	2301	2
	1984	0.330	0.230	0.025	0.102	0.065	70.90	264.65	2218	796
	1985	0.312	0.218	0.022	0.092	0.065	61.03	273.74	1824	22

Table 6.33
Measures of Inequality for Female Weekly Earnings
1976 - 1985

30 < = AGE < 60

	YEAR	GINI	RMD	THEIL	KAKAWANI	FRACTION	COEFF.VARIATION	MEAN	OBSERVS	KAPPA
NO HS DEGREE	1976	0.360	0.247	0.031	0.121	0.140	94.99	158.52	3465	9187
	1977	0.366	0.253	0.029	0.124	0.130	75.34	158.14	3972	58
	1978	0.357	0.247	0.028	0.119	0.125	78.34	161.87	3822	284
	1979	0.355	0.244	0.027	0.117	0.113	72.64	165.71	3561	34
	1980	0.350	0.242	0.026	0.115	0.105	69.99	165.38	3959	23
	1981	0.367	0.251	0.038	0.125	0.101	180.56	172.95	3863	958169
	1982	0.358	0.246	0.031	0.119	0.099	101.28	163.61	3392	58423
	1983	0.358	0.246	0.030	0.120	0.089	86.50	161.05	3042	2210
	1984	0.374	0.257	0.036	0.129	0.083	109.06	170.43	2844	7908
	1985	0.348	0.242	0.027	0.112	0.082	68.26	164.11	2304	15
HS DEGREE	1976	0.356	0.250	0.026	0.119	0.323	83.28	204.25	7985	12033
	1977	0.379	0.264	0.029	0.134	0.322	89.18	204.37	9796	3201
	1978	0.371	0.259	0.027	0.128	0.324	81.32	206.88	9869	2161
	1979	0.363	0.253	0.026	0.123	0.328	86.34	211.74	10290	17970
	1980	0.357	0.249	0.024	0.119	0.339	73.89	212.01	12771	129
	1981	0.361	0.252	0.025	0.120	0.343	79.33	212.25	13103	3870
	1982	0.357	0.250	0.024	0.118	0.351	71.97	210.32	12006	302
	1983	0.365	0.256	0.024	0.123	0.353	71.96	214.96	12042	25
	1984	0.363	0.255	0.024	0.121	0.362	75.93	220.30	12383	1034
	1985	0.363	0.256	0.025	0.121	0.370	79.29	217.05	10323	2736
COLLEGE GRADUATE	1976	0.381	0.259	0.040	0.137	0.070	107.84	332.73	1745	5297
	1977	0.360	0.252	0.031	0.124	0.074	77.02	318.17	2267	498
	1978	0.362	0.254	0.030	0.124	0.077	69.91	312.68	2359	15
	1979	0.367	0.256	0.032	0.127	0.083	84.33	314.29	2604	1828
	1980	0.359	0.251	0.028	0.121	0.090	70.17	321.02	3419	20
	1981	0.353	0.247	0.027	0.117	0.094	70.76	315.42	3607	129
	1982	0.357	0.248	0.028	0.119	0.100	78.49	312.21	3418	1386
	1983	0.354	0.247	0.028	0.119	0.109	81.12	322.21	3713	9383
	1984	0.351	0.244	0.026	0.116	0.119	67.46	334.33	4070	10
	1985	0.351	0.243	0.026	0.116	0.118	68.17	343.54	3308	7

Table 6.34
Measures of Inequality for Female Weekly Earnings
1976 - 1985

AGE >= 60

	YEAR	GINI	RMD	THEIL	KAKAWANI	FRACTION	COEFF. VARIATION	MEAN	OBSERVS	KAPPA
NO HS DEGREE	1976	0.426	0.312	0.044	0.161	0.037	79.62	119.47	937	3
	1977	0.474	0.343	0.059	0.193	0.035	114.01	128.61	1073	452
	1978	0.460	0.331	0.053	0.183	0.036	110.94	126.53	1100	81
	1979	0.450	0.326	0.048	0.177	0.032	99.58	128.59	1020	226
	1980	0.441	0.316	0.051	0.171	0.029	90.61	127.11	1117	23
	1981	0.447	0.318	0.051	0.175	0.028	99.56	126.68	1069	132
	1982	0.442	0.313	0.044	0.171	0.026	96.45	127.56	903	98
	1983	0.422	0.304	0.044	0.157	0.026	82.04	118.91	891	13
	1984	0.511	0.355	0.114	0.222	0.025	373.62	142.49	866	127001
	1985	0.429	0.306	0.047	0.161	0.026	86.40	118.84	749	27
HS DEGREE	1976	0.421	0.303	0.045	0.157	0.037	86.54	178.35	934	45
	1977	0.474	0.335	0.067	0.195	0.041	166.52	194.05	1261	20702
	1978	0.462	0.330	0.057	0.184	0.042	127.96	183.79	1290	3173
	1979	0.438	0.314	0.050	0.168	0.041	110.74	191.27	1295	2067
	1980	0.411	0.296	0.039	0.151	0.040	80.90	182.34	1534	13
	1981	0.421	0.304	0.041	0.156	0.040	83.14	183.44	1573	10
	1982	0.430	0.311	0.045	0.164	0.042	92.27	182.64	1445	211
	1983	0.427	0.309	0.043	0.162	0.043	83.14	186.49	1472	7
	1984	0.436	0.315	0.044	0.166	0.043	86.78	187.58	1473	16
	1985	0.440	0.317	0.050	0.170	0.045	114.49	186.38	1263	6266
COLLEGE GRADUATE	1976	0.436	0.316	0.060	0.177	0.010	78.66	294.56	256	1
	1977	0.467	0.331	0.073	0.198	0.009	106.54	301.89	288	214
	1978	0.458	0.346	0.064	0.190	0.008	83.74	270.69	253	2
	1979	0.449	0.340	0.061	0.185	0.008	81.74	275.03	276	2
	1980	0.474	0.352	0.066	0.201	0.009	93.14	271.13	366	10
	1981	0.428	0.315	0.054	0.168	0.009	81.30	290.34	344	6
	1982	0.458	0.330	0.068	0.188	0.008	104.09	297.01	301	248
	1983	0.515	0.370	0.101	0.229	0.010	195.15	293.64	347	8388
	1984	0.427	0.305	0.054	0.163	0.008	82.25	342.37	307	5
	1985	0.447	0.320	0.062	0.178	0.009	86.96	309.52	256	7

ENDNOTES

[1]We are grateful to Kin Blackburn for pointing this out.

[2]As Kin Blackburn reminds us, there is a problem with "individual income earners" since (say) a husband and wife may earn interest income but it is only reported for the husband. We ignored this distinction. We also dropped observations with values of zero for reported income.

Chapter 7

THE DISTRIBUTION OF EARNINGS ACROSS OCCUPATIONS

7.1 Introduction

If we attended a meeting of the American Economic Association and asked participants as they passed us in the hotel lobby to explain wage rate determination (and consequently earnings inequality), they would reply:

1) Age
2) Sex
3) Education
4) Experience
5) Luck
6) Ability
7) Hicks-Marshall laws of factor demand
8) Discrimination
9) Hedonic wage theory
10) Unions
11) Technology
12) Regulation
13) Occupational choice

and many more determinants. The reader sees immediately that these factors are not necessarily mutually exclusive and, in fact, many of these factors are highly correlated. For example, (13) may be highly positively correlated with (6) for white males but (8) may impede (13) for white females implying negative correlation.

Chapter 6 has shown us that age, sex and education impact earnings (income) distributions for families, households and individuals. In Chapter 7 we merely present inequality measures across occupations and attempt inference based on the labor market trends discussed in Chapter 2 using neo-classical economic theory as a guiding principle. We also will invoke theories from such authors as Lydall (1968) who believed that the distribution of earnings was proportional to how many people are under you in the firm's hierarchy and Creedy (1985) who models movement in the distribution through a mobility index recalling stochastic changes as one begins his/her ascent (descent).

We will not run regressions with the log of earnings, variance of earnings or variance of log of earnings on the left and our socio-economic factors on the right for several reasons. Firstly, we don't believe earnings are lognormally distributed **a priori** (without checking), we know that universal specification tests haven't yet been developed, we do believe in selectivity bias and most importantly, the data (from the Current Population Survey)· is sufficiently confused through "hot deck" imputations that running these regressions becomes highly problematic, cf. Lillard, Smith and Welch (1986). You may then consider the task of even examining the distributions fruitless, but we would argue that using this data to construct distributions is only a misdemeanor but to use it in earnings (causal) equations is a felony. Thus, we will suggest felonious behavior but try to only suggest it, not commit it. Finally, we also want to point out that human capital theory and human capital theorists have had a profound impact and made a major contribution to modern economic theory. The problem is, however, that the aforementioned theorists intended their models to explain investments by individuals in education, training and job search. They never intended for their models to explain wage determination, cf. Ehrenberg and Smith (1988).

For all of these reasons, we discuss the occupational aggregation selection in section 7.2 and discuss the earnings distributions in section 7.3. Section 7.4 summarizes this chapter of our book.

7.2 A Description of the Data

The data utilized to examine earnings distributions across occupations are from the March Current Population Survey which has already been discussed in Chapter 6. From nearly 1000 original occupational codes we recoded to fifty two and then again to fourteen. In Table 7.1 we report the fifty-two coded occupations and then follow this with fourteen classifications in Table 7.2. As can be seen from Tables 7.1 and 7.2, executives (01) includes managers and administrators and management related occupations. Professionals (02) includes doctors, scientists, professors, engineers and other professionals. Technicians (03) includes health and science technicians. Sales (04) includes sales reps, supervisors and commodity brokers. Administrative support (05) includes secretaries, stenographers, computer equipment operators and clerical staff. Private household support (06) includes gardeners, chauffeurs and domestics. Protective service (07) includes body guards, security guards and alarm system specialists. Other service (08) includes food servers, janitorial work and health service jobs. Farming (09) includes farmers, fishermen and lumberjacks. Crafts(10) includes carpenters, plumbers, mechanics and similar trades. Operators (11) includes machine operators, assemblers, production inspectors and samplers. Transportation (12) includes truck drivers and heavy equipment operators. Laborers (13) includes freight handlers, construction laborers and stock handlers. Finally, Armed Forces (14) includes individuals working in military support positions but not in the military.

While the aggregation from 52 to 14 groups should seem quite reasonable, several problems arise. The most obvious problem is that when we construct our inequality measures below, to some extent the dispersion in earnings will reflect the way that occupations were lumped together. This is exacerbated by the admittedly ad hoc method of aggregation. The aggregation is necessary in order to ensure that each cell (group) has enough observations to make comparisons valid, cf. West (1987) and Lerman and Yitzhaki (1988). Despite the obvious problems, we still can draw many conclusions from the data. The classifications still signal us about the relative skill levels involved and education attainment necessary to pursue particular trades. We can also make inferences about the hedonic nature and hierarchical structure involved. Therefore, we now examine the earnings distributions across these occupational classifications for the period 1976-1980 and 1984 and 1985. We also add that the data for Armed Forces support occupations wasn't collected until the early 1980's and therefore is not reported for the 1976-1980 period. We excluded 1981-1983 because we found problems with the data for those three years which we couldn't rectify even after several attempts at getting the data fresh and beginning all over again each time.

7.3 The Empirical Results

Tables 7.3-7.9 report summary information for the occupational groups discussed above. We examine the earnings distribution for each group for the years 1976-1980 and 1984 and 1985. For each occupational group, for each year, we report the Gini coefficient, Theil's entropy measure normalized, and several descriptive statistics of the distributions. Namely we report the mean, variance, skewness coefficient and kurtosis. These statistics will of course tell us if the earnings distributions across occupations have increased in magnitude (may be reflected in larger means), greater dispersion (larger variances), tending toward a Paretian distribution (skew is becoming more j-shaped) and whether or not they have become increasingly kurtotic (flatter or steeper).

From Table 7.3 we observe that in 1976 Technicians, Protective Services, Crafts and Transportation occupations had the lowest inequality levels in their respective earnings distributions. The highest levels of inequality were observed for Sales jobs, for Private Household jobs, for Other Services and for Farming. Explaining the reasons for high level-of-inequality occupations vis a' vis low level-of-inequality occupations is difficult to say the least. Recall that the category "Sales" represents occupations that might be expected to have relatively large differences in earnings. Many individuals do sales work part time and in relatively low paying positions such as store clerks and individuals that sell by phone. Concurrently, this category also includes stock brokers and supervisors. The nature of the aggregation may explain in part the high level of inequality for this category. Interestingly, we can see from Tables 7.3-7.9 that the relatively high inequality levels in sales jobs continue from 1976-1985. Recalling the trend in Chapter 2 of more women entering the labor market, we can also predict that since education levels have not increased commensurately with the increased LFP by women, we would predict many of these women to be entering jobs that don't require large investments in training or schooling. We would expect this since many of those increasing their LFP, are not in the younger age cohorts, cf. Chapter 2. If women are not in the younger cohorts then the discounted present value of net benefits won't be as large as for younger cohorts and we would expect these women to forego large human capital investments. One consequence of doing so is that they only qualify for relatively unskilled, low-wage occupations. The result of this process coupled with several high income sales jobs is a high level of inequality. Executives and professionals, on the other hand, appear to have remarkably stable earnings distributions over time. Their mean incomes are consistently the highest of all the occupational groups yet the dispersion of earnings rank below many other groups. One possibility for this phenomenon is the unfortunate fact that the data may be truncated so much at the "cut off" point (see Chapter 6) that the measure of inequality is biased downward. It also is well known that these two groups have large investments in schooling and training and the return on schooling decreases as the investment increases. While these individuals have steeper age/earnings profiles than lesser educated cohorts, since their returns are lower, we wouldn't expect larger variation. Lydall's (1968) theories are particularly relevant here since these groups are the "bosses" and supervise many employees. While earnings rise with increases in position, the national trend has also been towards earlier retirement and lower expected worklifes. The increases in lucrative fringe benefits and "golden parachutes" create pure income effects which tend to cause earlier departure from the labor force. Therefore the wage increases they experience as they oversee more of the firm's resources is offset by earlier retirement meaning these high wage individuals are replaced with lower wage neophytes. The net result of this process and the biased data result in the inequality measures which are consistent with the national averages (see Chapter 5) even using other data.

The farming cohort (recall this group includes forestry and fishing) exhibits a very high concentration of earnings which is due in part to the data lumping together farm workers, lumberjacks and fishermen with the individuals that run these concerns. A better reason for the high inequality level is probably easier to explain. The trend in all three occupations has been towards consolidation with economies of scale and scope looming large. The end result is huge farm concerns side by side with mom and pop farms. We see the same trends in fishing and forestry and would expect the high concentration of earnings we observe. The best test of this hypothesis would require earnings data going back twenty-five years before all this consolidation took place; unfortunately the government did not collect such data twenty five years ago, so no meaningful comparative study can be undertaken.

Transportation jobs, machine operators and administrative support jobs are predominantly occupations that don't require large investments in schooling and relatively short training investments. Primary causes for wage differentials in these jobs may be due to acquisition of supervisory positions. Again, the relatively stable earnings distributions in these occupations reflects that earnings in these occupations move with national productivity and technology change. We also note that these jobs are highly unionized and one impact of the union may be to limit the dispersion of wages. If the union is concerned with maximizing its membership with an eye on the wage bill, it may seek (and frequently does) across-the-board increases that prevent too much wage dispersion.

Crafts (which include carpenters, mechanics, etc.) showed a very stable level of inequality for the years 1976-1980. Suddenly in 1984 and 1985 the level of earnings inequality rose markedly. This would seem to be another case where consolidation has occurred. The U.S. economy has moved steadily away from gas stations where a mechanic was on duty to situations where 10 minute lube shops have sprung up all over. While most mechanics' wages won't change much, the supervisor of the shop and residual claimants of these businesses will see economic rents. The decline of unions in these occupations may also work towards increasing wage dispersion. One ironic factor is, that as more consolidation occurs, unions may make a comeback since collective bargaining is presumed to cut transaction costs for larger groups. Plumbers, electricians, and carpenters on the other hand, may be following a national trend towards more independent (individual) work effort. As they strike out alone we would expect wages closely tied to productivity and since productivity is quite disperse, so are earnings. Union effects towards less concentration are also at work here as independents shun the unions.

In terms of general trends, it does appear that inequality as measured by the Gini coefficient and entropy measure have been relatively stable with some occupations (executives, technicians, administrative support, private households, protective services, other services, transportation and laborers) experiencing increasing inequality and several occupations (professionals, sales, and farming) showing slight declines. Mean income rose for all groups, but comparisons are difficult due to data truncation.

The kappa values for executives, professionals, sales jobs, the service occupations, farming, transportation and laborers all fluctuated from negative to positive values. The skewness coefficient and kurtosis also vascillated greatly so the κ values aren't surprising. Recalling Chapter 4, as the kappa values fall to negative numbers, the Beta I distribution becomes the likely hypothetical statistical distribution to describe the empirical graduation and as the values got very large and negative the gamma distribution was the likely candidate, e.g., notice the κ values for farming in 1978, 1979 and 1984. It is also interesting that for administrative support services and crafts jobs, only the lognormal and Pareto distributions are viable candidates to describe the empirical earnings distributions (the κ values are all between zero and one).

Among the occupations with some negative κ values (signalling the Beta I distribution or gamma distribution for large values) sales jobs have the largest percentage of negative values (86%). The fluctuating values of the κ criterion for professionals and executives and other service oriented occupations is not surprising since to some extent the earnings in these occupations are tied to the economy, and since many of these individuals are self-employed we should expect some volatility.

Finally, we close this chapter by pointing out that the inequality measures (the Gini coefficient and Theil's entropy measure) maintained the same ranking throughout all the occupations over time. It is frequently asserted that one problem with inequality measures is that they violate this ordering. We did not observe any violations in this chapter. We now conclude and summarize our results in Chapter 8.

Table 7.1
Detailed Occupation Recodes
(01-52)

DETAILED OCCUPATION CODE	RECODE	OCCUPATION
ADMINISTRATORS AND OFFICIALS, PUBLIC ADMINISTRATION	01	3-6
MANAGERS AND ADMINISTRATORS, EXCEPT PUBLIC ADMINISTRATION	02	7-19
SALARIED	03	
SELF-EMPLOYED	04	
MANAGEMENT RELATED OCCUPATIONS	05	24-37
ACCOUNTANTS AND AUDITORS	06	23
ENGINEERS, ARCHITECTS, AND SURVEYORS	07	43-63
ENGINEERS	08	44-59
NATURAL SCIENTISTS AND MATHEMATICIANS	09	65-83
COMPUTER SYSTEMS ANALYSTS AND SCIENTISTS	10	64
HEALTH DIAGNOSING OCCUPATIONS	11	86-89
PHYSICIANS AND DENTISTS	12	84-85
HEALTH ASSESSMENT AND TREATING OCCUPATIONS	13	95-106
TEACHERS, LIBRARIANS, AND COUNSELORS	14	113-154 163-165
TEACHERS, EXCEPT POSTSECONDARY	15	155-159
OTHER PROFESSIONAL SPECIALTY OCCUPATIONS	16	166-199
HEALTH TECHNOLOGISTS AND TECHNICIANS	17	203-208
ENGINEERING AND SCIENCE TECHNICIANS	18	213-225
TECHNICIANS, EXCEPT HEALTH, ENGINEERING, AMD SCIENCE	19	226-235
SUPERVISORS AND PROPRIETORS, SALES OCCUPATIONS	20	243
SALES REPRESENTATIVES, COMMODITIES AND FINANCE	21	253-259

Table 7.1 (Continued)

OTHER SALES OCCUPATIONS	22	263-285
COMPUTER EQUIPMENT OPERATORS	23	308-309
SECRETARIES, STENOGRAPHERS, AND TYPISTS	24	313-315
FINANCIAL RECORDS PROCESSING OCCUPATIONS	25	337-344
OTHER ADMINISTRATIVE SUPPORT OCCUPATIONS, INCLUDING CLERICAL	26	303-389
PRIVATE HOUSEHOLD SERVICE OCCUPATIONS	27	403-407
PROTECTIVE SERVICE OCCUPATIONS	28	413-427
FOOD SERVICE OCCUPATIONS	29	433-444
HEALTH SERVICE OCCUPATIONS	30	445-447
CLEANING AND BUILDING SERVICE OCCUPATIONS	31	448-455
PERSONAL SERVICE OCCUPATIONS	32	456-469
FARM OPERATORS AND MANAGERS	33	473-476
FARM OCCUPATIONS, EXCEPT MANAGERIAL	34	477-484
RELATED AGRICULTURAL OCCUPATIONS	35	485-489
FORESTRY AND FISHING OCCUPATIONS	36	494-499
MECHANICS AND REPAIRERS	37	503-549
CONSTRUCTION TRADES AND EXTRACTIVE OCCUPATIONS	38	553-617
CARPENTERS	39	567-569
SUPERVISORS, PRODUCTION OCCUPATIONS	40	633
PRECISION METAL WORKING OCCUPATIONS	41	634-655
OTHER PRECISION PRODUCTION OCCUPATIONS	42	656-699
MACHINE OPERATORS AND TENDERS, EXCEPT PRECISION	43	703-779
FABRICATORS, ASSEMBLERS, AND HAND WORKING OCCUPATIONS	44	783-795
PRODUCTION INSPECTORS, TESTERS, SAMPLERS, AND WEIGHERS	45	796-799
TRANSPORTATION OCCUPATIONS	46	803-834

Table 7.1 (Continued)

MATERIAL MOVING EQUIPMENT OPERATORS	47	843-859
CONSTRUCTION LABORERS	48	869
FREIGHT, STOCK, AND MATERIAL HANDLERS	49	875-883
OTHER SPECIFIED HANDLERS, EQUIPMENT CLEANERS, AND HELPERS	50	863-888
LABORERS, EXCEPT CONSTRUCTION	51	889
ARMED FORCES, CURRENTLY CIVILIAN	52	905

Table 7.2
Major Occupation Group Recodes
(01-14)

OCCUPATION GROUP CODE	RECODE	OCCUPATION
EXECUTIVE, ADMINISTRATIVE, AND MANAGERIAL OCCUPATIONS	01	3-37
PROFESSIONAL SPECIALTY OCCUPATIONS	02	43-199
TECHNICIANS AND RELATED SUPPORT OCCUPATIONS	03	203-235
SALES OCCUPATIONS	04	243-285
ADMINISTRATIVE SUPPORT OCCUPATIONS, INCLUDING CLERICAL	05	303-389
PRIVATE HOUSEHOLD SERVICE OCCUPATIONS	06	403-407
PROTECTIVE SERVICE OCCUPATIONS	07	413-427
SERVICE OCCUPATIONS, EXCEPT PROTECTIVE AND HOUSEHOLD	08	433-469
FARMING, FORESTRY, AND FISHING OCCUPATIONS	09	473-499
PRECISION PRODUCTION, CRAFT, AND REPAIR OCCUPATIONS	10	503-699
MACHINE OPERATORS, ASSEMBLERS, AND INSPECTORS	11	703-799
TRANSPORTATION AND MATERIAL MOVING EQUIPMENT OCCUPATIONS	12	803-859
HANDLERS, EQUIPMENT CLEANERS, HELPERS, AND LABORERS	13	863-889
ARMED FORCES, CURRENTLY CIVILIAN	14	905

Table 7.3

Summary Statistics of Earnings Distributions for Various Occupations for 1976

Occupation	Number of Observations	Gini Coefficient	Entropy Coefficient	Mean Income	Variance	Kappa Criterion	Skewness Coefficient	Kurtosis Coefficient
Executives	4844	0.357	0.219	14285.8	96136900	2.062	1.597	4.593
Professionals	5235	0.385	0.258	12393.9	84928023	3.573	1.665	4.653
Technicians	1074	0.314	0.169	10481.8	38493991	0.727	1.406	4.538
Sales	3253	0.532	0.483	7425.1	64760584	-6.255	2.129	6.226
Administrative	7671	0.360	0.224	6779.6	20691714	-0.303	1.524	8.673
Private Households	568	0.531	0.480	1301.9	1950945	-2.405	1.943	4.535
Protective Services	724	0.315	0.176	1037.9	38082997	1.244	0.343	0.221
Other Services	4746	0.455	0.349	3930.1	11877068	0.954	1.900	8.226
Farming	1665	0.561	0.569	5703.9	54015575	5.570	3.905	27.950
Crafts	5827	0.302	0.161	10718.7	34133879	0.097	0.701	3.019
Operators	5089	0.368	0.226	7032.6	22277555	0.377	1.096	3.410
Transportation	2153	0.334	0.184	9574.4	33034373	0.324	0.956	2.708
Laborers	2401	0.399	0.267	6318.3	21150222	0.405	1.118	3.444

Table 7.4

Summary Statistics of Earnings Distributions for Various Occupations for 1977

Occupation	Number of Observations	Gini Coefficient	Entropy Coefficient	Mean Income	Variance	Kappa Criterion	Skewness Coefficient	Kurtosis Coefficient
Executives	6201	0.357	0.219	15030.8	104599600	1.999	1.504	4.061
Professionals	6589	0.391	0.266	13157.4	98925949	2.286	1.682	5.043
Technicians	1316	0.338	0.197	11056.3	50295915	0.845	1.521	5.140
Sales	4158	0.526	0.474	7884.4	73215737	2.969	2.446	10.897
Administrative	9262	0.365	0.232	7232.5	24258245	0.329	1.452	7.207
Private Households	690	0.521	0.461	1329.0	1957820	-4.895	2.029	5.558
Protective Services	867	0.332	0.192	11581.3	40119460	-0.468	0.687	1.142
Other Services	6446	0.456	0.350	4223.1	13682766	1.873	1.699	5.335
Farming	2318	0.562	0.569	6028.0	57263366	-15.592	3.122	11.833
Crafts	7154	0.371	0.168	11674.0	42585433	0.229	0.629	1.316
Operators	6133	0.371	0.229	7714.3	27440501	0.695	1.121	2.787
Transportation	2724	0.335	0.191	10767.2	44450501	0.469	1.179	3.629
Laborers	2814	0.399	0.269	6932.0	25767747	0.373	1.252	4.656

Table 7.5

Summary Statistics of Earnings Distributions for
Various Occupations for 1978

Occupation	Number of Observations	Gini Coefficient	Entropy Coefficient	Mean Income	Variance	Kappa Criterion	Skewness Coefficient	Kurtosis Coefficient
Executives	6324	0.365	0.226	16077.8	121755137	25.326	1.307	2.600
Professionals	6300	0.380	0.249	13954.9	102760667	9.070	1.490	3.475
Technicians	1299	0.323	0.177	12155.0	53076010	0.810	1.185	3.003
Sales	4055	0.533	0.485	8772.6	91138459	-30.423	2.162	6.892
Administrative	8988	0.362	0.225	7763.7	27383245	-0.673	1.290	3.832
Private Households	718	0.537	0.495	1455.2	2633021	5.719	2.433	9.875
Protective Services	825	0.347	0.208	11832.6	53575515	-6.514	0.567	0.470
Other Services	6230	0.456	0.349	4511.5	15523651	1.996	1.666	5.052
Farming	2021	0.540	0.518	6553.0	58834279	-26.445	2.880	12.094
Crafts	7032	0.313	0.170	12584.1	51903236	0.203	1.016	4.107
Operators	5819	0.370	0.228	8521.7	33020883	2.052	0.998	1.723
Transportation	2555	0.344	0.201	11522.6	53291192	0.370	1.194	4.186
Laborers	2803	0.399	0.265	7463.5	29445661	1.107	1.053	2.149

Table 7.6

Summary Statistics of Earnings Distributions for
Various Occupations for 1979

Occupation	Number of Observations	Gini Coefficient	Entropy Coefficient	Mean Income	Variance	Kappa Criterion	Skewness Coefficient	Kurtosis Coefficient
Executives	6288	0.358	0.214	17569.4	139177308	-8.219	1.277	2.345
Professionals	6620	0.379	0.247	14599.3	109775636	1.918	1.423	3.638
Technicians	1368	0.319	0.171	13149.4	59682192	1.044	1.081	2.304
Sales	4069	0.531	0.481	9078.4	96424515	-4.114	2.044	5.491
Administrative	9230	0.367	0.232	8352.3	33488507	0.362	1.746	11.086
Private Households	661	0.522	0.473	1656.8	3453539	4.325	3.127	17.682
Protective Services	829	0.351	0.217	12275.4	60649033	0.485	0.742	1.321
Other Services	5910	0.452	0.345	4988.2	19116374	1.744	1.884	6.788
Farming	1971	0.536	0.507	7791.4	79112017	11.084	2.769	12.275
Crafts	6968	0.310	0.165	13731.2	59028676	0.234	0.763	1.967
Operators	5882	0.374	0.234	9402.5	40917718	9.800	0.975	1.471
Transportation	2570	0.341	0.196	12659.8	62205512	0.823	1.011	2.126
Laborers	2674	0.406	0.274	7983.6	34621770	-2.330	0.962	1.207

Table 7.7

Summary Statistics of Earnings Distributions for Various Occupations for 1980

Occupation	Number of Observations	Gini Coefficient	Entropy Coefficient	Mean Income	Variance	Kappa Criterion	Skewness Coefficient	Kurtosis Coefficient
Executives	8012	0.356	0.211	18483.2	145947903	-1.324	1.021	1.193
Professionals	8255	0.379	0.245	16080.6	128748805	-2.385	1.169	1.761
Technicians	1717	0.320	0.175	14050.9	70753113	1.162	1.225	2.928
Sales	5026	0.520	0.461	9926.0	108961136	-6.558	2.006	5.577
Administrative	11356	0.369	0.236	9073.4	39663335	0.744	1.436	4.703
Private Households	799	0.571	0.580	1792.5	5348350	6.453	3.724	24.511
Protective Services	949	0.329	0.187	13836.8	67749101	0.290	0.801	1.951
Other Services	7551	0.451	0.345	5454.7	22702577	1.510	1.878	6.967
Farming	2548	0.537	0.506	8265.3	85029605	-3.959	2.261	6.563
Crafts	8735	0.314	0.169	14769.8	69016900	0.537	0.625	0.888
Operators	6759	0.364	0.221	10318.3	46741579	5.507	0.976	1.150
Transportation	3168	0.342	0.196	13455.5	68019121	-2.448	0.729	0.707
Laborers	3219	0.400	0.266	8755.0	40573940	4.172	1.018	1.674

Table 7.8

Summary Statistics of Earnings Distributions for Various Occupations for 1984

Occupation	Number of Observations	Gini Coefficient	Entropy Coefficient	Mean Income	Variance	Kappa Criterion	Skewness Coefficient	Kurtosis Coefficient
Executives	6311	0.365	0.223	25179.0	292600000	8.195	1.211	2.2920
Professionals	7712	0.380	0.249	21811.0	245600000	-3.146	1.311	2.2860
Technicians	1742	0.316	0.171	19026.5	130000000	1.175	1.443	4.1550
Sales	6637	0.511	0.444	14461.0	214300000	-2.203	1.795	3.8340
Administrative	9663	0.366	0.231	12242.8	69410000	0.626	1.278	3.8590
Private Households	622	0.577	0.578	2579.5	9655092	-13.084	2.339	7.8720
Protective Services	921	0.356	0.219	16870.8	114500000	-0.780	0.563	0.3190
Other Services	7182	0.458	0.356	6985.5	308500000	1.784	1.697	6.6540
Farming	2328	0.557	0.555	8486.2	1035000000	-25.195	2.764	11.1372
Crafts	7604	0.356	0.216	17827.2	133000000	-0.262	1.030	3.5980
Operators	4898	0.370	0.228	12724.5	74480000	-3.969	1.033	1.4740
Transportation	2704	0.367	0.228	16205.4	119200000	-0.930	1.098	2.4500
Laborers	2425	0.441	0.325	10065.7	66950000	-16.690	1.180	2.0490
Armed Forces	108	0.416	0.320	11384.6	117300000	-4.011	2.997	10.9848

Table 7.9

Summary Statistics of Earnings Distributions for
Various Occupations for 1985

Occupation	Number of Observations	Gini Coefficient	Entropy Coefficient	Mean Income	Variance	Kappa Criterion	Skewness Coefficient	Kurtosis Coefficient
Executives	6518	0.374	0.238	27113.3	383400000	3.335	1.6630	4.678
Professionals	7674	0.381	0.254	23501.6	303200000	2.434	1.7540	5.457
Technicians	1821	0.325	0.181	20410.7	161300000	1.134	1.6430	5.580
Sales	6643	0.510	0.446	15662.1	265900000	-7.999	2.1990	6.752
Administrative	9945	0.374	0.244	12995.8	85500000	-0.604	1.7130	7.567
Private Households	620	0.596	0.676	2702.8	19600000	137.908	8.4080	109.977
Protective Services	899	0.359	0.224	18575.1	141100000	-1.590	0.5620	0.401
Other Services	7060	0.462	0.366	7341.2	45300000	-1.520	2.2230	10.230
Farming	2059	0.557	0.562	8850.2	129700000	4.497	4.9530	52.553
Crafts	7586	0.343	0.200	19185.5	142700000	0.442	0.9250	2.177
Operators	4851	0.374	0.234	13758.8	90470000	0.930	1.2062	2.991
Transportation	2683	0.364	0.222	17103.0	129700000	1.008	1.0700	2.273
Laborers	2418	0.436	0.317	10801.4	76790000	-3.781	1.2550	2.148
Armed Forces	87	0.426	0.315	12616.8	120700000	-1.269	1.8550	3.366

Chapter 8

SUMMARY AND CONCLUDING REMARKS

8.1 A Review and Summary of Our Findings

We now briefly review our results and then suggest future research applications. In Chapter 2 we discussed recent trends in the labor force. We devoted considerable attention to this chapter because ultimately education, sex, race and age are all important determinants of labor supply behavior. Earnings are the primary component of total income so trends which affect earnings will affect the distribution of total income as well. The major demographic change in our economy is of course the substantial increase in the number of women entering the labor force. At the same time these women were entering in unprecedented numbers, men continued to retire earlier (even though legal mandatory retirement ages have been lifted). Concurrent with this labor market activity, the influx of baby boomers into the labor force began with an anticipated result of lower real earnings relative to peak wage-earners, cf. Ehrenberg and Smith (1987). This fact coupled with all these women of all ages entering, the labor force (and earnings structure) has changed considerably and will continue to. For some time, the distributions of earnings obviously have been affected. After discussing these trends we moved on to discuss their implications.

Chapter 3 reviewed the various theories of how observed income graduations are actually generated. Theories ranged from the "ability" theory of the 1930's to modern human capital models. While human capital models are now widely accepted, the problem remains that they inadequately describe the shape of the distribution of income. We also discussed the problems of choosing one measure of inequality as the most "appropriate" one. Different measures convey different information about the underlying income graduation. There is nothing wrong with this as long as individuals attempting to evaluate inequality in a given graduation are cognizant of the fact. We also discussed the relatively recent rise of theoretical work which advocates an axiomatic approach. The theorists following this route have laid out a set of criteria for the inequality expert to take as a list of necessary attributes to be fulfilled by the measure of inequality chosen. Theil's entropy measure is one case of the Generalized Entropy Class which does appear to satisfy the axiomatic criteria. Chapter 3 concluded with an examination of the major hypothetical statistical distributions which have been used to approximate the actual distributions observed. We saw later in Chapter 5 how one member of the Pearsonian family, the beta distribution of the second kind, allowed for meaningful comparisons between groups without the restrictive assumptions of (say) the lognormal distribution.

In Chapter 4 we discussed a technique from classical statistics, the Kappa criterion, which allows us to discern between various hypothetical statistical distributions as candidates to approximate observed income graduations. The usual procedure is based on goodness-of-fit techniques which take a long time to do and are tedious to utilize. The Kappa criterion is based only on the first four central moments and is relatively straightforward to apply. We utilize the technique in Chapters 6 and 7 in actual applications. Chapter 4 also presented a flow diagram of the relations between various well-known statistical distributions. The relationships are defined by the transformations of variables which are stated explicitly in the text.

In Chapter 5 we discuss the beta distribution of the second kind in considerable detail. The unique feature of this distribution function is not only that it provides a good approximation to actual observed income data, but also that the marginal distributions of income components maintain the same functional form as the joint distribution of total income. We applied the model to income data by states. We treated each state's distribution as a marginal distribution from the total income (joint) distribution for the United States as a whole. The beta distribution of the second kind is also a functional form of hypothetical distribution which allows us to discuss multidimensional inequality. The multidimensional approach is concerned with the notion that income is in fact merely one dimension of the inequality problem. By taking a joint distribution approach, we can look at income and other attributes (e.g. expenditures) simultaneously. Again, information content becomes an important principle. We discuss this below in more detail. Chapter 5 also presented a simple example to show how the joint distribution of labor and nonlabor income varies over the life cycle with an overlapping generations model. It was found that you can't unambiguously conclude one cohort is better off than another and thus, it remains an empirical question. The joint distribution approach we utilized yielded results consistent with the hypothesis that labor earnings' marginal

distributions have less inequality than the marginal distributions of
total or nonlabor income.

In Chapter 6 we discussed inequality across demographic groups. We
did so with a clear message in mind. It was perhaps not surprising that
the level of inequality (and shape of the income graduation as measured
by the Kappa criterion) varied across cohorts by age, race and sex. It
is probably no more surprising that the distributions reflected different
levels of inequality for different income receiving units (irus). What
is surprising is that many people (policymakers, a concerned citizenry
and religious groups, to name just a few) continue to ask the question,
"What has happened to the level of income inequality?" with little regard
for the complexity of the issue. It was and is our hope that our
analysis makes clear that there is no simple answer to that question.

Chapter 7 reiterates the lessons of Chapter 6 in light of Chapter 2.
The distributions of earnings do vary across occupations and they should.
As the labor force changes its demographic makeup and we switch to a
service-oriented economy, the distributions of earnings will continue to
change their shapes. In sum, this study has attempted to present a broad
discussion of the many empirical issues involved in analyzing income
inequality. It has been our purpose here to caution the reader that any
discussion of income distribution and redistribution stands on very
tenuous ground. The tenuous nature of the subject matter stems from the
fact that income itself is a concept of many meanings. Some lend
themselves to empirical scrutiny, some do not. We discussed a concept
that is becoming increasingly popular in the inequality literature, the
notion of multidimensional inequality. While a growing literature exists
on the theoretical aspects of multidimensional inequality, we have
attempted to show how one can actually go about doing empirical research
in a meaningful way on this important topic. We hope this book has
helped to clarify some of these issues as well.

8.2 Future Research Applications

Finally, we will close this book by suggesting areas of inequality
research that merit more attention in the future. We will follow the
same pattern that we did in the text in discussing these issues. We will
begin with some thoughts on the definition of and measurement of income.
It is well known that regardless of which definition of the income
receiving unit (iru) is chosen as the appropriate one, there is always

the problem of measuring income with some error, cf. Van Praag et al. (1983). The ramifications of this problem for making inferences about the level of inequality in a given income graduation should be obvious. It also calls into question any evaluations of current redistribution programs for the same reason. Aigner and Slottje have begun to explore this problem with the so-called DYMIMIC (dynamic multiple indicator multiple cause) models. There will be much fruitful research to do in the future on how best to deal with measurement error and the distributional consequences of such error.

Another area of empirical research on income inequality that has not been carefully explored is that of the relationship between various inequality measures. The author of this book and A. F. Shorrocks are currently engaged in research which attempts to find some summary statistics of inequality measurement that will serve as a basis for others. While it is well known that no single measure is an affine transformation of another frequently used measure, is it possible to find one that is a linear/nonlinear combination of several others? This may not be a question that is easily answered and may require much work in the future by many individuals. A related question concerns the optimal grouping of observations. Davies and Shorrocks have recently begun doing some work on this problem, but the problem of optimal grouping may require sensitivity analysis to see if the "optimal group" will be robust across data sources and different irus, as well as inequality measure.

Most empirical work that has been done on the impact of fiscal policies on inequality has implicitly assumed that their is no feedback, that is, these studies assume that fiscal policies cause change in the income graduation with no impact the other way. Hayes, Porter-Hudak and Slottje (1988) have recently studied the problem the other way by utilizing multivariate causality tests of the Granger-Sims variety. Balke and Slottje are currently engaged in research where we use VARs (vector autoregressions) to study the problem. The advantage of these models is that they allow us to study the problem without imposing a specific form on the structure. A related issue that has not received much attention is the relationship between monetary policy and inequality. Slottje, Russell and Haslag (1988) have discussed this issue, but much work remains to be done on monetary policy implications.

All of the above are empirical applications that deal with specific issues in the inequality literature. There also remains the fundamental problem of bringing econometric work on inequality into the future with respect to the philosophical underpinnings with which it is undertaken. Leamer (1978), Hendry and Richard (1982), Van Praag et al. (1988) and Theil (1988) among others are changing the way empirical work is done in econometrics. These econometricians realize that we must not only engage heavily in specification searches, but also admit that we are doing so. It is perfectly valid to "torture the data" but good science dictates that we report we are doing so and that we quit being obsessed with the "confessions" that are forthcoming. We must carefully consider the information content of the results we present. In other words, are any inequality measures a minimally sufficient set in a statistical sense? These are the sort of questions we must ask.

In summary, the young economist looking for an area of specialization would be well advised to take a serious look at income distribution questions. We began the book by noting that some earlier economists found the question of income distribution uninteresting, we hope that consideration of the issues discussed in this book have helped to persuade the reader otherwise.

APPENDIX 1

A Description of the Data

The data reported and analyzed in this book originated from four primary sources. The data in Chapter Five on various income components are from the

U.S. Department of the Treasury
Internal Revenue Service
Statistics of Income: Individual Tax Returns
1952-1981
Washington, D.C.: Government Printing Office.

In 1981, this data consisted of approximately 92,000,000 individual returns. The I.R.S. reports the data in the above publications in frequency form with the grouping somewhat consistent over time.

The data on states for 1960, 1970 and 1980 discussed in Chapter Five are from the

U.S. Department of Commerce
U.S. Bureau of the Census
1960, 1970 and 1980 Census of the Population:
Characteristics of the Population
Washington, D.C.: Government Printing Office.

The Census Bureau undergoes the exhaustive sampling and surveying of the U.S. population every ten years at tremendous costs. Individuals must respond to the survey by law.

The data utilized in Chapter Six on demographic characteristics and in Chapter Seven on occupational earnings are from the

U.S. Department of Commerce
U.S. Bureau of the Census
Current Population Survey: Annual Demographic March File
1975-1981
Washington, D.C: Government Printing Office.

These data are based on an annual sample done every March and consist of about 45,000 observations in the natural sample. Problems with the so-called "hot deck" imputations of missing observations have been well documented, cf. Lillard, Smith and Welch (1986).

The quintile data discussed in Chapter Six are from the

U.S. Department of Commerce
U.S. Bureau of the Census
Consumer Population Reports: Consumer Income
1947-1984
Washington, D.C.: Government Printing Office

These data are in quintile form and report the percent of consumer income in each of five classes. The definition of income is comprehensive in that it includes cash transfers but does not include transfers in-kind or taxes paid.

REFERENCES

Ahluwalia, M.S., J.H. Duloy and G. Pyatt (1980). Who benefits from economic development?: Comment. American Economic Review, 70, 242-245.

Aigner, D.J. and A.J. Heins (1967). On the determinants of income inequality. American Economic Review, 57, 175-184.

Aigner, D.J. and A.S. Goldberger (1970). Estimation of Pareto's law from grouped observations. Journal of the American Statistical Association, 65, 712-723.

Aitchison, J. and J.A. Brown (1957). The Lognormal Distribution. Cambridge, Massachusetts: Cambridge University Press.

Amoroso, L. (1925). Riceche in torno alla curva dei redditi. Annali di Mathematica pura ed applicata, Series 4-21, 123-59.

Ashenfelter, O. and G. Solon (1982). Employment statistics: the interaction of economics and policy. American Economic Review, 72, 233-236.

Atkinson, A.B. (1970). On the measurement of inequality. Journal of Economic Theory, 2, 244-263.

Atkinson, A.B. and F. Bourguignon (1982). The comparison of multi-dimensioned distributions of economic status. Review of Economic Studies, 49, 183-201.

Bach, R.L. and A. Ando (1957). The redistributional effects of inflation. Review of Economic Statistics, 39, 1-13.

Basmann, R.L., D.J. Molina, M. Rodarte and D.J. Slottje (1983). Some new methods of predicting changes in economic inequality associated with trends in growth and development. Issues in 3rd World Development, R. Sampath (ed.). Denver: Westview Publishing.

Basmann, R.L., D.J. Molina and D.J. Slottje (1984). Variable consumer preferences, economic inequality, and the cost-of-living concept: Part one. Advances in Econometrics, Vol. 3, R.L. Basmann and George F. Rhodes, Jr. (eds.). Greenwich, Connecticut: JA1 Press Inc.

Basmann, R.L., K. Hayes, and D.J. Slottje, (1988). Some New Methods for Analyzing Empirical Income Graduations. In progress.

Becker, Gary S. (1962). Investment in human capital: a theoretical analysis. Journal of Political Economy, 70, 9-49.

Becker, Gary S. (1967). Human Capital and the Personal Distribution of Income: An Analytical Approach, Woytinsky Lecture No. 1. Ann Arbor: University of Michigan, Institute of Public Administration.

Beckerman, P. and D. Coes (1980). Who benefits from economic development?: Comment. American Economic Review, 70, 246-249.

Berrebi, Z.M. and J. Silber (1987). Regional differences and the components of growth and inequality changes. Economics Letters, 25, 295-298.

Bishop, J., J. Formby and P. Thistle (1988). Statistical inference, income distributions and social welfare. Research on Economic Inequality. (forthcoming).

Black, D., K. Hayes and D.J. Slottje (1987). A joint distribution approach to analyzing the size distribution of labor and non-labor income simultaneously. Unpublished paper.

Blackburn, M. (1988a). Interpreting the magnitude of changes in measures of income inequality. Journal of Econometrics, (forthcoming).

_____ (1988b). The effects of sectoral shift and the baby boom on earnings inequality among males. Unpublished mimeo.

_____ (1988c). Differences in earnings inequality using the March and May current population surveys. Unpublished mimeo.

Blackburn, M. and D. Bloom (1987a). Earnings and income inequality in the United States. Population and Development Review (forthcoming).

_____ (1987b). The effects of technological change on earnings and income inequality in the U.S. N.B.E.R. Working Paper No. 2337.

Blackorby, C., D. Donaldson, and J. Auersperg (1980), A new procedure for the measurement of inequality within and among population subgroups. Discussion Paper 80-25, University of British Columbia, Canadian Journal of Economics, 14, 665-685.

Blinder, A.S. (1975). Distribution effects and the aggregate consumption function. Journal of Political Economy, 83, 447-475.

Blinder, A. and G. Esaki (1978). Macro-economic activity and income distribution in the post war U.S. Review of Economic Statistics, 60, 604-608.

Bowles, S. (1969). Planning Educational Systems for Economic Growth. Harvard Economic Studies, vol. 133, Cambridge, Mass.: Harvard University Press.

Brandt, W. (1980). North-South: A Program for Survival. Cambridge, Mass.: M.I.T. Press.

Bronfenbrenner, M. (1971). Income Distribution Theory. Chicago: Aldine Publishing Co.

Bronfenbrenner, M. and F.D. Holzman (1963). Survey of inflation theory. American Economic Review, 53, 593-661.

Brown, E.H.P. and Bernard Weber (1953). Accumulation, productivity, and distribution in the British economy, 1870-1938. Economic Journal, 63, 263-288.

Brown, J.A.C. (1976). The mathematical and statistical theory on income distribution. The Personal Distribution of Incomes, A.B. Atkinson (ed.). London: Allen and Unwin.

Burns, A. (1969). The Business Cycle in a Changing World, Studies in Business Cycles. New York: Columbia University Press.

Butler, R. and J.B. McDonald (1986). Income inequality in the United States, 1948-1980. Research in Labor Economics, 8, 85-140.

Campos, R. (1961). Two views on inflation in Latin America. In Latin American Issues (A. O. Hirschman, ed.), pp. 69-79. New York: Twentieth Century Fund.

Champernowne, D.G. (1937). The Distribution of Income Between Persons. New York: Cambridge University Press.

_____ (1952). The graduation of income distribution. Econometrica, 20, 318-351.

_____ (1953). A model of income distribution. Economic Journal, 63, 318-351.

_____ (1974). A comparison of measures of inequality of income distribution. Economic Journal, 84, 787-816.

Chiswick, B.R. (1974). Income Inequality: Regional Analysis Within a Human Capital Framework. New York: National Bureau of Economic Research, Columbia University Press.

Clark, J.B. (1899). The Distribution of Wealth. New York: MacMillan Publishing.

Cowell, F. (1977). Measuring Inequality. London: Phillip Allan.

_____ (1980). On the structure of additive inequality measures. Review of Economic Studies, 47, 521-531.

Cramer, J.S. (1964). Efficient grouping, regression and correlation in Engel curve analysis. Journal of the American Statistical Association, 59, 233-250.

Creedy, J. (1972). Economic Cycles in the Life of Individuals and Families. Thesis, Oxford University.

_____ (1985). Dynamics of Income Distribution. New York: Basil Blackwell, Inc.

Dagum, C. (1980). Inequality measures between income distributions with applications. Econometrica, 48, 1791-1804.

Dalton, H. (1920). The measurement of the inequality of incomes. Economic Journal, 91, 348-361.

Davis, L. et. al. (1972). American Economic Growth. New York: Harper and Row.

Dougherty, C.R.S. (1971). Estimates of labour aggregate functions. Harvard Center for International Affairs, Economic Development Report, No. 190, Cambridge: Development Research Group.

_____ (1972). Substitution and the structure of the labour force. Economic Journal, 82, 170-182.

Durbin, J. and G.S. Watson (1950). Testing for serial correlation in least-squares regression, I. Biometrica, 37, 409-428.

Edgeworth, Francis Y. (1924). Untried methods of representing frequency. Journal of Royal Statistical Society, 82, 170-182.

Ehrenberg, R. and R. Smith (1988). Modern Labor Economics, 3rd Edition. Glenview, IL: Scott Foresman and Co.

Élteto, O. and E. Friayes (1968). New inequality measures as efficient tools for causal analysis and planning. Econometrica, 36, 383-396.

Elderton, W.P. (1938). Frequency Curves and Correlation. Cambridge: Cambridge University Press.

Fase, M.M.G. (1970). An Econometric Model of Age-Income Profiles. Rotterdam: Rotterdam University Press.

Fei, J.C.H., G. Ranis and S.W.Y. Kuo (1978). Growth and the family distribution of income by factor components. Quarterly Journal of Economics, 92, 17-53.

Fields, G.S. (1977). Who benefits from economic development?--A reexamination of Brazillian growth in the 1960's. American Economic Review, 67, 570-782.

_____ (1979). Income inequality in urban Colombia: A decomposition analysis. Review of Income and Wealth, 25, 327-341.

_____ (1980). Who benefits from economic development?: Reply. American Economic Review, 70, 257-262.

Fisher, I. (1922). The Making of Index Numbers. Boston and New York: Houghton Mifflin.

Fishlow, A. (1980). Who benefits from economic development?: Comment. American Economic Review, 70, 250-256.

Fisk, P.R. (1961). The graduation of income distributions. Econometrica, 29, 171-185.

Frank, Robert H. (1984). Are workers paid their marginal products? American Economic Review, 74, 549-71.

_____ (1985). Choosing the Right Pond: Human Behavior and the Quest for Status. New York: Oxford University Press.

Friedman, Milton (1953). Choice, chance, and the personal distribution of income. Journal of Political Economy, 61, 277-290.

196   *References*

_____ (1975). <u>An Economist's Protest</u>. Glen Ridge, N.J.: Horton and Daughter's Publishing.

Galbraith, J.K. (1962). <u>The Affluent Society</u>. London: Pelican Publishing.

Gastwirth, Joseph L. (1971). A general definition of the Lorenz curve. <u>Econometrica</u>, 39, 1037-1039.

_____ (1972). The estimation of the Lorenz curve and Gini index. <u>The Review of Economics and Statistics</u>, 54, 306-316.

Gibrat, R. (1931). <u>Les Inégalités Economiques</u>. Paris: Sirely.

Gini, C. (1912). <u>Variabilita e Mutabilita</u>. Bologna.

Gisser, M. (1981). <u>Intermediate Price Theory</u>. New York: McGraw-Hill.

Grunwald, J. (1961). The 'Structuralist' school on price stability and development: the Chilean case. In <u>Latin American Issues</u> (A.O. Hirschman, ed.), pp. 95-123. New York: Twentieth Century Fund.

Hagen, E. (1980). <u>The Economics of Development</u>. Homewood: Richard Irwin.

Hayes, K., J. Hirschberg and D.J. Slottje (1987a). Computer algebra systems: Some economic and econometric applications. <u>Advances in Econometrics</u>, 6, (forthcoming).

_____ (1987b). Some further examples of computer algebra systems in econometric uses. SMU Working Paper #8713, Dallas, TX.

Hayes, K.J., S. Porter-Hudak and D. Slottje (1988). U.S. redistributive policies, Unpublished mimeo, S.M.U., Dallas, TX.

Hendry, D. and J.F. Richard (1982). On the formulation of Empirical Models in dynamic econometrics. <u>Journal of Econometrics</u> 20, 3-33.

Hirschberg, J., D. Molina and D.J. Slottje (1988). A selection criterion for choosing between functional forms of income distribution, the κ criterion. <u>Econometric Reviews</u>, (forthcoming).

Hirschberg, J. and D. Slottje (1988). Remembrance of things past: the κ criterion and earnings graduations by occupation. <u>Journal of Econometrics</u>, (forthcoming).

Hunt, J.M. (1961). <u>Intelligence and Experience</u>. New York: Ronald Press.

Iyenger, N.S. (1960). On a method of computing Engel elasticities from concentration curves. <u>Econometrica</u>, 28, 882-891.

Jencks, C. (1972). <u>Inequality: A Reassessment of the Effect of Family and Schooling in America</u>. New York: Basic Books.

Jenkins, S. (1987). "The measurement of economic inequality. <u>Readings on Economic Inequality</u>, Lars Osberg (ed.), Armonk, NY: Sharpe.

Johnston, J. (1963). Econometric Methods (2nd ed.). New York: McGraw-Hill.

Jorgenson, D.W. and D. Slesnick (1984a). Aggregate consumer behavior and the measurement of inequality. Review of Economic Studies, 51, 369-92.

_____ (1984b). Inequality in the distribution of individual welfare. Advances in Econometrics, 4, 70-121.

Kadiyala, D.R. (1968). A transformation used to circumvent the problem of autocorrelation. Econometrica, 36, 93-96.

Kakwani, N.C. (1980). Income Inequality and Poverty. New York and London: Oxford University Press.

Kakwani, N.C. and N. Podder (1973). On the estimation of Lorenz curve from grouped observations. International Economic Review, 14, 278-292.

_____ (1976). Efficient estimation of the Lorenz curve and associated inequality measures from grouped observations. Econometrica, 44, 137-148.

Kaldor, N. (1957). A model of economic growth. Economic Journal, 67, 591- 624.

_____ (1959). Economic growth and the problem of inflation. Economica, 26, 212-226, 287-298.

Kalecki, M. (1945). On the Gibrat distribution. Econometrica, 13, 1961-1970.

Kapteyn, J.C. (1903). Skew Frequency Curves in Biology and Statistics, Groningen: Astronomical Laboratory.

Kendall, M. and A. Stuart (1977). The Advanced Theory of Statistics, Vol. 1. New York: MacMillan Publishing Co., 3rd. Edition.

Kessel, R.A. and A.A. Alchian (1960). The inflation-induced lag of wages. American Economic Review, 50, 43-46.

Kosters, M.H. (1975). Controls and Inflation. Washington DC: American Enterprise Institute for Policy Reasearch.

Kuznets, S. (1953). Shares of Upper Income Groups in Income and Savings. New York: National Bureau of Economic Research.

_____ (1955). Economic growth and income inequality. American Economic Review, 45, 1-28.

_____ (1976). Demographic aspects of the size distribution of income: an exploratory essay. Economic Development and Cultural Change, 25, 1-94.

Lasswell, H.D. (1958). Politics: Who Gets What, Where, and How? New York: Meridian Books.

Leamer, E. (1978). Specification Searches in Econometrics, New York: J. Wiley Press, Inc.

Levine, D.B. and N.M. Singer (1970). The mathematical relation between the income density function and the measurement of income inequality. Econometrica, 38, 324-330.

Lerman, R. and S. Yitzhaki (1984). A note on the calculation and interpretation of the Gini index. Economics Letters, 15, 363-368.

_____ (1985). Income inequality effects by income source: a new approach and applications to the U.S. Review of Economics and Statistics, 76, 151-155.

_____ (1988). Improving the accuracy of estimates of Gini coefficients. Unpublished mimeo.

Lillard, L., J. Smith and F. Welch (1986). What do we really know about wages? Importance of nonreporting and census imputation. Journal of Political Economy, 94, 489-506.

Lluch, C., A.A. Powell and R.A. Williams (1977). Patterns in Household Demand and Saving. New York: Oxford University Press.

Loehr, W. and J.P. Powelson (1981). The Economics of Development and Distribution. New York: Harcourt Brace Jovanovich.

Lorenz, M. D. (1905). Methods of measuring the concentration of wealth. Journal of The American Statistical Association, 9, 209-219.

Lydall, H. (1968). The Structure of Earnings, Oxford: Clarendon Press.

_____ (1979). A Theory of Income Distribution, Oxford: Clarendon Press.

_____ (1986). The Structure of Labor Earnings. Oxford: Oxford University Press.

Maasoumi, Esfandiar (1986). The measurement and decomposition of multi-dimensional equality. Econometrica, 48, 1791-1803.

Macurdy, Thomas E. (1984). Distribution tests based on empirical moment generating functions. Unpublished Manuscript, Stanford University.

McAlister, D. (1879). The law of the geometric mean. Proceedings of the Royal Society, 29, 367-376.

McDonald, J.B. (1981). Some issues associated with the measurement of income inequality. Statistical Distributions in Scientific Work, 6, 161-179, C. Taille, Editor, New York: Reidel Publishing Co.

_____ (1984). Some general functions for the size distribution of income. Econometrica 52, 647-664.

McDonald, J.B. and D.O. Richards (1987). Model selection: Some generalized distributions. Communications in Statistics, 16, 1049-1074.

McDonald, J.B. and M. Ransom (1979). Functional forms, estimation techniques and the distribution of income. Econometrica, 47, 1513-1516.

Metcalf, C. E. (1972). An Econometric Model of the Income Distribution, Chicago: Markham Press.

Mincer, Jacob (1970). Investment in human capital and personal income distribution. Journal of Political Economy, 66, 281-302.

_____ (1970). The distribution of labor incomes: a survey, with special reference to human capital approach. Journal of Economic Literature, 8, 1-26.

_____ (1974). Schooling, Experience and Earnings. New York: National Bureau of Economic Research.

_____ (1976). Progress in human capital analyses of the distribution of earnings. The Personal Distribution of Incomes, A.B. Atkinson (ed.). London: Allen and Unwin.

Mirer, T.W. (1973). The distributional impact of the 1970 recession. Review of Economic Statistics, 51, 214-224.

Molina, D. (1982). The asymptotic properties of the Gini coefficient. Texas A & M University, mimeo.

_____ (1984). Extension of Dagum's inequality measure applied to Mexican expenditure data. Presented at the Second International Meeting of The North American Economic and Finance Association. Mexico City.

Molina, D. and D.J. Slottje (1987). The gamma distribution and the size distribution of income reconsidered, Atlantic Economic Journal, 15, 86.

Mood, A.M., F.A. Graybill, and D.C. Boes (1974). Introduction to the Theory of Statistics. New York: McGraw-Hill.

Morgan, J.N. (1962). The anatomy of income distribution. Review of Economics and Statistics, 44, 270-283.

Moroney, J.R. (1979). Income Equality. Lexington: Lexington Books.

Musgrove, P. (1980). Income distribution and the aggregate consumption function. Journal of Political Economy, 88, 504-525.

Nilsen, S. (1979). Employment and unemployment statistics as funding allocators for nonmetropolitan areas. In National Commission on Employment and Unemployment Statistics, Data Collection, Processing and Presentation, Washington, DC, 502-522.

1976/1984 Consumer Population Survey (CPS). U.S. Department of Commerce, Bureau of the Census, Washington, DC.

Ord, J.K. (1972). Families of Frequency Distributions. London: Griffin.

Ott, L. (1977). An Introduction to Statistical Methods and Data Analysis. Belmont: Wadsworth.

Pareto, V. (1897). Cours d'Economique Politique. Vol. 2, Part I, Chapter 1, Lausanne.

Pechman, J.A. and B.J. Okner (1974). Who Bears the Tax Burden? Washington, DC: Brookings Institution.

Pen, Jan (1971). Income Distribution. Translated from the Dutch by Trevor S. Preston, New York: Praeger Publishers.

Pigou, Arthur C. (1932). The Economics of Welfare, 4th edition. London: Macmillan.

Porter, P.K. and D.J. Slottje (1985). A comprehensive analysis of income inequality in the U.S. for the years 1952-1981. Southern Economic Journal, 52, 412-422.

Prais, S.J., and J. Aitchison (1954). The grouping of observations in regression anaysis. Review of the International Statistical Institute, 22, 1-22.

Psacharopoulos, G. and K. Hinchliffe (1972). Further evidence on the elasticity of substitution among different types of educated labor. Journal of Political Economy, 80, 786-796.

Pyatt, G., C. Chen and J. Fei (1980). The distribution of income by factor components. Quarterly Journal of Economics, 95, 451-474.

Ricardo, D. (1819). Principles of Political Economy. London: Cambridge A. Press.

_____ (1951-73). The Works and Correspondence of David Ricardo, P. Straffa (ed.) Vols. I-XI. Cambridge: Cambridge University Press.

Rutherford, R.S.G. (1955). Income distributions: a new model.Econometrica, 23, 277-294.

Sahota, G. (1978). Theories of personal income distribution: a survey. Journal of Economic Literature, 16, 1-55.

Salem, A.B.Z. and T.D. Mount (1974). A convenient descriptive model of income distribution: the gamma density. Econometrica, 42, 1115-1127.

Samuelson, P.A. (1977). Economics (11th ed.). New York: McGraw-Hill.

Savin, N.E. and K.J. White (1977). The Durbin-Watson test for serial correlation with extreme sample sizes or many regressors. Econometrica, 45, 1989-1996.

Schultz, T.P. (1965). The Distribution of Personal Income. Washington: U.S.G.P.O.

Schultz, T.W. (1961). Capital formation by education. Journal of Political Economy, 68, 571-583.

References   201

_____ (1963). *The Economic Value of Education*. New York: Columbia University Press.

_____ (1969). Secular trends and cyclical begavior of income distribution in the U.S., 1944-1965. *Six Papers on the Size Distribution of Wealth and Income* (L. Soltow, ed.), pp. 77-100. New York: Columbia University Press.

Sen, A. (1973). *On Economic Inequality*. New York: W.W. Norton.

Shackett, J. and D.J. Slottje (1987). Labor supply decisions, human capital attributes and inequality in the size distribution of earnings in the U.S.: 1952-1981. *Journal of Human Resources*, 22, 82-100.

Shorrocks, A.F. (1973). *Aspects of the Distribution of Personal Wealth*, Ph.D. dissertation, London School of Economics.

_____ (1978). Income inequality and income mobility. *Journal of Economic Theory*, 19, 376-393.

_____ (1980). The class of additively decomposable inequality measures. *Econometrica* 48, 613-26.

_____ (1982). Inequality decomposition by factor components. *Econometrica*, 50, 193-211.

_____ (1983). The impact of income components on the distribution of family income. *Quarterly Journal of Economics*, 98, 311-326.

Shuettinger, R.C. (1978). Four thousand years of price controls. *Policy Review*, Summer, 73-78.

Silber, J. (1988a). Factor components, population subgroups and the computation of the Gini index of inequality. *Review of Economics and Statistics* (forthcoming).

_____ (1988b). Growth, inequality change, permutations and the measurement of change. Unpublished mimeo, Bar-Ilan U.

Simons, H. (1948). *Economic Policy for a Free Society*. Chicago: University of Chicago Press.

Singh, S.K., and G.S. Maddala (1976). A function for the size distribution of incomes. *Econometrica*, 44, 963-970.

Slottje, D.J. (1984). A measure of income inequality based upon the beta distribution of the second kind. *Economics Letters*, 15, 369-375.

_____ (1987). Relative price changes and inequality in the size distribution of various components of income: a multidimensional approach. *Journal of Business and Economic Statistics*, 5, 19-26.

Slottje, D.J., W. Russell and J. Haslag (1988). *Macroeconomic Activity and Income Inequality in the U.S.*, Greenwich, Ct.: JAI Press, Inc.

Smith, A.[1776] (1979). The Wealth of Nations. Penguin Books Ltd.,
Harmondsworth.

Steindl, Josef (1965). Random Processes and the Growth of Firms; A Study
of the Pareto Law. New York: Hafner Press.

Stephenson, S. (1979). The impact of alternative poverty definitions on
the interstate allocation of federal funds. Review of Regional
Studies, 9, 31-46.

Stockfisch, J.A. (1982). The income distribution effects of a natural
gas price increase. Contemporary Policy Issues, 1, 9-25.

Taubman, P. (1975). Sources of Inequality of Earnings. Amsterdam:
North-Holland.

Taussig, M.K. (1976). Trends in inequality of well-offness in the United
States since World War II., Rutgers College, unpublished.

Theil, H. (1967). Economics and Information Theory. Chicago: Rand
McNally Co.

_____ (1979). The measurement of inequality by components of
income. Economics Letters, 2, 197-199.

_____ (1988). The development of international inequality.
Journal of Econometrics (forthcoming).

Thurow, L. (1970). Analyzing the American income distribution. American
Economic Review, 60, 261-269.

Tinbergen, Jan (1975). Income Distribution: Analysis and Policies,
Oxford: North-Holland.

Tintner, G. (1965). Econometrics (Science ed.). New York: John Wiley
and Sons.

Tobin, J. (1972). Inflation and unemployment. American Economic Review,
62, 1-18.

Underground economy's hidden force. Business Week, 5 April 1982, pp. 64-
70.

United States Government Superintendent of Documents. (1975). Historical
Statistics of the United States: Colonial Times to 1970.
Washington, DC: Government Printing Office.

_____ (1980). Statistics of Income - 1952-1979. Washington, DC:
Government Printing Office.

_____ (1982). Economic Report of the President 1981.
Washington, DC: Government Printing Office.

Van Praag, B.M.S., A. Hagenaars and W. van Eck (1983). The influence of
classification and observation on errors in the measurement of
income inequality. Econometrica, 51, 1093-1108.

Van Praag, B.M.S., J. de Leuw and T. Kloek (1988). Large sample properties of method of moment estimators under different data generating processes. Journal of Econometrics, 37, 157-170.

Weisskoff, R. (1970). Income distribution and economic growth in Puerto Rico, Argentina, and Mexico. Review of Income and Wealth, 16, 303-332.

West, S. (1987). Measures of central tendency for censored earnings data from the current population survey. Procedings of the American Statistical Association, (forthcoming).

Zellner, A. (1979). Statistical analysis of econometric models. Journal of the American Statistical Association, 74, 628-642.

204

INDEX